Social Regulation: Strategies for Reform

SOCIAL REGULATION:

STRATEGIES FOR REFORM

Eugene Bardach, *Editor*

Robert A. Kagan, *Editor*

Lawrence S. Bacow

Paul Danaceau

George C. Eads

Joseph Ferreira, Jr.

Thomas P. Grumbly

William R. Havender

Michael H. Levin

Michael O'Hare

Stuart M. Pape

Timothy J. Sullivan

Institute for Contemporary Studies
San Francisco, California

Distributed by Transaction Books
New Brunswick (U.S.A.) and London (U.K.)

Library of Congress Catalog No. 81—85279.

Social regulation.

  Bibliography: p.
  Includes index.
  1. United States—Social policy—Addresses,
essays, lectures.   2. Safety regulations—United
States—Addresses, essays, lectures.   3. Environmental
policy—United States—Addresses, essays,
lectures.   I. Bardach, Eugene.   II. Kagan, Robert A.
III. Bacow, Lawrence S.
HN65.S577   361.6'1'0973   81-85279
ISBN 0—917616—47—2   AACR2
ISBN 0—917616—46—4 (pbk.)

CONTENTS

III

Private Sector Alternatives to Direct Regulation

IV

Conclusion

CONTRIBUTORS

LAWRENCE S. BACOW
Assistant professor of law and environmental policy,
Massachusetts Institute of Technology

EUGENE BARDACH
Professor of public policy, University of California, Berkeley

PAUL DANACEAU
Consultant, U.S. Regulatory Council

GEORGE C. EADS
Senior economist, The Rand Corporation

JOSEPH FERREIRA, JR.
Associate professor of urban studies and operations research,
Massachusetts Institute of Technology

THOMAS P. GRUMBLY
Senior consultant, Temple, Barker and Sloane, Inc.

WILLIAM R. HAVENDER
Research biochemist, University of California, Berkeley

ROBERT A. KAGAN
Associate professor of political science,
University of California, Berkeley

MICHAEL H. LEVIN
Chief, Regulatory Reform Staff, Office of Policy and Resource
Management, U.S. Environmental Protection Agency

MICHAEL O'HARE
Lecturer in public policy, Kennedy School of Government,
Harvard University

STUART M. PAPE
Associate, Patton, Boggs & Blow

TIMOTHY J. SULLIVAN
Assistant professor of public policy,
University of California, Berkeley

PREFACE

The decade of the 1970s brought two major trends in government regulation of the private sector—an explosion of new "social" regulation of health, safety, and the environment, and a growing awareness that many of the older economic regulations of specific industries were counterproductive and in need of reform or repeal.

The Institute for Contemporary Studies has published a number of specific studies on the older economic regulations, two books on energy, two on land use controls, and one on credit allocation. *Regulating Business*, edited by Donald Jacobs and published as a joint project with Northwestern University's Graduate School of Management in 1978, was our first broad study of economic regulation, focusing especially on economic and political problems of reform in different sectors of the economy. Following that was *Bureaucrats and Brainpower*, edited by Paul Seabury in 1979, which touched a broad range of social issues.

By the end of the 1970s, it was clear that the new social regulation was having an enormous impact on the U.S. economy at a time when the economy was experiencing its worst performance since the 1930s. Moreover, a growing number of studies showed that many of the new regulations, based on direct attempts to "command and control" behavior, were imposing costs far exceeding reasonable estimates of their benefits. Thus, it is not surprising that demands for reform have grown.

With a new presidential administration committed to regulatory reform, the Institute asked Eugene Bardach and Robert Kagan, both political scientists at the University of California, Berkeley, to put together a study of social regulation focused on strategies for reform. In choosing political scientists who are sensitive to the economic issues involved, we have a study that brings together both economics and politics in the search for reforms that make political and institutional, as well as economic, sense. This, after all, is the special burden of the policy analyst—in contrast to the more ideal and rarified world of the pure economist or political scientist. Few areas of public policy offer as much opportunity for reform, with as much economic and social impact.

We hope this study will expand understanding of options for reform in this critical policy area.

A. Lawrence Chickering
Executive Director
Institute for Contemporary Studies

San Francisco, California
March 1982

I

The Problems of
Social Regulation

1

EUGENE BARDACH

ROBERT A. KAGAN

Introduction

The change in regulatory reform. Imposed costs of current regulation. Why excessive regulation occurs. Three forms of excessive control. Technical difficulties. CYA behavior. The need for discretion and flexibility.

Only ten or fifteen years ago the phrase "regulatory reform" generally meant making regulation more *effective* in controlling socially harmful behavior. Economic regulation, as in the transportation or utilities fields, was usually said to have been "captured" by the industries being regulated. Most "social" or protective regulation—as in the areas of worker safety, antidiscrimination, pollution control, fire prevention, product and housing quality—was then conducted at the

3

state or local level by agencies often thought to be weak, understaffed, and unduly inclined towards cooperative rather than coercive modes of enforcement. Regulatory reform, therefore, meant making regulation "tougher." From the reformers' standpoint, legal standards were to be raised and tightened, enforcement needed to be intensified, and penalties had to be increased in severity and frequency. Citizen complainants and watchdogs needed to be given more power to influence both policy and enforcement.

This basic reform strategy strongly animated the growth of federal protective regulatory programs in the 1960s and 1970s. During this period Congress created a thicket of new agencies, including the National Highway Traffic Safety Administration (NHTSA), the Environmental Protection Agency (EPA), the Occupational Safety and Health Administration (OSHA), the Consumer Product Safety Commission (CPSC), the Equal Employment Opportunity Commission (EEOC), and the Office of Surface Mining (OSM); it also augmented the legal powers of existing agencies such as the Food and Drug Administration (FDA), the Federal Mine Safety and Health Administration (MSHA), the Federal Trade Commission (FTC), and the meat and poultry inspection units of the Department of Agriculture (USDA).

The new federal regulatory statutes behind these agencies defined ambitious health, safety, and equity goals and in some cases established strict deadlines for attaining them nationwide. The statutes frequently restricted agency discretion to moderate regulatory standards in view of economic or other social considerations. They empowered citizen complainants and advocacy groups to sue agency officials for failure to promulgate strict implemental rules or to enforce them aggressively. Regulated enterprises and their officers were subjected to much higher criminal and civil penalties for violations. Firms were obligated to seek agency permits in advance for a wide range of new facilities, and were required to undertake extensive recording and reporting of their compliance efforts and of the social and environmental consequences of their operations. Local governments, school districts, health care facilities, and business corporations failing to meet federally prescribed regulatory requirements concerning affirmative action and other goals were threatened with debarment from federal grants-in-aid and contracts.

Perhaps understandably, in the late 1970s and early 1980s "regulatory reform" has taken on an entirely different meaning than it had in the 1960s and early 1970s. Today's reform usually implies moderating the "excesses," the "over-regulation" attributed to the effectiveness-enhancing regulatory reforms of the 1960s and 1970s. The regulatory pendulum, it is argued, has swung too far, has reached the point of diminishing (or negative) returns, and must be pushed back a bit, at least until the economy as a whole has regained its forward momentum. Thus President Reagan campaigned in 1980 against "unreasonable" and "excessive" regulation, and there appeared to be widespread support for this position.

Certainly one important source of discontent with the new and tougher protective regulation is its substantive economic cost. According to the U.S. Council on Environmental Quality (1979), for example, in 1978 alone regulation-imposed costs for air and water pollution control totaled $26.8 billion. In some industries—such as electric power generation, steel production, foundries, copper smelting, electroplating, and automobile manufacturing—pollution control and in-plant emission reduction expenses dominated many firms' capital investment portfolios in the mid-1970s, displacing their capacity for investments in more modern production facilities.[1]

The less tangible social and psychological costs of regulation make up another important source of discontent. Even managers who share the goals of regulatory policy dislike the government's eagerness to specify for them the detailed means of achieving protective objectives and to require constant assurances, in reports and other forms of paperwork, that compliance in fact is taking place. Alienation is further increased when government officials—even if only a minority of them—seem to be narrow-minded or highhanded. It is no accident that public discussion of regulation is dominated by "horror stories" about supposedly rigid or antagonistic officials. Because people fear that regulatory encounters *could* be this bad, they become wary of regulation generally, even if it has not yet (or never will) become so.

These costs might be tolerable if the offsetting social benefits of regulation were evidently very large. But in a great many cases it is clear that they are, at best, modest by comparison. By 1985 water pollution control regulation will impose about $18–$19 billion per year in compliance costs, while the best estimate of benefits is only $12.3 billion (U.S. Council on Environmental Quality 1979).[2] Despite hundreds of millions of dollars spent in response to OSHA-mandated worker safety rules, several studies have indicated that the program has had, at most, only a small effect on workplace accident rates (see Bacow 1980, Mendeloff 1979, Nichols and Zeckhauser 1977). President Ford's Council on Wage and Price Stability and President Carter's Regulatory Analysis Review Group (see chapter 8 by Eads) called attention to numerous proposed regulations—such as some strip-mining restoration controls and OSHA rules requiring employers virtually to eliminate (rather than reduce) certain workplace emissions—that would entail massive compliance costs while yielding benefits only slightly above the level that would have been provided by far less costly alternatives (see Miller and Yandle 1979; *American Petroleum Institute* v. *OSHA*, 581 F.2d 493 [5th Cir. 1978]).

Not surprisingly, then, the new call for cost-cutting regulatory reform inspires many cheers. Unfortunately, it is a lot easier to cheer than to know exactly how to go about the reform itself. In the realm of economic regulation, it has been apparent that out-and-out deregulation is a good policy. The idea, for instance, that a regulatory bureaucracy could rationally set railroad and truck rates for millions of transactions and allocate service routes is absurd on the face of it. Whatever its minor imperfections, "the market" in the surface transportation sector can certainly perform a lot better than an administrative apparatus; and the case thus can easily be made to allow the market to work once again unimpeded by government regulation. Our focus in this book, however, is exclusively on protective regulation, and in this case out-and-out deregulation is not nearly so appealing. It is easy to believe that beneficent market forces will rush in spontaneously to perform *price-setting* functions that government regulators had hitherto performed, but it is a very different matter to believe that they will provide incentives for politically acceptable levels of pollution abatement, nondiscrimination, and control of waste disposal sites. After all, most protective regulation originally came into being because society's first lines of defense—market pressures and privately activated lawsuits for damages—had not been effective in deterring certain harms. Neither market mechanisms nor the slow, costly, and uncertain processes of liability law had prevented growing air and water pollution, high death rates in highway accidents, shabby treatment of the aged poor in nursing homes, or invisibly developing lung disease among many cotton mill, asbestos, and coal mine workers; thus neither mechanism now seems capable, on its own, of fully displacing direct regulatory rule making and surveillance.

Reforming protective regulation also presents more difficult challenges—technically, philosophically, and politically—than the effectiveness-oriented reform movement of years past. In the heady, low-inflation days of the late 1960s and early 1970s, the costs of compliance were not a serious concern for regulatory reformers. Industry, it was thought, could well afford to provide higher levels of protection: it could pay for the required abatement measures out of profits or pass them on to consumers (who would hardly know the difference). The necessary regulatory techniques, from this perspective, could be determined straightforwardly: establish (via technical or scientific analysis) a level of safety or purity necessary to protect human health (allowing a margin of error); mandate the devices or tests or procedures likely to guarantee attainment of that level; deploy enough inspectors and agency attorneys armed with sufficient sanctions and remedial powers to provide a strong incentive to compliance; insulate the regulators from political pressures by highly specific statutes and guaranteed participation rights for beneficiary groups. Deciding what level of enforcement, sanctions, or standards is sufficient to achieve the goals would not be simple, of course, but experience would show how much further the screws would have to be tightened.

By contrast, reforming protective regulation to excise the component that is "excessive" is intellectually more complicated, bedevilled by troublesome moral and institutional questions. How far, and in what particular areas, can "deregulation" occur without pushing the pendulum too far and unduly impairing regulatory effectiveness? How far is "too far"? That is, assuming that a totally risk-free society is neither attainable at a tolerable cost nor desirable, and that some curtailment of absolute rights to safety and health and equality is necessary, what is the appropriate stopping point? How much *should* we spend—as a society—to save a life, to increase access for the physically handicapped, to make a river or bay clean enough for edible shellfish and human recreation? Assuming that such questions about objectives can be clarified, are our administrative and political institutions capable of implementing more fine-tuned regulatory policies? Can regulators be expected to have the competence and integrity to take selective and appropriate steps toward leniency without a great deal of error, or without being subjected to devastating charges of having "sold out" or of violating citizens' human rights? What are the most cost-effective regulatory strategies and techniques (other than traditional, deterrence-oriented, legalistic enforcement) for achieving whatever level of protection we decide upon?

It must be recognized, after all, that even though curing "overregulation" currently dominates the reform agenda, political pressure for effectiveness-enhancing regulatory reforms will not simply fade away. Opinion polls continue to reveal high levels of support for protective regulation. In a highly complex and technologically dynamic economy, it is inevitable that new chemical hazards, unexpectedly dangerous new production techniques and services, and new varieties of social injustice periodically will emerge. Catastrophic accidents will slip through the gaps in existing regulatory programs to fill the evening television news, shock the national conscience, and stimulate legislative hearings that call for new preventive laws and enforcement techniques. Environmental and consumer protection groups, labor unions, and investigative reporters will continue to watchdog agencies for signs of ineffectiveness (sometimes exposing dramatic failures). Along with business firms that would profit from stricter rules for their competitors, they will also sue agencies in court and lobby for new legislation to control newly discovered hazards. The staffs of regulatory agencies, too, constantly detect gaps in their data base, ways in which some firms make end runs around existing controls, and weaknesses in their system of sanctions, and they will propose new regulations to deal with these flaws.

The tide of regulation, therefore, will continue to flow in, even if it does so with a somewhat reduced force. Thus one major challenge, addressed by the chapters in this volume, will be to devise subtle ways to keep essentially humanitarian and admirable regulatory impulses from being transformed into excessively costly and legalistic regulatory techniques; or perhaps more realistically, to hold the quantum of "excess" to a reasonably acceptable level.

WHY REGULATION TENDS TO
BECOME EXCESSIVE

Regulatory requirements can be characterized as excessive or unreasonable to the extent that (1) compliance would not materially reduce the harms in question (as when government-mandated, computer-assisted braking systems for tractor-trailer trucks generally worked poorly and failed to improve highway safety); (2) compliance would produce some additional protection (as compared, say, with a somewhat less stringent regulatory requirement) but only at disproportionately large additional cost, diverting the extra capital and human energy required from more productive uses; (3) less costly alternative requirements would be of comparable effectiveness.

All three forms of excessive regulation can occur at the level of regulatory effects considered in the aggregate (as in the case of the mandatory brake rules); or excessiveness can occur in particular sites by reason of mechanical application of a generally "good" but overinclusive rule (as when an OSHA regulation requiring certain protective clothing for workers exposed to molten metal was enforced in a humid Louisiana smelter where the company had a good burn prevention training program and the thick protective clothes would have increased the more salient health risk of heat exhaustion).

There exists no well-developed theory of when and why regulatory excessiveness is likely to occur—and hence, how it might best be avoided.[3] Our own view emphasizes the essential mismatch between the formalism of government— which we impose because we demand equal treatment before the law, due process, and the trappings of rationality—and the thriving diversity of everyday life in the great wide world. In the short space of this introduction we obviously cannot elaborate much on this very large theme, and in any case, we have done so in our recent *Going by the Book* (Bardach and Kagan 1982). We shall restrict our comments here to just two subtopics, and each of these comments will itself be brief. They concern the technical problems in implementing protective regulation and the defensive behavior of regulatory agencies and officials that exaggerates the already prevailing commitment to formalism.

TECHNICAL PROBLEMS: COMPLEXITY OF THE REGULATORY TASK

Each regulatory agency confronts a different population of regulated enterprises and a different array of potentially harmful conditions. The difficulty of the regulatory task — and hence the degree to which the agency risks being accused of ineffectiveness or unreasonableness — increases to the extent that the harms to be prevented are of uncertain degree or origin, and secondly, to the extent that the regulated enterprises to be controlled are diverse (in technology, cooperativeness, and ability to afford compliance).

Consider first the characteristics of the harms to be prevented. As noted above, the impulse to control hazards through regulation usually arises precisely because it is intrinsically difficult for citizens themselves to detect the dangers in question and to exert effective pressure for their elimination via the marketplace, collective bargaining, or lawsuits. Workers cannot tell whether the fumes they are exposed to will ultimately make them ill or at what level of control they will become safe. The woman denied a promotion cannot tell whether the supervisor's decision was based on legitimate job-related factors or on sexist prejudice. Yet, as several authors in this volume note, regulators may not be able to resolve such uncertainties either. William Havender's article, for example, describes the manifold ambiguities in determining whether chemical substances in the air or in our foods are carcinogenic, and if so, at what level they are safe.

Once we leave the laboratory, the problems may be even more ambiguous, especially at the level of individual enterprises. Just how dangerous to human health, if at all, is a particular storage site for chemical wastes, with its own unique constellation of containment methods, geological conditions, type of wastes, proximity to population centers or underground aquifers, etc.? How dangerous is the novel construction technique proposed by a particular architect? Is an electric utility's use of a standard psychological or intelligence test a *bona fide* way of assessing job applicants or is it a hidden method for continuing racial discrimination?

Nor can regulators always prescribe effective technologies for controlling certain kinds of pollution, accidents, or injustices. The greater the uncertainty concerning the degree of risk or appropriate control technology, the greater the potential for legislators and regulatory officials to resolve the uncertainty by erring on the side of "prudence," as Havender puts it—that is, by promulgating mandatory protective requirements designed to provide a "margin of error" on the side of safety, health, or equity, but a margin that in fact may be unnecessarily wide and costly to maintain.

A related technical problem involves the recurrent mismatch between standardized regulatory tools and the diversity of regulated enterprises. In a political system dedicated to "the rule of law," "due process," and "equal protection," regulators' powers of intrusion and coercion must be bounded by fixed legal rules, applicable uniformly and equally to entire classes of enterprises and operations. Even if scientific questions concerning risk and appropriate abatement methods are fairly well understood in general, in many programs the sheer diversity of enterprises to be regulated makes it almost impossible to devise a single regulatory rule or standard that will "make sense" in scores of different copper smelters, nursing homes, and food processing plants, each of which employs a somewhat different technology or mode of worker supervision. A regulation requiring the "best available control technology" for every source of air pollution in a large steel mill or chemical complex, as Michael Levin's article on EPA's "bubble policy" indicates, will be vastly more expensive and produce less reduction for some sources than for others.

Laws also must focus on objective, measurable phenomena. The ultimate goal in many social regulatory programs, however, is to induce a general attitude of "social responsibility" whereby plant managers or nursing home administrators are continually alert and sensitive to all of the diverse harmful acts that may result from their technologies and their employees' activities. A regulation that would instruct a plant manager, say, to "be alert to previously unrecognized sources of danger to employees and instill in employees a positive attitude toward safety" would clearly be unenforceable, and would probably violate due process norms as well. Instead, regulations are directed to things the enforcement official can measure or see on his intermittent visits to the site or whose absence can be easily proved—enduring physical features (such as machine guards or sulfur dioxide scrubbers), fixed inputs (such as maintenance of a specified patient/staff ratio in a nursing home, or a designated number of minorities in a work force), and permanent records (such as mandatory charts kept by nurses or quality control engineers, documenting their activities). These specified facilities, ratios, and signatures, however, are only proxies for—rough correlates of—the underlying attitudes of carefulness, attentiveness, cleanliness, fairness, etc., that we actually care about. And inevitably those correlations will be imperfect. Some nursing homes will be just fine regardless of their patient/staff ratio—and some will not (see Vladeck 1980). A certain wire-stranding machine may be entirely safe, even if it fails to comply with a general rule that re-

quires double-interlock guards for all moving machinery in
all factories, or it might be dangerous for reasons not specified in any regulations (see Bardach and Kagan 1982).

Similarly, the law usually is blind to the fact that regulated
enterprises often differ greatly in their attitudes toward regulation, in their ability to afford specialized compliance
staffs, and in the quality of their maintenance and super-
visory systems. Hence mandatory precautions and documentary reports A through M, elaborated by an agency step
by step in response to accidents or risks detected in a few
manufacturing plants, will end up being overelaborate for
better plants, some of which could safely eliminate steps H
through L because of the protections provided by their quality control or accident prevention system taken as a whole.
Unannounced inspections and automatic penalties, as prescribed by law, may be necessary for a small proportion of
recalcitrant firms, but not for the much larger proportion of
firms disposed to respond more cooperatively to regulatory
initiatives. The greater the diversity of regulated enterprises—in terms of technology, attitudes toward cooperation, and organizational or financial capacity to control the
risks in question—the greater the probability that regulatory requirements and penalties will be overinclusive and
hence excessive in a considerable proportion of cases.

CYA BEHAVIOR

The diversity of regulated enterprises and uncertainty about
the risks they pose do not necessarily lead to excessive regulation. In theory, legislators could decide to do nothing until
more definitive information about risks had accumulated.
They could grant enforcement officials discretion to apply
general regulatory standards in a flexible manner, as Paul
Danaceau's chapter suggests, tailoring regulatory require-

ments to the particular combination of risks and costs present in each enterprise. But such a cautious and flexible approach to regulation, while reducing the possibility that regulation will be *excessively strict*, increases the probability of the opposite error—the regulators may later be shown to have been *inappropriately lenient*. For example, a regulatory agency that declines to recall a possibly carcinogenic pesticide (or a possibly defective automobile model), on the basis of preliminary but inconclusive research or reports, is exposed to the possibility that research completed three years later will show conclusively that the substance probably caused an estimated number of cases of cancer or chromosomal damage (or so many highway deaths) that could have been prevented by an earlier recall.

When confronted by such a choice, regulators are inclined, as William Havender puts it, to a "worst case" analysis of the situation; that is, to prevent the worst—even if the most improbable—outcome for which they could be held accountable. They take this stance because the political environment of regulators typically punishes them more for failing to prevent harms to life and limb than for failing to permit innovation or to facilitate food production or to lower the cost of automotive transportation. An agency's primary mission is to prevent harm, and its "worst case" is therefore to appear to have acted so as to *permit* harm rather than prevent it. Indeed, the nightmare of most regulatory agencies is a scandal revealing that enforcement officials have been dilatory about enforcement, too accepting of industry-supplied data or technical excuses, or involved in outright corruption—a particularly embarrassing form of the "inappropriately lenient" error.[4]

The best defense against scandal is an administrative style whereby enforcement officials are expected to prove their diligence by logging a high number of inspections, citations, abatement orders, and other enforcement actions. Inspectors are instructed to guard against co-optation by adhering strictly to the formal steps or checklists prescribed in their manual of regulations, rather than negotiating with representatives of regulated entities. In bureaucratic argot, this is the "cover your ass" (CYA) syndrome whereby bureaucratic defensiveness leads to an ostensibly aggressive insistence on literal compliance with regulations, submissions of formal documentation to support any factual claim or discretionary act (such as issuing a permit or allowing an exception), and extensive reporting and data-gathering requirements—much of which is in fact unnecessary to provide added protection for the public in the particular case, and hence is experienced as "red tape" or as "nit-picking."

By contrast, agencies find it difficult to establish bureaucratic measures of how "reasonable" they have been. Few agencies publish annual reports showing how much money and aggravation they have saved individual enterprises by extending a deadline here, expediting a permit application there, or waiving a legally required report or test or protective device that is unnecessary under certain circumstances. Indeed, for an agency to encourage such informal exceptions or modifications would be to subvert legal and bureaucratic norms of regularity while providing an opening for the exercise of discretion, which sooner or later may lead to the very kind of error, co-optation, or corruption that is the stuff of scandal—and scandal, in turn, threatens the tenure of the agency's top officials.

Moreover, agencies typically have few positive organizational incentives to favor "reasonableness" over stringency. Avoiding regulatory unreasonableness entails new costs for the regulators. For example, a commitment to flexible regulation, whereby regulatory officials would selectively relax requirements for less risky situations or more reliable enterprises, means that the agency would have to win appropriations for—and recruit—a more highly trained and carefully supervised staff. To grant exceptions or devise more finely tuned regulatory categories, as Timothy

Sullivan's article indicates, imposes costly information-gathering, administrative, and documentary burdens on the agency.

Yet as an organization, the agency typically will receive few benefits in return for assuming such additional burdens. The unreasonableness that stems from excessive regulation creates thousands of small bits of unnecessary expense for hundreds of regulated enterprises. For the agency to seek to reduce those costs via more flexible regulation would benefit those enterprises and the nation as a whole, but would create concentrated costs (as well as risks of undue leniency errors) for the regulatory organization itself.

From time to time these perverse incentives can perhaps be mitigated or reversed by capable organizational leaders concerned about curtailing the excessive portion of regulation. They may be able to combat entrenched bureaucratic insistence on administrative consistency and convince regulatory staffs that there are real benefits to be garnered from a more flexible and cost-conscious regulatory style — principally, less wasteful conflict and costly litigation and more opportunities to advance social goals by constructive, cooperation-eliciting exchanges with regulated enterprises.

Nevertheless, any reform strategy that depends on "leadership" rests on a weak reed. Under conditions where external advocacy groups and legislative overseers suspect that a regulatory bureaucracy is susceptible to corruption or to co-optation by regulated enterprises, there will be strong pressures on regulatory leaders to guard that flank by insisting on a more inflexible regulatory style that creates at least the appearance of toughness.

TWO REFORM STRATEGIES

Much that is excessive about protective regulation springs, at one level, from the overinclusiveness of centrally formulated rules applied broadly to enterprises that differ in technology, attitudes, capabilities, potential for harm, and costs of abatement. In some degree this problem arises, as we have said, from the sheer technical difficulty of writing suitably differentiated rules, and in some degree it arises from the inflexibility that our legal and moral norms impose on governmental conduct. Whatever the constellation of causes, though, one obvious remedy for the problem is to institutionalize a certain amount of official discretion to mitigate the effects of overinclusive rules either at the field enforcement level or in the course of higher-level appeals and reviews. This could mean creating explicit legal authority for inspectors to overlook certain violations, authorizing enforcement officials (in conjunction with regulated parties) to work out alternative means of reaching regulatory goals, introducing more explicit bargaining over compliance schedules, transforming inspectors from "cops" into "consultants" in some areas, or any of a number of other things. Most of the chapters in part II of this book search for ways to introduce more flexibility and discretion into conventional, command-and-control, protective regulation. Some, like those by Levin, Grumbly, and Danaceau, emphasize action at the field level. Sullivan and Pape, on the other hand, explore the more traditional avenue to differentiating and customizing regulation, that is, writing better rules in the first place. Eads's chapter 8 reviews recent attempts to improve "regulatory oversight," the process whereby particular proposed regulations can be blocked or modified if reviewers outside the proposing agencies find them unreasonable or ill advised.

We have also emphasized the political aspects of excessive regulation, in particular the constraints on flexibility that we identify with CYA behavior on the part of regulatory officials. It does no good to endow regulators with discretion, after all, if they are too intimidated to use it. One way to solve this problem is to shield regulatory officials from the rather stringent demands for accountability to which the public sector is presently subjected. But what sort of shield would be strong enough—and at the same time would be permeable enough—to leave just the right residue of accountability? The chapters in part III explore the possibilities of privatization, of removing certain regulatory functions from the public sector altogether and permitting private parties to perform them. Bacow writes about collective bargaining over worker health and safety; O'Hare, about the potential for government to mandate disclosure of information that consumers, workers, and citizens could then use to protect themselves; and we ourselves write about the regulatory potential of litigation and the threat of litigation under improved institutions of the liability law. Ferreira examines the role of insurance industry practices as a form of private regulation, and Eads charts the rise of quality control units within corporations that also act as regulators. Bardach concludes the section with some observations about the dilemma of exchanging a lesser burden of inspectorial visits under direct command-and-control regulation for a potentially greater paperwork burden under various forms of privatized regulation.

Of course, no reforms are initiated or implemented in a political and organizational vacuum. At present there is widespread agreement that regulatory reform is desirable. But this agreement remains at the level of principle only. When it comes down to details, consensus decays and impediments loom in every direction. Our concluding chapter discusses how prevalent images of social responsibility and a pervasive emphasis on accountability pose significant political and bureaucratic obstacles to reform. Rather than ending on a pessimistic note, however, we add as a postscript a "Regulatory Reform Wish List" that reflects the more optimistic and constructive spirit of the earlier chapters.

2

WILLIAM R. HAVENDER

Assessing and Controlling Risks

Research on health hazards: epidemiology, animal bioassays, short-term tests. Centralized regulatory agencies. The nature of regulation: lethargy, maximin thinking, costs, increased risks, the information gap, agency myopia and redistributionism, premature judgments. The need for alternatives in the private sector.

The last ten years have witnessed a florescent concern with hazards to our health and with the regulatory measures instituted to deal with them. In fact, it seems almost daily that something else in our food or water or work environment is found to cause cancer (today's newspaper, for example, reports that newspaper ink does so [*San Francisco Chronicle*, 17 August 1981]), and these alarms frequently serve as the basis for increased government action to "protect" the public. At the same time, the public is growing weary of this ceaseless crying of "wolf" and impatient with science, which seems able only to raise the alarm but never to solve the problem. This discussion focuses on what science can tell us about these hazards, why science cannot, in truth, presently solve them, and how regulatory agencies handle the problem of decision making in the context of these uncertainties.

Health risks are commonly divided into acute and chronic. Acute risks are those that result from one or a few exposures, and in which the health effect is apparent immediately or shortly after exposure occurs; poisoning is an instance. Acute hazards do not usually pose intractable problems of public policy because the connection between cause and effect typically is clear, allowing us to assign responsibility for the hazards and to learn relatively quickly how to avoid or minimize them. Chronic hazards, on the other hand, are those where the health effect shows up only after many years of exposure. Examples are lung cancer, which develops only after decades of smoking, and bladder cancer, one main cause of which is thought to be occupational exposure to certain industrial chemicals over a score of years or so. The policy situation with regard to chronic health hazards is very different than with acute hazards since, as we shall see, the area of uncertainty is much, much larger.

CANCER

The chronic hazard of greatest current concern is cancer (although another that is starting to emerge in public discussion is mutagenicity—the long-term harm to generations yet to come). Several factors account for the urgency of this concern and for the difficulty in developing a consensus on cancer policy. First, cancer is a common disease, and is largely incurable. Some 20 to 25 percent of us can expect to develop cancer of one type or another. This is a much higher proportion than used to be the case, although this increase is *not* due to there being a sudden epidemic of cancer attributable to our industrial society. Rather, it is a consequence of the great reduction in mortality from infectious diseases (tuberculosis, diphtheria, pneumonia, smallpox, polio, and others) that public health measures and modern medicine (especially antibiotics and vaccines) have achieved in this century. Almost everyone now expects to reach the age when cancer, which is largely a disease of the elderly, can develop. Cancer incidence figures that have been corrected for the larger numbers of people living into old age (this is called "age-adjusting") show that, with one exception, the overall incidence of cancer has been rather steady or slightly decreasing since 1933, the first year for which all states had to notify the causes of all deaths centrally (Doll and Peto 1981, section 4.1 and appendix D). The exception has been the large rise in respiratory cancer, for which smoking, not "modern industrial pollution and chemical exposures," is by far the largest cause. Still, the fact that one in four of us will now, in the absence of infectious diseases, get cancer accounts for a large part of the enhanced public concern.

Second, it is now well established that our chances of getting cancer are highly influenced by environmental agents. This proposition is deduced from the fact that the incidences of particular types of cancer vary greatly from place to place around the globe, and also from time to time. Liver cancer, for example, is common in parts of sub-Saharan Africa, but is rare in the United States. Breast cancer is common here but rare in Japan, whereas stomach cancer is common there and uncommon here. That this is not due to a genetic difference is shown by the fact that Japanese immigrants within one generation develop the cancer patterns typical of the United States. Lung cancer, seldom seen at the turn of the century, is now the leading cause of cancer death among men and is rapidly on the rise among women as well, reflecting the historic smoking patterns among the sexes. Persons of Scandinavian and Celtic descent do not have high rates of skin cancer when living in Northern climes, but they do when they move to the tropics where they are exposed to more sun. By a careful comparison of such variations, the World Health Organization concluded in 1964 that "the majority of human cancer" was influenced by "extrinsic factors" (World Health Organization 1964). This early estimate has been updated and confirmed; currently the best estimate is that 75 or 80 percent of human cancer in the United States is susceptible to environmental factors (Doll and Peto 1981, p. 1205). This fact raises the hope that cancer, if not curable, might be preventable, and it has led to extremely diligent attempts to identify the causative agents.[1] It has also resulted in a vast expansion of the regulatory apparatus set up to deal with these hazards.

The third distinguishing feature about cancer (and this is where most uncertainties arise in trying to devise reasonable policies) is that its causes are not usually easy to identify. Despite the diligence of the effort to find causes, only limited (though extremely important) success has been achieved. Consensus has been reached on the main cause of lung cancer (namely, smoking) and on a variety of occupational cancers (Doll and Peto 1981, tables 11, 19), but in these cases the proportional increase caused by single factors has been quite large, and this does not seem to be the case for many common cancers (e.g., breast and colon cancer). Another difficulty is the stochastic, or statistical, nature of cancer; that is, among a group of similarly exposed persons, only some of them—seemingly at random—will actually develop cancer. Not every smoker of high-tar cigarettes contracts lung cancer (in fact, only about one in five does), and not every worker who worked with asbestos comes down with mesothelioma (a form of cancer associated almost exclusively with asbestos exposure). An even greater problem in connecting causes and effects is posed by the long latency of cancer, where a period of one or more decades passes between the commencement of exposure to a causative agent and the manifestation of symptoms. This makes it difficult not only to tease out true causes and hence to assign responsibility, but also to see improvements as a consequence of policy changes. Low-tar cigarettes, for instance, have been available now for many years, and yet there is still no proof that they do in fact reduce the occurrence of lung cancer by a substantial degree. (This is by no means a trivial point, since we don't know yet whether the right things were taken out, nor do we know that the flavoring agents added back in won't themselves prove to be carcinogenic.) Dealing with these uncertainties can result in enormous costs to society if unbounded "prudence" is the tactic chosen to deal with them.

There are three main kinds of evidence that are used to try to establish whether or not a chemical poses a cancer hazard to humans—namely, epidemiology, animal bioassays, and short-term tests. Each has advantages and disadvantages.

EPIDEMIOLOGY

Epidemiology is the study in humans of the patterns of occurrence of disease and of exposure to various suspect agents. This tool has the great virtue that it directly identifies *human* risk factors, and once a carcinogenic agent has been identified, there are no further fundamental problems of interpretation as there are with animal bioassays and short-term tests. But it suffers from several inherent defects. It is,

for one thing, not a very sensitive technique, which means
that it is difficult to establish small effects with statistical
confidence ("small," of course, means proportionally; this
could still translate into many thousands of cases annually
for a sizable population). Partly, this is due to the difficulty of
assembling reliable information on large numbers of people,
whether by means of interviews or examination of medical
records. Partly, it is due to the difficulty of eliminating "confounding variables" from the comparison groups (i.e.,
eliminating those differences between the groups to be compared that may be spuriously generating or concealing a
causal correlation). This can be a problem even when the
carcinogenic effect under investigation is large, but when it
is at best small (such as the suspected effect of saccharin on
bladder cancer or of hair dyes on breast cancer), the problem
can be insuperable. Using large numbers of subjects and taking great care in matching up the comparison populations
can reduce the problem. Epidemiology's usefulness is also
diminished by the difficulty of assembling true zero-dose
control groups. If we wanted to test, for example, the hypothesis that caffeine is carcinogenic, it would be hard to find
a sizable group of people with *no* exposure at all to caffeine,
since it is a constituent in coffee, tea, Coke, and other common foods as well. One would have to look at groups like the
Seventh-Day Adventists, but since they would differ from
other people on many additional variables, confounding
might occur.

Complicating the limited sensitivity of epidemiology is
cancer's long latency, which means that to study people who
currently have cancer entails asking questions about their
personal habits and occupational and medicinal exposures
two or three or four decades in the past. People's memories
that far back are not usually very accurate — (How many
diet pops did *you* drink in 1957? What hair coloring did you
use in 1960? Was that dental X-ray in 1962 or 1963? Were
you drinking chlorinated water in 1964? Oh, you moved to

New Jersey in 1968 and lived near a chemical dump? What, you did *all* of these things?)—and estimates of dose tend, of course, to be even less reliable. Multiple exposure to suspect agents is common (so would it be the saccharin in 1957, the hair dyes of 1960, the X-rays of 1962—1963, the trihalomethanes of 1964, or the dump seepages of 1968 to which the breast cancer of 1981 should be attributed?). The picture can become even more complex because of the possibility of interaction between suspect agents (smoking, for example, greatly increases the already elevated chance that asbestos workers will develop lung cancer, so should we attribute it to the smoking or to the asbestos?).

A final, serious limitation of epidemiology is that it cannot, of course, help us with new chemicals to which humans have never before been exposed. About a thousand new ones are introduced into commerce each year; hence, this is a significant limitation.

Despite these shortcomings, epidemiology can be used—even when it has yielded a negative or marginal result—to set an upper limit on the risk to humans of substances to which they have been exposed for adequately long periods. For there would be certain levels of carcinogenic effect that *could* have been seen in the study with statistical confidence had they been present. Not seeing these levels, then, at least says that the suspect substance is not a "strong" carcinogen; it is at most "weak." The actual meaning to be attached to the words "strong" and "weak" would, of course, depend on the details of the particular study.

Finally, it must be noted to epidemiology's credit that every human carcinogen now known has been identified by means of epidemiology. This tool has established the very phenomenon of human cancers resulting from environmental exposures commencing decades before clinical symptoms were evident.

ANIMAL BIOASSAYS

Because of the ineluctable limits of epidemiology, surrogate means are sought for identifying human hazards, and the predominant surrogate currently in use is animal bioassays. These are studies where the suspect chemical is administered to laboratory animals, usually rats or mice, and the animals are then monitored for the growth of tumors. Typically, the chemical is given to the animals in their food or water (or by stomach tube if the substance is unpalatable) for long periods, often for their entire lifetime. The key advantages of bioassays are that rodents live only about two years, reducing the time involved to see a tumorigenic effect from decades to two or three years, and that one can deliberately test any specific chemical of interest—in particular, new chemicals under consideration to be introduced into commerce. The disadvantages of bioassays, however, are substantial. Even these tests, for example, are not inexpensive—$1,000 an animal for a lifetime study is a typical cost —so that a standard-sized test on a single chemical involving an untreated (control) group and low- and high-dose groups with 50 animals of each sex at each dose (300 animals in all) will cost well in excess of $250,000. Yet even such a test would have limited sensitivity; it would probably never pick up a chemical that caused a 1 percent incidence of tumors in high-dose males, and such a chemical might well be declared "safe" even though it would be capable of causing many tens of thousands of cases of cancer a year in humans.

It is to compensate for this limited sensitivity that high doses are commonly employed in animal bioassays. In general, the incidence of cancer will rise as the dose increases, up to the point where the animals are dying off prematurely from simple poisoning. Therefore, to make a bioassay as sensitive as possible, a dose will be included that is the maximum the animals can tolerate over their lifetimes without succumbing early from poisoning. This is the so-called "maximum tolerated dose" (MTD).

But while this procedure undoubtedly maximizes the chance that even a weak carcinogen will be picked up, it introduces other sources of uncertainty, particularly when the only dose yielding tumors is the MTD. Perhaps the physiological events taking place in dose-stressed animals do not occur at all—or at least not in proportion—in normal animals, so that the outcome observed in high-dose animals would not be valid at the much lower body doses common in human exposures.

This reasoning leads us directly to the vexing problem of dose response; specifically, to the question of whether the risk at low dose can be estimated by simple extrapolation downwards along a straight line from the risk observed at high dose. Such a risk/dose relation is called a "linear" dose response. And while this may be a reasonable guess when the extrapolated dose is not very far from the experimentally observed dose, most scientists are very uncomfortable with relying on such an estimate when extrapolating to doses one hundred or one thousand times smaller than the experimental dose, as is often the case. The critical question is whether one or more inflection points (or a threshold) exist in the dose-response curve, in which case the true low-dose risk could be much smaller than under the linear assumption.[2]

In theory, one can readily design experiments to find out what actually happens to the cancer rate at low doses comparable to human exposures; but the incidence of tumors would shrink, and much larger numbers of animals would have to be used in order to detect these tumors with statistical confidence. This would mean testing with thousands of animals and with multiple doses ranging down to the dose of interest, a procedure which would be prohibitively expensive, not to mention logistically difficult (e.g., acquiring thousands of animals of identical genetic background and age all at more or less the same time, labeling them and maintaining records, and so forth). In any case, the test would pertain only to the chemical of immediate interest, so it would have to be repeated for every chemical investigated. This is clearly infeasible on a regular basis, and so we are reduced for practical purposes to making extrapolations—i.e., guesses —about the expected risk at low doses.[3]

Many thousands of words have been devoted to the problem of estimating low-dose risks from limited high-dose data, and some highly sophisticated statistical models for extrapolation have been advanced. The hard fact remains, however, that the verifiable dose effects are similarly compatible with all of them (not surprising, since the models were developed to fit the available data) and thus cannot distinguish between them; yet the models differ by factors of hundreds or thousands in their estimates of the size of the risk to be seen at very low doses. Of all the various models, the linear one is not only by far the simplest mathematically, but it also has the virtue of being the most "prudent"; that is, if its estimates are in error, they are virtually certain to err on the side of overpredicting the true risk. This means that if a low-dose risk estimated by means of the linear model is considered to be negligible, then one can feel quite secure in this judgment. For this reason, the linear model is often adopted as a prudent way of dealing with this profound uncertainty. When, however, the estimate yielded by the linear assumption is not so negligible (as is the case with saccharin, where the Food and Drug Administration [FDA] estimated an annual incidence of about 1,200 cases of bladder cancer per year in the U.S. population [Office of Technology Assessment 1977, p. 88]), the procedure leads to dispute.

The other intractable problem with animal bioassays concerns whether rats and mice can be regarded simply as "little men," or whether there can be, in any specific instance, an important physiological difference in the way rodents and higher primates handle a carcinogen. This uncertainty concerns, as does the dose question, both the qualitative outcome (is or is not this chemical a carcinogen in humans?) and the quantitative outcome (can we assess the degree of risk to humans from the degree of risk seen in rodents?). Again, because of the limitations of epidemiology discussed earlier, arguments run on both sides of this question, with science not being able to offer a definitive judgment. The fact that all but one of the proven human carcinogens (the exception is arsenic) have been found also to cause cancer in laboratory animals favors the "little men" argument, at least qualitatively; but the crucial question is, of course, the reverse: can we expect, just because we have found conditions under which a chemical will cause cancer in rodents, that it will pose a true risk in man? There are by now several instances in which epidemiology has been unable to confirm cancer risks to humans suggested by rodent tests (e.g., saccharin, hair dyes, DDT),[4] although because of the limited sensitivity of epidemiology the possibility of small elevations in risk cannot be ruled out. The question becomes even more unsettling when one cogitates upon the peculiarities of the experimental conditions under which carcinogenicity in animals has often been established (e.g., high-dose regimens or, as in the saccharin experiments, *in utero* exposure). Hundreds of chemicals, including table sugar, pepper, eggs, and Vitamin D, have by now been shown to cause cancer in animals under one or another set of experimental conditions.[5] Is it really reasonable to assume on this basis that these substances imperil mankind?

One would feel more confident in making such a prediction if a chemical had been tested in several mammalian species and were carcinogenic in all of them; that is, the qualitative result in any one of them could be used to predict correctly the results in the others. It is uncommon, however, to have results on the same substance in more than two species (usually rats and mice), and even for these two species, discordant results are often seen.[6]

Nevertheless, animal bioassays are the best means we have for assessing a chemical's carcinogenic hazard in those instances where we have only poor epidemiologic data or none at all. Some chemicals are such strong and reproducible animal carcinogens that there is consensus among scientists about their hazards, but in general there is a continuity of results grading smoothly down to situations at the margin of statistical significance, or where there is reason to believe the MTD has been exceeded, or where there is dispute among pathologists whether the growths seen should be classified as tumors or not.

One highly important fact to come out of animal tests, and one that has yet to be incorporated into routine regulatory decision making, is that the relative potencies of different chemicals—defined as the dose needed to produce cancer in half of the test animals—vary over a millionfold range (Ames et al. 1982). In other words, a dose of aflatoxin (the strongest animal carcinogen yet found) would cause a million times as many cases of cancer as the same dose of saccharin (the weakest carcinogen so far detected in animals). That chemicals' intrinsic carcinogenic hazard can vary over this enormous scale is a fact of central importance for sensible policymaking, since it forces one to set priorities and to pay attention to considerations of cost-effectiveness.

SHORT-TERM TESTS

In the last few years a new group of human surrogates has been under development—namely, bacteria and mammalian cells in tissue culture. These are used in "short-term" tests that examine the capacity of the test substances to induce mutations or other genetic damage. These tests have a vast advantage over animal bioassays in that they take only a few days or weeks to carry out and they cost only a few thousand dollars per chemical. By far the best known and best validated of these is the so-called "Ames" test (named for its inventor, Bruce Ames), which seems to detect some 90 percent of chemicals that have been shown to cause cancer in animal bioassays and to have a low incidence of "false positives" (i.e., the obtaining of positive Ames test results for a substance that has been adequately tested in animals and found not to be carcinogenic [McCann and Ames 1976, pp. 950−54]). Still, certain classes of chemicals are missed by the Ames test, such as hormonally active carcinogens like diethylstilbestrol (DES), carcinogens that act by means of chronic physical irritation like asbestos, and some chlorinated hydrocarbons (which category includes many pesticides such as DDT) that are proven carcinogens in animal tests or humans. Dioxin, for instance, which is the highly dangerous contaminant in Agent Orange and the banned herbicide 2,4,5−T, is an extremely potent carcinogen in rodent tests but is Ames negative. Some short-term tests detect substances missed by others, so that a carefully assembled "battery" may be the best way of utilizing them. But just what the best composition of the battery should be is a matter still under discussion (Hollstein et al. 1979, pp. 289−356). Currently, the prime utility of short-term tests is in preliminary screening of large numbers of chemicals for exceptionally mutagenic (hence, presumptively carcinogenic) ones, particularly those contained in complex mixtures of chemicals (such as urine, cigarette smoke, drinking water, air pollutants, foods, or cosmetics). Once suspicions have been raised by such a screen, full-scale animal tests can be scheduled.

These are the main sorts of evidence, then, that are used for inferring whether a chemical poses a carcinogenic risk to humans. Currently, short-term tests are in use in thousands of industrial and university laboratories, and the National Cancer Institute has a vast testing program under way in rats and mice, with a hundred chemicals placed under test each year. In addition, industry is carrying out a large number of animal tests, as marketing approvals are sought for new drugs and other consumer products. And, of course, a great variety of epidemiology studies are in progress at any given time. Thus, decision makers are faced with a large and steadily growing volume of information, with only some of it (namely, positive epidemiology findings) capable of establishing human risk unambiguously, and the bulk of it raising questions about the imminence of human hazard but not clearly proving it. This evidence forms a continuum, without clear decision boundaries, ranging from chemicals that show strong carcinogenic activity in several species to disputed results in others, frequently with discordant results between species or sexes or strains, or between animal tests and short-term tests, or between suggestive animal results and decades of safe use in human experience. Science is really at its limits in most of these cases and cannot yield a single, clear verdict concerning human risk. Decision-makers must cope with this reality.

It may be that the best use of scientific evidence will not be for yes/no decisions but will be for *ranking* hazards — that is, one might use uniform assumptions for the dose and species extrapolation problems, assign weights to the various kinds of available evidence, and then rank chemicals in terms of intrinsic hazard. This could then be combined with estimates of current human exposure to get a rough sense of the *relative* human hazard posed by different chemicals. Uncertainties would exist, of course, even for this limited interpretation of the evidence, but one's chances of establishing sensible priorities would probably be higher than if these relative differences were ignored altogether.

A LOOK AT THE REGULATORY RECORD

Given these uncertainties, but given also the urgent need to do something prospectively to guard against hazards from the great numbers of new chemicals, what institutional means will work best? The reflex response of the past years has been increased surveillance and rule making from Washington in the form of various agencies—the FDA, the Occupational Safety and Health Administration (OSHA), the Environmental Protection Agency (EPA), the National Highway Traffic Safety Administration (NHTSA), the Consumer Product Safety Commission (CPSC), and the like. This is not necessarily the only way these problems can be dealt with, although—with the characteristic mix of hubris, naiveté, and zeal to do both good and well that is endemic to social planners—this was the general approach that was favored. Identifying a problem (usually precipitated by a crisis) led reflexively to setting up an agency authority to deal with it (clean air, clean water, toxic chemicals, toxic dumps, food additives, new drugs, worker safety, and so forth), but with little thoughtful examination of what spontaneous corrective mechanisms might already be in place or how their effectiveness might be increased by comparatively modest reforms, and also without much thought given to the actual probability that Washington bureaus *could* and *would* solve the problems. Besides, there was also the strategic difficulty of contrasting a known flawed condition (the crisis did, after all, occur) with a hypothetically flawless unknown condition (the new agency). But now we have had a decade's experience (or more) with these bureaus, and there is a fair-sized body of practical fact that we can use to test the hypothetically ideal against the real. As we shall see, these facts feed the growth of doubt and lead to speculation about the possible role of alternative institutions in handling these problems. Could insurance companies become major factors in monitoring and reducing public risks? Could the courts? Could the prospect of being sued so wonderfully "concentrate the mind" as to lead corporate decision-makers to take optimal account of prospective public risks, including chronic ones? These questions will be examined fleetingly here, and in more detail by other contributors to this book.

The last decade's experience with regulatory agencies has made clear certain features about the true nature of regulation:

(1) It is typically slow.

(2) Agencies tend to deal with uncertainty by a "maximin" strategy, i.e., by imagining the worst case that could possibly occur and devising a regulation to minimize the damage from this worst case.

(3) Economic considerations tend to be resisted.

(4) *Increases* in risk that are brought about by delay tend to be ignored, as are increases in risk that result *from* new regulations, particularly when these risks fall outside the authoring agencies' mandated purview.

(5) Agencies tend to ignore information that cannot readily be analytically or scientifically articulated, even when this information may be highly relevant to the issue in question.

(6) Agencies' perspective tends to be central, and hence utilitarian. This can lead to lumping some persons' risks with other persons' benefits, hence obscuring great diversity in individual circumstances, and also to deliberate efforts at redistributing costs and benefits.

(7) Agencies are prone to basing regulations on premature and unconfirmed science.

The first of these points—that regulatory decision making is characteristically slow—is richly documented. For example, a typical review period for a "New Drug Application" (NDA) at the FDA (a formality required before a new drug can be marketed, and which is submitted after several years of previous research and clinical trials have been completed to support the drug's safety and efficacy in humans) is two to three years, despite a nominal legal limit of 180 days. This is two to three years during which patients are denied the benefits of the new drug, and it is also two to three years during which the patent clock is ticking (Quirk 1980, pp. 226–32). And OSHA, in its ten years of existence, has developed standards for only 20 carcinogens, though several hundred suspected carcinogens are in industrial use and many questionable new ones are introduced each year. The process of developing a rule has typically taken three to five years from first announcement to the end of judicial review. And while the Clean Air Act, passed in 1970, required the EPA to list and then regulate all hazardous air pollutants, it has so far regulated only 4 (asbestos, beryllium, mercury, and vinyl chloride) and listed 3 others (benzene, arsenic, and radionuclides). The Toxic Substances Control Act (TOSCA) of 1976 gave the EPA authority to regulate the uses of the 55,000 chemicals currently in industrial and commercial use. But of a priority list of 42 substances selected for EPA review, only 3 have so far been considered by EPA.[7]

Part of the reason for this apparent lethargy is procedural. OSHA, for example, issues regulations by means of a process that is "Byzantine in its complexity," and that is very open and full of points of access and challenge. Having gathered the information to support a rule, OSHA publishes a proposed regulation in the *Federal Register*. Both environmental and inflationary impact statements must be drafted (the latter under executive orders from presidents Ford and Carter). Public hearings are then held at which any interested party may appear, and afterwards there is a period during which "posthearing comments" may be filed. Then OSHA, on the basis of this record, must determine a final regulation to be filed in the *Federal Register*, together with a "statement of reasons" detailing the rationale behind each clause. This final regulation then typically must undergo court review, possibly up to the Supreme Court (Kelman 1980, pp. 244–46). Comparable procedures are required of the other regulatory agencies as well.

But another cause of the characteristic delay is the sheer

mass of the information that must be transmitted to these agencies and evaluated by them. Much of this information has to do with ascertaining the existing "state" of affairs. OSHA's mandate, for instance, covers *every* firm with at least one employee, from great factories to the corner grocery. Some 4 million establishments are covered (Kelman 1980, p. 246) and, in theory at least, all of these must be inspected and monitored for hazards and for continuing compliance with regulations. The TOSCA requires the EPA to inventory the 55,000 existing chemicals in use and the 1,000 or so new ones added each year—together with information on their toxicity, carcinogenicity, mutagenicity, and teratogenicity (capacity to cause birth defects) — and to monitor their production, use, and disposal. Under the provisions of the 1970 Clean Air Act and the Federal Water Pollution Control Act of 1972, the EPA must set standards and monitor air and water effluents from tens of thousands of factories across the country. Pesticide use by farmers must be monitored and controlled.

Added to this enormous informational task in simply ascertaining the state of things is the collection and evaluation of all the—typically ambiguous—scientific information concerning each of these chemicals in order to determine tolerable exposure standards. Much of this scientific information has to be generated by requiring experiments to be done, so another reason for delay enters. A typical NDA for the FDA can involve some 200 volumes (and may require several revisions) that must be evaluated before marketing approval can be granted (Quirk 1980, p. 207). Clearly, attention can be paid to only a small subset of the submitted information, and even so, delay is usual.[8]

A second feature of regulatory decision making is that it does not really deal with the true ambiguities of many issues. Instead, a simplifying strategy is used that resolves disputed issues on the side of what is called, to describe it by its hoped-for results, "prudence." That is, the worst possible alternative is assumed on every disputed point and the regulation is framed to palliate this worst case. The problem with this strategy is that instances where the evidence for human hazard is extremely weak but where there is a large range of uncertainty are treated with the attentiveness and determination properly reserved for serious, imminent hazards. A blatant example of this tendency is OSHA's "generic" carcinogen policy that aims to diminish the scientific basis for challenging its rulings by declaring certain recurring, fundamental scientific issues to be "settled" on the side of "prudence." Such general determinations are not challengeable in the course of a specific rule making, no matter what pertinent evidence might be available in a specific case, and the agency hopes thereby to speed rule making along. OSHA thus recognizes no such thing as an overdose in animal tests; benign growths are given equal weight with malignant tumors; rats and mice are considered comparable to humans in their response to a carcinogen; "safe doses" for humans are presumed not to exist; a single positive test in any species outweighs any amount of negative evidence in other species or from actual experience in people; and substances that merely "promote" are regulated as though they were as dangerous as totipotent chemicals (*Federal Register*, 22 January 1980, pp. 5001–296; *Regulation*, March/April 1980, pp. 4–7). The sum of such decisions will, of course, inflate both the number of substances determined to present a hazard and the perceived degree of that hazard (and hence the costs of protecting against it). The EPA has indicated that it will follow OSHA's lead in these matters.

While such an attitude is understandable from the point of view of the agency decision-maker (and indeed it is arguable in the abstract that, given the inherent uncertainties, it is better to err always on the side of prudence), it is by no means clear that ignoring true ambiguities and treating every case as though it were a great hazard will lead to optimal public policy. For one thing, assuming the worst on every disputed point means that substances whose hazards are merely unclear will get lumped with those that *are* serious dangers, thus causing limited regulatory resources to be scattered rather than concentrated on the most urgent needs. For another, the strategy leads to great expense.

Dependence upon maximin thinking in the regulatory process is common. A recent article in *Science* describes the battle over approval of a new artificial sweetener, aspartame, which was finally approved by the FDA in the summer of 1981 after eight years of effort by its manufacturer, G. D. Searle & Company. This substance is composed of two amino acids, aspartic acid and phenylalanine, both of which are naturally occurring, ubiquitous components of the proteins in our diet. Why did it take so long to gain marketing approval for a substance whose constituents are *already* a normal part of our food supply? The reasoning is instructive. There is a rare, inborn ailment called phenylketonuria, which is an inability to metabolize phenylalanine. Ingestion of foods containing this amino acid by people with this condition leads to brain damage and mental retardation, and such persons must be placed on a phenylalanine-free diet immediately after birth and throughout life in order to avoid this outcome. About 15,000 people in the United States currently suffer from this disorder. Special labeling of products sweetened with aspartame should be sufficient to warn these people away. But what about an unborn fetus suffering from the condition, which would normally be diagnosed only at birth? Could aspartame ingested by its unsuspecting mother harm the fetus? Well, in most instances a pregnant woman would have to consume huge amounts of aspartame-sweetened soft drinks, some 28 quarts at a time, to jeopardize her fetus—an unlikely event. But there are several thousand women reaching childbearing age each year who suffer from *another* rare condition where their natural blood level of phenylalanine fluctuates wildly and in whom, should they be carrying a phenylketonuric fetus, a smaller dose could endanger the fetus. Of course, such women would already be exposed to other sources of phenylalanine such as milk or meat and, if no special effort were exerted to discourage these women from ingesting these foods while pregnant, it would be hard to make a case for treating aspartame differently. In a few cases, of course, it may indeed be the aspartame that provides the straw pushing the mother's blood level past a critical threshold where it might harm her fetus. This incredible argument, concerning at worst a vanishingly small fraction of the population, was, according to *Science*, the prime point in dispute contributing to the eight-year delay in approval (Smith 1981*a*, pp. 986–87). This is a clear case where the worst imaginable situation was the determining factor in a regulatory process. (As it happened, no breakthrough of a scientific nature on these issues finally brought about approval; rather, a change of administration did so.)

Other instances of maximin thinking are EPA's attempt to devise air pollution standards designed to ease the plight of the most sensitive fraction of the population—namely, asthmatics—and the insistence by federal agencies that even quadriplegics have full access under their own steam to subways, buses, libraries, and all other public facilities.

A third characteristic of regulatory decision making is the tendency to overlook considerations of cost and economic rationality. Numberless disputes arise between regulators, whose decisions impose costs, and businessmen who, as proxies of the public, have to pay them. Much effort has been expended by scholars of regulation in proselytizing on behalf of cost/benefit analysis, cost-effectiveness considerations, and risk assessment. These ideas seem to be making headway within the agencies, to be sure, but the fact remains that the estimated costs involved in saving a human life vary over a huge range from decision to decision, even within the same agency (Graham and Vaupel 1981, pp. 89–95). This clearly indicates the remaining scope for the implementation of cost-effectiveness techniques since, at least in principle, more lives could be saved with the same limited regulatory resources by "buying" more of the "cheaper" lives and fewer of the "dearer" ones.

Fourth, there is a clear tendency for agencies to ignore risks occasioned by *delay* in decision making, as well as *increases* in risks resulting from regulations that occur outside the mandated purview of the agency. An astonishing instance of the first is related by Carl Djerassi in his recent fine book about oral contraceptives. Rare side effects among users of "The Pill" began to appear in the 1960s from the doses then in use, but no reduction in dose was allowed until the FDA had completed its review (of efficacy as well as safety) of the new lower-dose formulation. It was not until 1974 that the FDA began approving low-dose contraceptive pills, some five to six years *after* women in Communist China, of all places, had switched to them. In short, millions of American women were needlessly overdosed for half a decade as a direct result of the FDA's dilatoriness. This was not without adverse public health impact, since virtually all the risks associated with oral contraceptives stemmed from the early high-dose pill (Djerassi 1979, pp. 63–65, 194).

Another instance is the well-documented phenomenon of "drug lag" whereby, as a consequence of the FDA's laborious requirements to win marketing approval, new and effective drugs enter clinical use much more slowly than they do in other countries. In the meantime, of course, patients who might benefit from a new drug must do without it (Wardell and Lasagna 1975). This zeal had its origin in the worthy desire to avoid a repeat of the thalidomide tragedy. But the opportunity cost of forgone health benefits that is ineluctably bound up with a "go slow" attitude to new drug introduction has largely been ignored by the agency; at least one attempt at estimating these opportunity health costs and comparing them to the health benefits of avoiding future "thalidomides" concluded that the public would benefit on balance from a much speedier process of drug approval (Peltzman 1974).

A similar situation obtains at the EPA; approval is needed, for example, even for plant modifications that *reduce* emissions. In one case, an oil refiner wanted to modernize a sulfur-recovery plant in a way that would decrease emissions of sulfur dioxide, but this modernization was delayed for eighteen months during EPA review of the plans (Lee 1981, p. 19).

DDT illustrates how agencies tend to ignore increases in risks brought about by their decisions when these increases take place outside the scope of their regulatory attention. This pesticide is, as far as acute hazards are concerned, extremely safe for farm workers and consumers to use (indeed, one of its common uses was to kill body lice on humans). Substituting other pesticides for DDT, as became necessary after the EPA banned it, meant that farm workers often must use more acutely toxic substances and apply them more frequently (since one of DDT's virtues, from the point of view of a farmer, is that its effectiveness is long-lasting). So the acute risk to *the workers* goes up. But that is not EPA's concern; it is OSHA's.

Again, this tendency is exhibited in the Delaney clause, which has as an explicit feature that the only health risks it considers are cancer risks from *using* a food additive, not the health risks of *not using* it. Thus it would not matter even if saccharin and nitrites did, indisputably, have unsubstitutable health benefits far outweighing their cancer risk. They would still have to be banned on the showing of cancer causation in animal bioassays, even though this action *raised* the net risk to the public's health.

Yet another instance is the trade-off between fuel economy and safety. Mandating fuel economy means making cars much smaller and lighter, but this makes them much less safe in the event of a crash (Lave 1981*a*, p. 897). The EPA mandates fuel economy, but the exacerbated safety problems end up in NHTSA's lap.

Fifth, the entire process of gathering information to the center, and evaluating it in order to make a regulatory decision, puts a premium on scientifically articulated and documented evidence—that is, on evidence that can be put into an analytical form that an expert can understand. Information that does not lend itself to analytical articulation, however significant, tends to be ignored. A perfect instance of this is supplied by the saccharin controversy, where the bioassay information concerning the risks of saccharin, however slight, was stated in scientific terms but the information on the benefits was entirely anecdotal and experiential. There was no controlled study, after all, to prove that the voluntary use of saccharin-containing foods by consumers actually did yield measurable health benefits. Instead, there was only a mass of personal testimony; much of it, to be sure, from people who should know—namely, diabetics and doctors. There was also evidence in the form of the market actions of consumers after saccharin's possible cancer risk was publicized (namely, continued demand for artificially sweetened products and occasional hoarding), and finally, there was the blizzard of letters opposing a saccharin ban that buried Congress and the FDA. But none of this really "counted" with the decision-makers at the FDA who, in the absence of "scientific" proof, in effect assigned a value of zero to the alleged health benefits of saccharin.

A sixth feature of regulation is this: implicit in a regulator's *Weltanschauung* is his perspective from the "center" of things. On one hand, this can lead to adding someone's costs in with someone else's benefits, possibly maximizing thereby the sum of public welfare, but also obscuring the wide diversity in individual cost/benefit circumstances. On the other hand, this can lead to active efforts to redistribute costs and benefits. The point of view of individual consumers is very different, and for good reason. One perennial theme in the saccharin debate, for instance, was how young children and the fetuses of pregnant women might be especially at risk.

The concern with fetuses arose because of the necessity for *two-generation* rat studies in order to see any carcinogenic effect; *in utero* exposure evidently magnifies this activity. The concern with young children was generated because a child weighs less than an adult, hence the per-pound dose from drinking a diet pop would be much higher than that for an adult doing the same; also, children have a much longer life expectancy ahead of them in which cancer could develop from a childhood exposure. But obviously, neither of these concerns applies to the elderly who are husbanding their weight and who might want to sweeten their morning coffee with saccharin in order to be able to enjoy a cocktail at night without a steady weight gain. Here the calorie reduction would be immediate, while the possible cancer risk would be far beyond their expected time horizon. From their point of view, they could only lose from a saccharin ban, no matter how much the society as a whole, when risks and benefits were centrally summed, might benefit.[9]

In the same way, the FDA faced a dilemma over the drug phenformin, which is an oral antidiabetic drug that has a lifesaving capability for a small number of patients but that also has fatal side effects in some cases. In practice, in addition to the small number of patients for whom the drug was strictly necessary, it was overprescribed to millions of others. In 1978 the FDA withdrew approval of the drug for this reason, despite the clear need for it by certain patients. Once again, the utilitarian calculus of central decision-makers overruled the individualized benefits to particular persons (Quirk 1980, p. 206).

And concerning the redistributionist potential of a central viewpoint, OSHA's many attempts to protect workers by imposing costs on industry (bounded only by the consideration of avoiding bankruptcy and hence causing unemployment) often exhibit redistributionist motivations. A clear example is OSHA's resistance to allowing the use of economical personal protective equipment as one means of assuring worker safety; instead, costly "engineering controls" are preferred (Nichols and Zeckhauser 1977, p. 61). No case has been made that personal protective devices cannot be made perfectly effective with the proper incentives for workers (such as a pay supplement) to use them. The main reason for OSHA's preference is simply that it is not as comfortable for workers to use respirators, earmuffs, and so forth.

Another redistributionist instance is the 55 miles per hour speed limit. This is alleged to save lives, but it does so only at the cost of delay to millions of drivers. Charles Lave calculated that, ignoring the monetary costs and looking only at the costs in terms of man-years of delay to save a life, it "costs" 102 years of extra time riding around in one's automobile to save one life (Lave 1978, p. 37). Since the average age of a saved life would be about 30, with a further life expectancy of some 40 years, this particular safety measure costs more than twice as many life-years as it saves. This is a strikingly perverse result.

A seventh serious problem with regulatory decision making is that new scientific findings that happen to relate to a current regulatory situation are hastily used to influence decisions before the result has been confirmed by the normal process of replication and peer review. These findings often turn out to be invalid. One instance is the so-called Califano report, which purported to prove that as much as 38 percent of all cancer in the United States could be attributed to occupational exposures. This report was generated within a government agency and offered during testimony to OSHA; but it was never peer reviewed, nor was it published in a scholarly journal, and it had no listed authors (although it had ten listed "contributors," at least seven of whom have since disavowed the claims made therein). The prestigious medical journal *Lancet* deplored this report. Sir Richard Doll, one of the world's great experts in epidemiology, called it "scientific nonsense" and, in collaboration with another renowned expert in statistics and epidemiology, Richard

Peto, mopped up the floor with this report for its mortally flawed methodological defects in a recent article in the *Journal of the National Cancer Institute* (Doll and Peto 1981, pp. 1240–41, appendix F). Yet, like an ever-resurrecting creature from the dead, this report continues to rattle around government agencies, wholly unkillable, influencing regulatory policies.

Another scandalous instance of the use of faulty science to sway policy is the study, released in May 1980, of chromosome defects among the residents of houses near the Love Canal in Buffalo, New York. Apparently due to a management blunder by the EPA, which had hastily commissioned it to develop data for forthcoming litigation, this study overlooked the detail of a matched control group without which it would be impossible to determine whether the observed frequency of chromosomal aberrations really was abnormal and, if so, whether it could be attributed to the toxic seepage from Love Canal. It could, after all, also be due to smoking (tobacco smoke abounds in mutagens), alcohol consumption, medication (including X-rays, which are proven mutagens), or job-related chemical exposures. Despite this fatal defect, the preliminary results were interpreted as possibly suggestive of hazard, and President Carter, four days after this news hit the headlines, decided to evacuate some 700 families to temporary quarters at a cost to the taxpayers estimated by *Time* to be some $30 million. Of more lasting significance is the fact that legislation setting up a "superfund" to deal with the hazards of toxic-waste disposal sites was passed by Congress very shortly thereafter, almost certainly due in part to the publicity generated by this report. Yet an EPA panel set up to review the results of this study, viewing photocopies of the original chromosome slides, disagreed with the preliminary interpretation and concluded that no indication of excessive chromosome abnormalities was present (Kolata 1980, pp. 1239–42).

A further example concerns nitrites. Two years ago Paul

Newberne of the Massachusetts Institute of Technology announced that the incidence of lymphomas (a type of cancer)
among rats fed nitrites was twice as high as among controls.
This was the first study to implicate nitrites directly in
cancer, and then Commissioner Donald Kennedy of the FDA
credulously acclaimed it: "We know more than enough about
the Newberne study to be convinced that it is well done and
strongly supports the hypothesis that nitrites are carcinogenic *per se.*" One year ago, however, the FDA announced that it had reviewed the same data Newberne had
used and found his interpretations of pathology to be flawed;
the experiment had in fact shown no increase in lymphomas
or any other kind of cancer that could be attributed to the
nitrite treatment (Hilts 1981, pp. 18ff.).

Yet another instance is the Canadian epidemiology study
announced four years ago that related the use of artificial
sweeteners by men to a 60 percent increase in the risk of
bladder cancer. While there were serious grounds for doubt-
ing this conclusion (such as the fact that *no* other study of
this much-investigated chemical, saccharin, had ever shown
such an indication), Commissioner Kennedy, already
embroiled in the effort to ban saccharin on the basis of suggestive rat studies, hailed the result, saying: "[This study]
makes it virtually certain that saccharin is a human carcinogen." Yet this "virtually certain" result has since been
decisively refuted by a giant project carried out by the National Cancer Institute, its results reported in December
1979. The NCI research, carried out with vastly larger numbers of subjects, found no elevation in risk among typical
users of normal amounts of artificial sweeteners. Two additional studies confirming this result were reported shortly
thereafter (Hoover and Strasser 1980, pp. 837–40; Wynder
and Stellman 1980, pp. 1214–16; Morrison and Buring 1980,
pp. 537–41).

There are still other cases in which poor science has influenced regulatory policy. The original rat study allegedly

showing that cyclamates caused cancer has not been confirmed upon further investigation, and Bernard Oser, who
conducted the study, disclaims that result. Yet cyclamates
remain banned. And the Alsea II study of the effect of
2,4,5–T spraying on the incidence of miscarriages and birth
defects among residents in and around the town of Alsea,
Oregon, has been shown to be invalid. But the EPA ban on
virtually all uses of 2,4,5–T, for which this study was directly
responsible, remains in effect (Hayes 1981, pp. 75–77,
92–93). The frequency of such examples shows that this
problem is pervasive and systemic, not anecdotal.

In conclusion, the actualities of regulatory decision
making are a "fer piece" away from what was ideally envisioned in the enabling legislation and the preceding agitation
to set up these agencies. Regulatory decisions are often not
demonstrably effective, not timely, not in the interest of
substantial classes of individuals, not conclusively in the
public interest either, and not even predicated on good
science. One is led, therefore, to reexamine the question of
whether there is a true need for the sort of regulation we
have, and to look at other social mechanisms and institutions
for ways to secure safety. Could there be existing means, for
instance, either in the market or in the liability law, that act
in a decentralized, prompt manner to foster good safety practices or that could be encouraged, with a modest amount of
tinkering, to do so? One is also led to question the interpretation put upon the classic "impelling events" that have mid-
wifed the birth of the "new" regulation in the first place.

And it doesn't take much in the way of skepticism to dis-
cover that many of the celebrated impelling events that led
to the setting up of regulatory authorities were *not* due to
negligence or deliberate sloppiness on the part of companies,
but were due to genuine ignorance. Others, it turns out, were
self-correcting. For example, the thalidomide tragedy, which
was instrumental in securing the passage of the 1962
amendments to the Food, Drug and Cosmetics Act of 1938,

was wholly caused by the fact that primates have a peculiar
sensitivity to the teratogenic effect of this drug. Thalidomide
does *not* have this effect on the usual animal test species, i.e.,
rats and mice. The testing done before it was released was
entirely consistent with what was understood to be safe practice at the time. Two points really are pertinent here: first,
this drug *was* kept off the American market by *already* existing legislation, so there was no need to pass even more legislation (which imposed more extensive costs and delays in
new drug introduction); and second, the many millions of dollars paid by the responsible firms to the victims of this disaster as a result of lawsuits supply a stiff incentive for the
management of these and all other drug firms to increase
their safety testing in the future.

Likewise, the diethylstilbestrol (DES) calamity—in which,
in the years following World War II, this artificial hormone
was administered to pregnant women thought to be at high
risk of miscarriage (e.g., diabetics)—was at the time recommended by leading medical researchers at Harvard University. That this would lead, two or three decades later, to a low
incidence (about 0.1 percent) of a rare cancer in the
daughters born to these mothers was something that could
not have been foreseen in animal tests. Even to this day
there are medical experts still recommending the use of such
hormones for particular high-risk pregnancies (Furman
1979, p. 141). It was not negligence, then, that led to this sad
outcome, but an absolutely unforeseeable consequence of our
best medical science. The companies that manufactured DES
are currently being sued under a novel legal doctrine that
relieves the plaintiffs of the burden of having to demonstrate
that the product of a specific manufacturer resulted in their
cancer; i.e., the manufacturers are being held collectively
responsible. Such an evolution of the law can be expected to
increase the caution with which companies offer products to
consumers in the future.

The Love Canal episode is another that did not result

from gross negligence on the part of the Hooker Chemical Corporation. The wastes were disposed of in a manner that not only complied with all regulations and good practice at the time but that *did*, in fact, successfully contain them until the barriers were disturbed by the home construction and road building in the area, which included the laying of sewer lines right through the Love Canal (Zuesse 1981, pp. 16–33). Far from being an instance of crass corporate insensitivity and shortsightedness, and hence a prime example of the pressing need for more regulation by disinterested public agencies, the interpretation is much more complex. Hooker is, not surprisingly, being sued by residents and state and federal government agencies for some $12 billion (*Newsweek*, 14 September 1981, p. 14).

INSTEAD OF REGULATION

Even this cursory glimpse, then, of impelling incidents shows that they are not at all what they seem, and that they do not lead simply to the interpretations that have traditionally been put upon them. This fact, combined with the defects in actual regulations that we have seen above, leads to the question of whether there are other, less defective, means of securing the safety of the public. These need not be perfect, since we now know that the true comparison should be between imperfect regulatory mechanisms and imperfect market and liability institutions, not between perfect regulation and a be-warted market. Two of the most important of these institutions pertinent to the problem here under review are tort law and liability, and insurance. Both of these will be examined in more detail elsewhere in this volume but, as William F. Buckley might say, "Concerning which, a few observations."

The notable fact about the impelling incidents mentioned

above is that the corporations involved did not get off scot-free but were held accountable for their actions by the courts in ordinary damage suits. And the sums involved have been enormous—so enormous that many, many years of routine operations would be needed to generate the profits to pay off these claims. This means that foresighted management will find it worthwhile to spend nearly as much time in avoiding the risk of suits as in ordinary profit-making activities. Several recent quotes from the popular press illuminate the fact that these incentives are having the desired effect:

As doing business has grown more legally perilous, staff lawyers have also come to the aid of their companies by practicing preventive law. Allied Chemical has assigned counsel to follow its products even after they are in the hands of other manufacturers. They watch for potentially hazardous uses and, in the process, build a record of responsible action. (*Newsweek*, 24 August 1981, p. 72)

There is only one way that you can get societal safety and that's out of liability—making it more expensive to do it in the unsafe way. . . . The Federal Government's efforts in getting a safer society are infinitesimal compared to what we do. It's the difference between a million-dollar verdict and a $500 fine,

says Harry M. Philo, past president of the Association of Trial Lawyers of America, a group whose members, according to the *New York Times*, spend "most of their time suing manufacturers of automobiles, airplanes, collapsing buildings, toxic chemicals and other products described as dangerous and defective in behalf of injured persons" (Taylor 1981).

That statement—"the difference between a million-dollar verdict and a $500 fine"—puts it in a nutshell, since regulatory agencies' sanctions are in fact rather modest. And with the recent growth in litigiousness, and in the sorts of liability claims being entertained by the courts, these incentives are growing ever more formidable. Courts are more and more adopting the rule of strict liability, which means that negligence need no longer be shown in consumer injury cases. This, together with the vast increases in personal awards by juries in recent years, suggests the enormously increased incentive that the liability process has had and will have on decision making by private business. It is true, to be sure, that the liability process may not work very efficiently or justly in particular instances (Bardach and Kagan 1982), but the system as a whole seems to be developing ever more powerful incentives for avoiding situations that cause injury to the public and hence expose corporations to lawsuits.

Nevertheless, certain problems are evident in the use of liability as a general cure-all. One is Workers' Compensation, which strongly limits a worker's right to obtain full damages from his employer for harm he suffers from hazardous working conditions. In particular, he cannot recover for pain and suffering, but only for direct medical costs, lost wages, and impaired future earning capability. This limits the effectiveness of the fear of being sued as an incentive influencing management decisions in the area of worker safety. Another problem is that the proof-of-harm standards that Workers' Compensation tribunals and the courts have developed to deal with ordinary worker safety issues are not necessarily adequate for dealing with hazards that operate statistically— that is, where only a few out of a group of similarly exposed workers actually develop a disease. As noted, this is the usual case with cancer where, with a type of brain cancer usually found in no more than 1 person among 100,000, a finding of 5 cases in a group of 100 workers would be considered conclusive by an epidemiologist while a jury or judge might wonder why the other 95 workers did not get the cancer. To the extent that courts do not accept epidemiologically persuasive but not traditionally causal evidence, the risk of liability will not be feeding back to influence safety decision making.

Another difficulty with relying on liability as the full answer to securing justice is the large cost in money, time, and personal commitment required to pursue a lawsuit. This means that the liability system has limited effectiveness where the damages sought are modest. If these weaknesses could be overcome—by reforms that reduce the costs of bringing suit and that establish presumptions or evidentiary rules that would facilitate proof—then liability law could become an efficient inducement indeed.

The other institution that might exercise a substantial role in public safety (especially if the liability system were made smoother and more reliable) is the insurance industry. The essence of the insurance business is to maintain a careful balance between premiums and payouts, with the premiums having to be set at a level that will cover claims but not so high that business is lost to competitors. Risk identification and assessment is therefore something that casualty insurers do every day, and their profits and losses depend on doing it as accurately as possible. More important, such firms can substantially reduce the chances that they will have to pay out claims during a term-insurance contract if they provide safety improvement advice to their insurees. Making safety improvements helps everyone in this transaction, since a better safety record will permit lower premiums in the next contract period. Thus there is a joint interest between insurer and insuree to improve safety, rather than the adversarial relation that currently obtains between regulator and regulated party. This structure of incentives favors, at least in principle, the effectiveness of the insurance mechanism as a means of fostering safety consciousness.

Both the insurance and liability institutions would, with reference to the problems of central regulation, share certain advantages. For one, the informational problem would be reduced, since information about the "state" of things would not need to be funneled to a central agency in far-off Washington for decision; local courts, and insurance companies on the spot, would assess the circumstances and make decisions. For another, since the decision-making units would be much smaller, the scope of aggregate, utilitarian thinking, with its obliteration of individually varied risk/benefit situations and redistributionist temptations, would be lessened. Since delay in implementing sensible safety measures would have costs (because of the liability exposure or high premiums during the implementation period), the adoption of safety measures should be speeded. Bad science would be penalized by means of financial losses. Because the incentives guiding decision making would be to a large degree financial, non–scientifically documented information (such as the experience and opinions of consumers) would be incorporated through consumers' market choices.

Concerning the problem of dealing with scientific uncertainties, a reasonable alternative to the maximin strategy would be to let local decision units differ in their assessments of those uncertainties (and in particular, to allow them to distribute themselves among uncertain alternatives in accordance with local or even individual risk/benefit circumstances), so that when mistakes were made, their harmful effects would be limited to the local area and not spread across the country (for example, banning saccharin could well lead to a public health disaster, if saccharin actually is currently lowering health risks for millions of diabetic and elderly overweight people). And finally, resistance to economic concepts such as cost/benefit analysis, cost-effectiveness, and risk assessment should be lessened, since these techniques are already in wide use by businesses.

There is, then, ample reason for thinking that these institutions, though by no means either perfect or frictionless, could, by careful reforms, have their effectiveness in the task of risk reduction strengthened. These could complement (and to some extent, replace) the regulatory structure now in place.

II

Reforming Direct Regulation

3

MICHAEL H. LEVIN*

Getting There: Implementing the "Bubble" Policy

Two market approaches to air pollution control. Evolutionary change v. revolutionary change. Conflict between proposals and assumptions. Advantages of the bubble concept. Opposition and compromise. The OPM task force. EPA's internal debate. State implementation plans. The controlled trading concept. The 1980 EPA conference. Incentive-based reforms.

*Chief, Regulatory Reform Staff, U.S. Environmental Protection Agency. The views in this chapter are the author's attempt to assess his own activities objectively and should not be attributed to EPA or any other government entity.

In July 1981 General Electric's (GE's) Louisville appliance plant discovered that it could not install a new plastic-parts line in time to meet Kentucky's October 1981 compliance deadline for emission control. The line's late arrival meant that GE could either risk noncompliance (and substantial penalties) for two years, shut down its old metal-parts coating line with its heavy emissions (and with large production losses), or buy a $1.5-million emissions incinerator that would be worthless when the old line was replaced in 1983. Instead, GE leased several hundred tons per year of emission reductions that had previously been deposited by International Harvester in the Louisville "emissions bank." GE paid $60,000 for its two-year lease, and used the leased emission reduction credits to meet regulatory requirements on the old line. The transaction produced faster compliance, saved GE more than $1.8 million in capital and operating costs, and produced healthier air than conventional controls, since the "banked" reductions contained a toxic component that continued emissions from GE's old line did not.

This emissions trade was made possible by two incentive-based reforms first allowed, then actively encouraged, by the U.S. Environmental Protection Agency (EPA): the Bubble Policy for existing sources of air pollution, and the Emissions Banking Policy, which lets emitters create surplus emission reductions and store or "bank" them for later use or sale. This chapter describes the existing regulatory system, and why previous proposals for incentive-based alternatives failed. It then sets the stage for these reforms, and traces both the strategies of those charged with implementing them and the shifting attitudes, within and outside the agency, that implementation evoked. Finally, it offers some guidelines for successful implementation of major substantive reforms in complex bureaucracies, using the Bubble Policy as a model.

Like other incentives approaches, the bubble inevitably implied structural changes in the way regulations are applied and enforced. These implications evoked massive resistance from the agency's Air Programs and Enforcement offices with large investments in the status quo, direct accountability to suspicious environmentalists, and perspectives formed by past dealings with recalcitrants. When their veto efforts failed, these offices attempted to use potential bubble savings as a lever to force applicants to correct larger program defects. Once the agency was firmly committed to the policy, however, it also had to make the policy work. That commitment eventually compelled agency change on more fundamental issues. Those changes forced EPA to become a manager auditing state programs rather than a direct regulator involved in every case, laying the basis for still broader reforms.

WHY MARKET-BASED PROPOSALS FAILED

The decade-long debate over the relative merits of emission fees and marketable permits has largely ignored the fact that *neither* appears workable, given the real-world constraints under which air pollution programs must operate. Both approaches would replace direct "command-and-control" regulation, with fees setting a market-clearing price per unit of pollution or permits setting a total pollution amount. Both approaches would theoretically produce the desired level of ambient air quality for the least cost. Both promise streamlined enforcement, continuous incentives for better voluntary control by emitting sources, and government ability to respond to new knowledge without cumbersome case-by-case rule making. Each sprang from a conviction that pollution control should focus on results (healthy air) rather than on compliance with detailed requirements.

Each was rooted in the belief that emission standards entail enormous unnecessary control costs, that "technology-forcing" requirements tend to freeze rather than promote innovative control technology, and that an incentives approach could cut these costs by harnessing industry's superior knowledge of local opportunities for equivalent emission control.

Under either approach, the profit motive of regulated firms would be put to work for (rather than against) pollution control. Innumerable variations in control opportunities that centralized agencies cannot take into account would effectively be incorporated. Companies would be able to plan how much to control and how much to allocate for permits or fees, secure in the knowledge that fees could be paid or permits bought if control efforts did not work as planned. Hard-pressed state agencies would only be required to monitor a plant's emissions and determine if it paid enough fees or held enough permits to cover them. Decisions about control methods would ultimately rest with plant managers, who know best how to reach stated goals.

Unfortunately, these scenarios generally overlooked the mechanisms by which their results would also have to be obtained. Under the Clean Air Act's bewildering array of acronyms, *EPA* was charged with setting (a) health-based maximum ambient concentration standards for specified "criteria" pollutants, as well as (b) nationwide technology-based emission limits for certain categories of major new stationary sources or modifications (the New Source Performance Standards [NSPS]), and (c) still more stringent limits for all major new sources in areas that met or did not meet the ambient standards, respectively.[1] But the *states* were responsible for designing EPA-approvable state implementation plans (SIPs) to assure that ambient standards were "attained and maintained" through control of *existing* sources, and were required to do so by compiling a quantified inventory of all emitting sources in their "nonattainment" areas, by relating those emissions to ambient violations, and by imposing source- or process-specific control requirements sufficient to make those violations disappear.

There were some facially good reasons for this approach, including the states' long (if spotty) history of direct air pollution regulation, a desire to prevent the flight of new plants to "pollution havens," and strong congressional belief that new sources should be stringently controlled at the design stage. But the approach posed critical implementation problems for any incentive-based alternative. The Clean Air Act implied uniform maximum pollutant concentrations, above which adverse health effects would occur, for every cubic meter of air throughout the nation. It assumed specific air quality effects from each required set of controls, based on mathematical dispersion models designed to relate emissions from particular plants to ambient pollutant levels. It relied heavily on government engineering expertise and standardized end-of-pipe control technology, both for economies of scale in setting emission limits and for ease of enforcing them. It contained short deadlines backed by severe penalties for SIP submittal and approval, for industrial compliance with emission limits, and for areawide attainment of ambient limits. It implied further control if the SIP was not enough to attain ambient air standards. It seemed to require every change in emission limits to be processed as an individual SIP revision, entailing notice, comment, hearing, and review at both state and federal levels.

Given these boundaries, how could any incentives approach let plant managers make "economically rational" decisions to pay fees or buy permits instead of install controls, where the change in emissions might cause new ambient violations because the location of those emissions was critical? What plant manager would risk the uncertainties of an untested control strategy, faced with short compliance deadlines and the danger that success might become a regulatory requirement? Absent continuous emissions monitors (which often were technologically infeasible), how could fees or permits be enforced without simultaneous tests of every stack or vent in a plant — a strategy that was itself unenforceable?[2]

If these problems were arguments for changing the legal framework to accommodate new approaches, they were also evidence of how much that framework would have to change. And beyond them lay other implementation issues. How would short-staffed state agencies acquire and use the detailed knowledge of potential industry cost curves needed to set *emission fees* that would not drastically overcontrol or undercontrol? How would they adjust fees that their legislatures would see as taxes and would insist on setting legislatively? How would they administer different fees for each geographic area where the level of pollution (and required cleanup) differed? Most important, how could they credibly enforce fees, which required both accurate measurement across the whole emissions spectrum (rather than a narrow band around a standard) and audits of every source obliged to pay a fee?

Permits offered more environmental certainty because they could set the total pollution amount. But if inventories had to be redone across the board to determine this total, no state would adopt permits. Assuming this hurdle was passed, how would permits be allocated? Grandfathering them to existing firms based on historical emissions would grant an economic windfall and might discourage geographic entry by new competitors. Auctioning them would entail huge payments to continue established production activities. Most important, the efficiency of permits rested on an easily used market in which firms could control up to the permit price, then sell excess permits to those whose control costs were much higher. How would states screen sales for ambient effects, assure that the same permits were not sold twice, and allow smooth permit transfers without prohibitive transaction costs?

Overhanging these issues was the stark fact that no major interest group wanted a wholesale shift to incentives. For industry, permits and fees posed increased uncertainty, plus double payments for control and the reform. For large firms with established environmental staffs—the only industry voice usually heard in Washington on air pollution matters—current problems were minor annoyances compared to the investment needed to learn a wholly new system. They had spent years learning to deal with the old system and could easily meet most technology requirements. Indeed, they had discovered that uniform technology requirements could increase their market shares.[3] They would stick with the devil they knew. For state air agencies, permits and fees represented huge restaffing and reeducation investments for potentially uncertain gains. For national environmental groups—many of whose leaders had been trained in early, bruising compliance battles with Pennsylvania steel mills—market-based incentives evoked both enforcement loopholes and the shibboleth of a "license to pollute" under which firms could simply pay to keep emitting. These groups had helped draft the Clean Air Act not merely to clean the air, but to punish: to force firms that for decades had used the atmosphere as a free dump to pay the maximum amount for past sins.

In short, proposals for permits or fees threatened to expose the gross defects in air quality management that direct regulation had largely swept under the rug—large gaps in inventories of actual emissions; huge inefficiencies of politically expedient engineering requirements that treated similar industrial processes identically; poorly understood relations between emissions and air quality; inadequate SIPs that EPA was compelled to approve in order to avoid writing local plans itself. Moreover, that threat was posed by the very economic benefit these proposals advanced: their ability to make extra pollution reduction financially rewarding. For if "legitimate" reductions in inventoried actual emissions

were valuable, costless "illegitimate" reductions in phantom
emissions from plants operating far below their permit
amounts, or from facilities due to close anyway, were still
more valuable and would leave polluted areas even farther
from attainment. If fees or permits could save local firms
millions in conventional control costs, it would be difficult for
states to deny these savings based on air quality models with
a 100 percent error factor.

Ultimately, proposals for permits or fees collided with
assumptions on which Congress and EPA had long operated:
that mandated technology would solve every problem; that
government had a monopoly on pollution control knowledge
and could do the job better; that the states required a strong
federal presence to avoid succumbing to developmental pressure; that rules must be written to exclude most firms as bad
actors, rather than to assume good faith and leave bad actors
to enforcement. Through October 1981, not a single jurisdiction had adopted a fee or permit system in lieu of direct
regulation, though some brave souls were still attempting
designs to overcome these barriers.[4] The economists' vision
was no one else's dream.

SETTING THE STAGE

Thus the threshold reform issue—whether movement
towards more flexibility, less government intrusion, and
reduced costs should come through evolution or revolution—
was settled at the start in favor of nonthreatening incrementalism. Any successful reform would have to change fundamental attitudes by fitting *within* the existing system and
demonstrating that reliance on market mechanisms rather
than marching orders could produce both savings and clean
air. It would have to rest on concrete benefits to key participants, not on abstract efficiency claims. It would have to

start small but encourage increased use that would pressure constraints and broaden its appeal. It would have to promise returns large enough to outweigh the disruption costs to EPA regions, states, and industries asked to do business differently. It would have to be easy to understand and use, producing short-run success stories that others would seek to imitate. Above all, it would have to be put on the streets to be used and marketed to insure its use. For though regulated firms remained the prime beneficiaries of market-based approaches, there were ten years of bad blood between industry and environmental agencies. And no matter how large the potential benefits to others, state agencies with shrinking budgets would not adopt any reform unless firms eager to use it forced them to respond.

This incrementalism was directly responsible for the birth of the "bubble" concept. For under the existing system, firms were required to meet uniform statewide or nationwide emission limits for identified industrial processes (e.g., no more than 75 tons per year of particulate matter from blast furnaces or 25 tons per year from cast houses). But the cost of removing 1 ton of particulates from adjacent processes could vary by over 100:1. Why not let plants—or groups of plants—treat all their emission points as though they were enclosed by a giant bubble and rearrange controls to remove more $1 tons and fewer $100 tons, so long as air quality remained the same? This "bubble" approach would *use* (rather than replace) existing regulations and procedures by letting plant managers counterpropose more efficient permit limits tailored to the unique age, size, and configuration of processes in specific plants. It would let firms trade increased control on processes where the cost of control was low for decreased control where the cost of controlling the same pollutant was high. It would give managers a balance sheet incentive — potential savings of millions of dollars per year —to seek new chances for cheaper control, and to justify those expenditures to corporate cost centers. It would reduce government intrusion, delegate more responsibility for individual control decisions, and make it easier for firms to plan compliance. It would also promote faster compliance and better emission measurement, since only quantified reductions below current requirements could be used to meet or avoid requirements elsewhere. As a voluntary program, it would neither require all firms to participate nor force state agencies to make massive structural adjustments. Indeed, it offered those agencies a painless way to upgrade their inventories and correct other deficiencies on a gradual basis, as individual bubble applications arrived. Most important, it could begin to change the beliefs that standardized engineering was the only way to assure environmental progress and that firms should rely solely on approved technology rather than on reductions produced by others or other means.

GETTING STARTED

Unlike some other successes, the origins of the bubble concept are not clouded with claims by competing proud parents. It began in 1972–1973 with suggestions from major smelters and the Nixon administration that EPA redefine "sources" subject to NSPS to include entire plants. This change would excuse plants undertaking major modifications, reconstructions, or expansions from stringent NSPS controls so long as total emissions from the plant did not increase. The proposal came from a heavily polluting and recalcitrant industry, appeared to contravene the Clean Air Act's directive that better controls be designed into new facilities, and was fiercely opposed by EPA's Air Programs and Enforcement offices on enforceability and equity grounds.[5] Under continuing pressure—and counterarguments that this bubble approach would produce better control on dirty *existing* sources, without overall increases in emissions—EPA ultimately proposed to allow plantwide bubbles for modifications but not for wholly new or reconstructed facilities (40 *Federal Register* 58416 [1975]).[6]

This result was immediately appealed by environmental groups asserting its illegality, as well as by smelters asserting that it should cover all three types of "new" facilities. On 27 January 1978 the District of Columbia Circuit Court struck it down in a notably formalistic decision, holding in the case of *ASARCO Inc.* v. *EPA* (578 F.2d 319 [C.A.D.C.]) that EPA lacked statutory authority generally to define "source" as a plant *by the form of words it had chosen,* though it might reach the same result for individual industries by different means.[7] In the two and one-half years this bubble approach had been on the books, not a single plant had tried to use it.[8] The agency had adopted no strategy for marketing the reform or promoting its use by industries identified as good actors.

However, the bubble concept immediately reappeared in another context, having been embraced as a *cause célèbre* by the agency's Office of Planning and Management (OPM). The 1970 Air Act banned all new construction that might cause or contribute to air quality violations in nonattainment areas after 1977. By 1976 it was clear that many industrialized areas would not meet this deadline. To avoid prohibiting economic growth, EPA issued a 1976 "Offset Ruling" that allowed major modifications, expansions, or wholly new sources to construct in such areas so long as they installed very stringent controls and secured sufficient extra reductions from nearby existing sources to produce a net decrease in emissions.[9] In 1977 Congress confirmed and required revisions in this rule, raising the possibility of a plantwide bubble to avoid these new emission requirements. This issue was a central point of EPA's internal debate during 1978, with the Air Programs and Enforcement staffs insisting *first,* that any such bubble was illegal after *ASARCO,* and *second,* that every available reduction should be seized in nonattainment areas, regardless of its small size or high cost. EPA's Office of General Counsel (OGC) supported a broad bubble, noting that Congress had arguably ratified EPA's plantwide approach *before ASARCO*, that NSPS would still apply to new facilities within plants, and that bubbles would assure no increases in emissions while providing an incentive for existing sources to do more than the minimum required.[10] Again, no economic data were advanced to support these asserted benefits. Again, policy debate was cloaked in legal terms to give it more force.

The final "compromise," issued in January 1979, explicitly banned bubbles in areas subject to the federal ruling, but permitted *states* to allow them—for modifications only—in their new nonattainment SIPs due to be approved by that July.[11] But this was a compromise in name only, for as Air Programs staff already knew, most SIPs for significant nonattainment areas would not be fully approved for years. Moreover, the new SIPs were statutorily required to be submitted by 1 January 1979—two weeks *before* the date of this ruling. Many had already gone to state-level rule making, and word of the availability of state bubble options did not reach most affected industry in time. Concerned with their SIPs' approvability in light of these negative signals, the states declined this ambiguous invitation.

The 1979 Offset Ruling did, however, establish two principles that would later prove important. It indicated that surplus emission reductions for bubble purposes might legitimately be created in nonattainment areas so long as they did not *interfere* with progress toward attainment. And it explicitly stated that such reductions could be "banked" or stored for future use. This banking provision was particularly crucial. It laid the basis for readily available reductions that could facilitate interplant bubbles and encourage firms to meet emission requirements through trades. It also enlarged opportunities for bubble savings, since cost-effective combinations of emissions increases and decreases seldom occur at the same time.[12]

Meanwhile, OPM was moving to consolidate the bubble concept and co-opt internal opposition on several other fronts. In the spring of 1978 an agencywide task force headed by OPM was formed, with the administrator's blessing, to examine the legality and technical feasibility of new and existing source bubbles for both air and water pollution. The impetus for this task force was again a recalcitrant industry (steel). But the industry was led by Armco, Inc., which had both a reputation as a "good actor" and the willingness to produce detailed studies of the bubble's economic, energy, and environmental benefits at its plants. Moreover, the association with the steel industry was diluted by the task force's decision to focus on benefits for all industries. It was also diluted by a presidential task group (the Solomon committee) that had found steel to be financially troubled and involved three important outside bodies in bubble development—the Treasury Department, the Council of Economic Advisers, and the regulatory reform arm of the White House Domestic Policy Staff. For the first time, the bubble concept had an external constituency that could neither be identified as industry shills nor easily charged with evading legitimate compliance.

The OPM task force progressively focused on a bubble for existing air pollution sources as the most feasible alternative, discarding objections that would have trivialized the concept's economic benefits or destroyed its acceptability to potential users. These objections were: *legal or enforcement arguments* that would, for example, have barred any relaxation of SIP requirements as part of a bubble; *technical arguments*, such as those that would have limited bubbles to precisely the same type of emission point and pollutant (e.g., no bubble between stacks and vents, or between SO_2 and SO_3); and attempts to use the bubble to *correct perceived defects in the current regulatory system*, such as proposals that mandatory state operating permit systems for existing plants be required by EPA before any bubble could be approved. A fourth line of argument suggested that bubble savings be "plowed back" into better mandatory control by applicants as a prerequisite to approval. The drafting process began to force a gradual split between Air Programs staff—who became increasingly committed to making the bubble work—and the program's senior managers, who were prepared to accept some form of bubble but were more concerned with multiple safeguards to prevent potential abuse.

The task force's September 1978 report recommended that bubbles for existing sources be endorsed by EPA but that a variety of eligibility requirements and safeguards be adopted to assure prompt compliance and environmental equivalence. Bubbles, it said, (1) should incorporate specific emission limits reflecting rearranged controls; (2) could not allow air quality to deteriorate; (3) should not allow trades between toxic and nontoxic pollutants, or between stacks and vents, unless emissions from the latter could acceptably be quantified; and (4) could not be used unless applicants met current emission limits or were on an enforceable compliance schedule to meet them. To conserve state resources, the report envisioned bubbles' being approved through normal state permitting processes. To further conserve resources, it recommended that the burden of proof on air quality and enforceability be placed on applicants, and that applications be limited to single plants. It explicitly noted that bubbles would encourage plants to disclose all their emission points (thus improving inventories) and adopt innovative control strategies that *would provide information leading to more stringent regulation.* Finally, the report identified several "major" unresolved issues, including whether EPA should actively encourage bubble applications, and whether bubbles should be floated on a trial basis before national endorsement. The legal arguments had been removed by perhaps the shortest opinion memorandum in government history, a July note from EPA's General Counsel that stated in full: "Is the bubble legal? Yes."[13]

The report produced a flurry of activity that was remarkable both for how quickly these "major" issues disappeared and for how fast internal attitudes began to converge. To this point, the program offices were principally concerned that bubbles not result in unenforceable emission limits or otherwise undermine past regulatory progress, while OPM and OGC believed new approaches were needed to assure future air quality improvement. Now, under pressure from a variety of external factors, these views began to coalesce. The Air Act would be reauthorized by Congress in 1980; the country was becoming more conservative; public attention had discernibly shifted from support for air quality regulation to more immediate concerns like nuclear safety and hazardous waste (see, e.g., Resources for the Future, Inc., 1980, summarizing trends). How could EPA continue to insist on point-specific regulatory requirements that involved the most rather than the least cost for air quality compliance? How could it demand that state agencies—faced with shrinking budgets, growing developmental resistance, and hostile legislatures—continue to regulate more and more small businesses while cranking down further on previously regulated ones? With some exceptions, direct regulation was starting to look as though it had reached the point of diminishing returns, and as though it were poor environmental management as well.

Beyond these factors lay the stark difference between the "ideal" regulatory world posited by environmental defenders and the real one. In that ideal world, states had comprehensive emission inventories; prompt compliance with state-imposed requirements based on those inventories and backed by EPA would produce clean air by fixed national deadlines; and state plans offered clear guidelines citizen groups could enforce. In the real world, inventories were grossly inadequate; all requirements were subject to negotiation; no one knew how to control many emission points; "compliance" was largely determined through unaudited self-certifications by regulated firms; states simply imposed requirements on industries that could bear the cost; the air quality effects of genuine compliance were uncertain; and a state plan could be ten file cabinets that no one had fully read. Industry and state agencies were already beginning to argue to Congress that the system was overloaded with expensive, unnecessary requirements that produced little real environmental benefit. These issues would have to be faced soon in any event; the bubble offered a way to begin to address them through gradual nonregulatory means.

In November 1978 Air Programs developed its own draft Bubble Policy for existing sources. While the draft emphasized possible burdens on state agencies and the use of bubbles for more stringent regulation, it generally tracked OPM's version and was quickly applauded by that office. It did contain some new wrinkles that could effectively have prohibited bubbles,[14] but these wrinkles quickly became bargaining points, not absolute demands. Moreover, OPM was under pressure, too, for the lead time required to order, install, and de-bug new control equipment required the policy to be issued as soon as possible to be usable by affected plants.

After a last-minute skirmish over whether the proposed policy should be issued before or after the 1 January due date for the new SIPs—a skirmish that involved the symbolic issue of whether the policy would be perceived as required in those SIPs or as merely a state option—the proposal was published on 18 January 1979 (44 *Federal Register* 3740). It "encouraged" states to allow bubbles for all existing sources, though it asked states to comment on resource drains and retained language about using bubbles for further regulation. Among other things, it would have limited bubbles to single plants; prohibited all bubble trades between toxic and conventional pollutants; prohibited trades between industrial process emissions and difficult-to-quantify emissions from storage piles, haul roads, or other "open-dust" sources; and barred extensions of existing compliance dates as a result of any bubble application. But it officially and freely permitted bubbles in all areas with approved SIPs, subject to air quality and enforcement tests, and it allowed increased controls on other production processes to meet requirements for process-fugitive emissions that were notoriously difficult and expensive to control.

More important than this content, however, was the fact that the agency had made the proposal public and committed itself to further publicity. For the first time, a rudimentary implementation strategy would accompany a proposed systemwide reform in environmental regulation. Comments were sought and received throughout that spring in a series of nationwide public meetings jointly run by the affected offices, as well as through the *Federal Register* proposal.

The comments were predictable. Environmental groups feared a political signal to relax regulation and continued to urge additional constraints to make sure the policy did not "call forth innovations in evasion [rather] than in technology."[15] State agencies saw resource drains behind every rock and asserted that they already possessed SIP authority to use bubble approaches, ignoring the fact that previous bubbles had been used solely as bargaining chips that rewarded recalcitrant firms engaged in drawn-out compliance negotiations. A score of regulated industries contended the policy was a "good idea" but that proposed constraints must be eased. Armco, in particular, noted that allowing open-dust trades would save it tens of millions of dollars while *improving* air quality. Indeed, it asserted, requiring process-fugitive controls without bubbles would *degrade* the air, since the electricity needed to operate those energy-intensive controls would significantly increase emissions from nearby power plants. It filed detailed studies to support these claims, which were paralleled by leading firms in chemical, petrochemical, refining, automotive, and other industries.

The comment *process*, however, served the more critical purpose of identifying and building a strong constituency of potential bubble proponents for the first time. Environmental groups would remain suspicious until demonstrated economic *and* environmental successes began to appear. State agencies (and most EPA regional offices) would process individual bubbles, but had no independent motive to go out on a limb by stimulating demand. Only if industry began using the bubble successfully would the proposed policy become real. However unsatisfactory and small a step towards use of incentives the proposed policy represented, getting it out was beginning to work. By the summer of 1979, states were already complaining about the volume of industry requests to use the bubble, and an internal Air Programs report had raised "the specters of bureaucratic strangulation" if constraints founded on mere suspicion were not eased (Standley 1979, p. 5).

This new impetus forced the agency to respond and paved the way for final policy resolutions that fall. Bubbles would still have to be individual SIP revisions, but EPA would speed their approval by helping its regions evaluate proposals and by proposing approval simultaneously with the states. The disquieting threat of further regulation and the ban on multiplant bubbles would be dropped. So long as the applicant demonstrated equivalent enforceability and air quality impacts, EPA would approve bubbles that used open-dust controls in lieu of process-fugitive equipment, provided the plant first installed those controls and verified their results; bubbles between toxic and nontoxic pollutant streams, provided the toxic stream decreased; even some bubbles that produced emissions increases—though it bluffed that, because of long-range pollution problems, it would "not approve such SIP revisions consistent with its current legal authority [to deny them]" (none). It would let states guarantee bubble applicants against more stringent future requirements derived from their applications so long as general SIP requirements were met. Plants that were entitled to statutory compliance extensions for any other reason (such as for installation of innovative control technology) could also get extensions to implement bubbles (see 44 *Federal Register* 71780 [11 December 1979]). EPA would affirmatively encourage states to approve bubble proposals in the interest of economic efficiency, while Air Programs would designate bubble coordinators in each region to respond to inquiries and facilitate requests. And these changes would be supported by recently completed analyses suggesting that bubbles might save very large amounts without adverse environmental effects—35 to 50 percent of conventional control costs for electric utility installations, for example; 60 percent of conventional control costs, or $80 million, for 35 domestic duPont plants; and 90 percent of duPont's costs if multiplant bubbles were allowed (U.S. Environmental Protection Agency 1979; Maloney and Yandle 1979; also Maloney and Yandle 1980, pp. 49–52).

The final Bubble Policy was signed by then EPA Administrator Douglas Costle on 29 November 1979. The event was marked by various forms of hoopla, including statements that the policy would produce "less expensive pollution control, not less pollution control," and a press conference that was treated to competing impromptu addresses on the need for safeguards and flexibility by the agency's assistant administrators for Air Programs and Policy. Key agency participants were also treated by the administrator to an evening bubble reception that appropriately featured a champagne toast. Unfortunately, the champagne was cheap and symbolic; for the agency had formally assigned just three staffers to implement the policy, had made no organizational or funding changes to back its rhetoric, and had only the foggiest notion of the resources that full-scale national implementation might entail. The policy was to become a major reform through $50,000 in emergency funds and the efforts of a competent economic analysis branch that was neither inclined to implementation nor organized for it.

GETTING GOING

One month before the final Bubble Policy, a new Regulatory Reform staff (RRS) within OPM had been created and charged with "coordinating" effective implementation of the bubble, emission banking, and related incentive-based reforms. It soon became apparent that "coordination" would not work where these projects were in separate divisions, were not answerable to the coordinating office, and were composed of close-knit staffs who viewed coordination as interference. The clean answer was a reorganization to bring these projects under common control. But reorganization was complicated by the fact that it would enlarge one OPM division at the expense of two others, as well as by the chicken-and-egg reluctance of OPM management to commit more resources until it was clear the bubble would succeed.

There were two interim answers, however. A common language could be created that emphasized the similarities and interrelations between these historically haphazard reforms. RRS could use that language to assume the marketing aspect of implementation—as a simple conceptual framework to explain to industrial groups, state personnel, and other actors how these reforms could profitably and predictably be used. Once that constituency was built and RRS was identified as the agency's public contact and application facilitator, reorganization would flow logically from the way EPA would have to respond.

The vague concept of "controlled trading" was duly given content to describe how all these reforms made extra control profitable by letting firms trade inexpensive reductions created at one emission point and time for expensive regulatory requirements on other points at different times, under controlled conditions to assure air quality and enforceability. In January 1980 implementing controlled trading was made a top regional priority in the administrator's budget guidance for fiscal year (FY) 1981. On 18 January the new chief of RRS and the head of the Bubble Project embarked on a cross-country series of double-barreled workshops for regional personnel, state agency staffs, and industrial representatives in which he explained the integrated trading concept while she described the Bubble Policy and where it fit in. Between March and July RRS and the bubble staff made nearly three dozen speeches embellishing these themes before trade associations, development groups, and air pollution professionals. A series of documents, ranging from elementary through technical, was developed to help leverage this effort and conserve manpower while responding to growing requests. RRS began to cultivate key press and trade journal contacts, sending them these materials and giving hundreds of hours of background interviews to explain the approach's importance and help spread the word to likely users.

In June the first bubble applications began to arrive and the bubble project was transferred to RRS, which began to act as a line Air Programs office to track these applications, provide technical assistance, and expedite approvals. This function proved to be particularly critical. It not only made RRS a central part of the agency's decision making, with strong necessary ties to state and regional officials; through individual applications it pinpointed ways the policy should be liberalized and provided vehicles for doing so. Moreover, it did so on potential opponents' own grounds, for applicants documented their arguments to show that liberalization would produce environmental as well as economic improvements.

But if issuance of the policy seemed a major victory to OPM veterans scarred by nearly two years of internal negotiation, it was soon apparent that despite initial interest the subject of this marketing effort would not sell. The final policy was a significant advance over the proposal. But it was not available in heavily industrialized areas without ap-

proved SIPs demonstrating attainment by December 1982—
areas that included most major urban zones, that contained
the widest mix of industry subject to the most stringent control requirements, in which the policy was most needed and
could most cost-effectively be used. Even where the policy
could be used, all bubbles had to be SIP revisions, and applying plants had to be on compliance schedules with old emission limits—a combination whose delays and short deadlines
virtually forced plant managers to start investing in conventional controls. And as several applications had unfortunately demonstrated, the requirement that air quality
equivalence be shown through detailed, site-specific dispersion modeling tended to "incriminate" applicants by predicting ambient violations not disclosed through the less fine-
grained modeling appropriate for general areawide SIPs.
Such results required not merely denial of the bubble application, but imposition of more stringent controls—though
these bubbles actually produced better air quality than the
SIP. Moreover, EPA would not have discovered the chance
for improvement without them.

By the summer of 1980 over 40 bubbles were being actively
developed by American industry, many promising large environmental as well as economic benefits. But influential
state officials were already insisting that these applications
were the crest of the wave rather than the tip of the iceberg,
and that the policy left them far less discretion to implement
bubbles than they had had before it was issued. For major industry, it had become conventional wisdom that the bubble
was a good idea that had been killed by agency suspicion—
that the policy was impractical because it viewed corporate
managers as criminals and contained too many needless procedural hoops.

GETTING THERE

In September 1980 RRS convened a national conference of 250 senior EPA, state, and industry officials whose stated theme was "Getting More for Less: Regulatory Reform at EPA." The conference's formal purpose was to give these officials a shirt-sleeves chance to tell EPA what was right or wrong with its trading reforms and which directions the agency should pursue. Its secondary goal was to start a genuinely constructive dialogue between EPA and hostile constituencies. Its ultimate aim was to bring sharply to the attention of top EPA management the need for drastic liberalization if the bubble—and the agency's credibility—were to survive: to accelerate the momentum for constructive change begun by individual applications, confront the most critical constraints created by conservative interpretations of enabling legislation, and bring home the common perception that the policy was a public relations gesture because too few resources had been allocated to make it real.

The conference succeeded beyond its sponsors' dreams. In open sessions and closed workshops, official after official came forward to excoriate the agency for its narrow-minded suspicion and lack of responsiveness, blast EPA's insistence on direct involvement in every air pollution permit, provide detailed examples of how they and the environment could benefit if illogical bubble constraints were removed, and urge that EPA give states more latitude and rethink its whole approach to air quality management. The consistent underlying message was that the bubble was important to responsible industrial managers, but that EPA seemed ready to see it—and the whole incentives approach—fail for fear of phantom abuses that, if they materialized, could be corrected by less prohibitory means. At the conference's close, David Hawkins, then assistant administrator for Air Programs and a died-in-the-wool environmentalist, publicly promised to find some legal way to approve most bubbles without case-by-case SIP revisions or federal review.

Within a month the agency's bubble staff doubled and the bubble's technical assistance budget quintupled. In October the banking project was reorganized into RRS. That same month the agency agreed on a three-tiered modeling screen that would prevent bubble applicants from incriminating themselves and would sharply cut the prohibitive expense of full-scale modeling demonstrations. If bubbled emission points were similar and close together, an even emissions trade without modeling would suffice. If those points were distant or dissimilar, a limited model that showed no significant increase in ambient concentrations would be sufficient. Only if the bubble produced a net increase in emissions or a significant increase in ambient concentrations would full-scale modeling still be required.[16]

In November the agency reversed a prior decision and proposed to endorse a "generic" New Jersey SIP rule that would let that state approve hydrocarbon bubbles without EPA review. The block here had been legal: to assure air quality attainment, the Air Act required federal notice, comment, and approval for every local change in emission limits, and the legislative history showed that Congress had inserted this provision to prevent the agency from approving any "secret" relaxations. But the question was what constituted a "change in emission limits." If the state had a SIP rule that assured that every bubble that met its terms also preserved air quality, EPA could approve all those bubbles in advance merely by approving the rule. The emission limits *authorized by the SIP* would not change (45 *Federal Register* 77459 [24 November 1980; proposal]; 46 *Federal Register* 20551 [6 April 1981; final approval]).

This was easy for hydrocarbons, which did not require modeling; within broad geographic limits, a pound of hydrocarbons from one source was equal in ambient effect to a pound from any other source, and bubbles could be approved under generic rules so long as permit totals were the same. But in December the agency went further and agreed to extend this generic approach to several classes of bubbles that normally required modeling. It also agreed to extend the policy to industrial areas without approved SIPs, so long as attainment would not be jeopardized.[17] Sources would also be given more time to implement bubbles, either through generic rules where the statute allowed it, or through discretionary case-by-case deferral of penalties where it did not. In all these situations, a state that adopted a generic rule as a one-time SIP revision could avoid further federal review.

The significance of these decisions was that, for the first time, they gave *all* relevant actors a substantial stake in the policy's success. For state agencies, generic rules offered escape from the uncertainty, delays, and resource drains of hydra-headed federal review—drains far more massive than resources needed to evaluate bubbles at the state level alone. For EPA regions—especially industrial regions overwhelmed with long backlogs of individual SIP revisions— they offered similar benefits. For industry, they held the clear prospect of a predictable alternative that fit corporate planning cycles, without hidden penalties or the dangerous fiction of having to agree to a compliance schedule with short milestones before more cost-effective emission limits could be proposed.

Because of the pending shift in administration and the six-month paralysis in agency rule making that would inevitably follow, the vehicle for these decisions became a press release. After a last-minute scramble, the release emerged on 16 January 1981, the Friday before the inauguration. It rested on EPA's good experience with actual bubble applications as its primary justification, admitted past excesses of caution, and carefully stated the rationale for its announcements, characterizing them as agency intent but noting that they were not meant to preclude even broader changes.[18] The next week RRS convened a nuts-and-bolts conference for consulting engineers, development firms, and other potential brokers of surplus emission reductions. The conference made front-page financial headlines and created a new nucleus of credible industrial advisers to press for trades and generic rules. Articles triggered by this conference generated more than a dozen major stories on controlled trading, the new Bubble Policy, and use of incentives between January and July, and made bubble developments regular fodder for the influential business press.[19]

In March EPA reversed another past decision and proposed to let modifying or expanding sources in nonattainment areas use a bubble approach to "net out of" preconstruction permits and other burdensome new pollution source review requirements, so long as plantwide emissions did not significantly increase (see 46 *Federal Register* 50766 [14 October 1981; final rule]). In April the New Jersey generic rule was approved and EPA's Seattle region hosted the first regionally sponsored conference on controlled trading for industrial and state representatives from California and the Northwest, focused on the scope of generic rules and the uses of surplus reductions for bubbles and netting. In May the agency's Steering Committee approved a draft Controlled Trading Policy Statement meant to supersede and liberalize the original Bubble Policy, and set clear guidelines for when surplus emission reduction credits (ERCs) could be created, stored ("banked"), and legally protected for use in any trade. In June/July RRS held the first regional workshops on generic rules for state personnel in the industrial Midwest.

By October 1981 three formal banking systems were operating, with more than a dozen others close behind. Firms had paid others $1,000 per ton for surplus particulate reductions and over $500 per ton for surplus hydrocarbon reductions, even in the absence of formal banks. Over 90 bubbles were being developed for federal approval; these *averaged* $2 million in savings over the cost of conventional controls, with many producing environmental improvements and energy benefits. EPA had approved 12 of these bubbles and proposed to approve about 6 more, with 30 others pending approval after state endorsement. They (and their state relations) included the following examples:

- Narragansett Electric of Providence, Rhode Island, is burning high-sulfur domestic oil at one generating station and natural gas at another, in lieu of low-sulfur oil at both. The bubble reduces overall sulfur dioxide emissions by 10 percent and ambient concentrations by 30 percent, while saving Narragansett and its customers over $3 million per year in imported oil.

- Can-coating facilities are saving $107 million in capital costs and $28 million in annual operating costs under an approved bubble approach that lets them average plant-wide hydrocarbon emissions on a daily basis, instead of having to meet emission limits for each line throughout the day. The approach lets these plants avoid installation and operation of energy-intensive gas incinerators, promotes innovative low-solvent technology, and sets a precedent for other coating operations, such as those for appliances and wire.

- 3M's Bristol, Pennsylvania, tape-coating plant will save $3 million capital and $2 million in annual operating costs under an approved bubble that uses innovative low-solvent and solventless technology on three lines in exchange for not controlling seven others. The bubble will reduce net hydrocarbon emissions by about 10 percent more than the Pennsylvania SIP.

- Armco's Middletown, Ohio, steel plant will save $15 million capital and $3 million in annual operating costs through a bubble that allows it to control particulate emissions from ore piles, haul roads, and other open-dust sources in lieu of expensive conventional controls for cast-house emissions. Despite its location in a nonattainment area and the limits in the original Bubble Policy, Armco secured approval by installing open-dust controls and demonstrating that they would bring *the area of its emissions' impact* into attainment. The bubble will improve air quality, eliminate six times as many emissions as conventional controls, and provide data that may make constraints on future open-dust trades unnecessary. Armco will save about $42 million in capital and $10 million in annual operating costs—almost 25 percent of the parent corporation's pretax profits—if pending applications are also approved for two other company sites.

- E. I. duPont's Chambers Works in Deepwater, New Jersey, will save about $10 million in capital plus several million dollars in operating costs by controlling hydrocarbon emissions to 99 percent at seven large stacks in lieu of state-required 85 percent control at several hundred vents, pumps, and seals. The bubble will improve air quality more than conventional controls and produce quicker compliance as well as easier enforcement, since only seven sources need be controlled and inspected.

- Another New Jersey bubble would let Johnson & Johnson overcontrol a newer plant in exchange for not retrofiting a marginal older one several miles away, preserving a positive cash flow and 150 jobs.

- The same month as the transaction in the headnote, Borden Chemical used the Louisville bank to buy 25 tons of hydrocarbon reductions from B. F. Goodrich for $1,000 per ton. Borden used the credits in a multiplant bubble that produced the same emission reductions as state-required methanol tank controls costing $5,800 per ton.

However, attention had already shifted to generic rules, which at least 15 areas—including Illinois, Oregon, Wisconsin, Massachusetts, Maryland, Pennsylvania, Maine, Ohio,

Michigan, Florida, Oklahoma, and the Los Angeles Basin —
were developing. Many of these rules covered all pollutants
and were at or through formal rule making; most included
banking as well as bubble provisions. New Jersey had extended its generic rule to allow multiplant trades and was
predicting several dozen state approvals by early 1982. Two
more regional conferences were scheduled for Dallas and
Philadelphia before the end of the year. Major accounting
and management consulting firms were beginning to high-
light descriptions of controlled trading opportunities in
monthly bulletins to their clients. The agency had approved
informal circulation of the draft Controlled Trading Policy
Statement for comment by states, industry, and environmental groups, and RRS was revising it for final agency review.
Guidelines for regional audits of state actions under generic
rules were also being developed, with strong emphasis on
checks of approval procedures rather than individual results.
Air Programs had asked to assume day-to-day implementation of controlled trading and had begun friendly negotiations on that point. Bubble and trading approaches were
being actively explored for water pollution and mobile source
regulation, and had led to preliminary marketable permits
proposals for non-aerosol chlorofluorocarbons and asbestos
(see 45 *Federal Register* 66726 [7 October 1980; CFCs]; 44
Federal Register 60056 [17 October 1979; asbestos]).

The Bubble Policy had forced the agency to face and resolve larger program issues: to make modeling a decision tool
rather than a decision rule; to delegate more responsibility to
the states; to conceive SIPs as collections of approved procedures for developing or changing emission limits rather
than collections of fixed limits; to start becoming a manager
who audited state programs instead of a regulator directly
involved in every case. By the fall of 1981, the bubble was
almost routinized within the agency, an automatic first response when difficult problems had to be resolved.

CONCLUSIONS

The bubble is not yet institutionalized, though the principal dangers now are conflicting perceptions within the new administration that (a) it is solidly established and needs no more visible support, (b) it is a Democratic smoke screen to divert attention from the "real issues" of federal intrusion and overly stringent regulation, and (c) its effectiveness may undermine the administration's program for revising the Clean Air Act. The ill-defined tension between "regulatory relief" (with overtones of deregulation) and "regulatory reform" has further muddied the outcome. But it seems fair to say that this, too, shall pass. For this trading approach is starting to produce real state delegation and very large savings that the administration can accelerate and take genuine credit for; and after all cost-ineffective regulations are adjusted, there will remain a large body of uniform rules whose inefficiencies can be reduced only through individual trades based on knowledge no centralized agency can afford to acquire. Moreover, industry knows—and is beginning to say—that imperfect but predictable administrative solutions are better than grand designs sought through an uncontrollable legislative process.

It also seems fair to say that controlled trading has made it possible to think about practical implementation of marketable permits for air pollution control. That possibility exists not just because threshold problems have been faced and multiplant bubbles have begun to convince industry that reliance on reductions produced by others may make solid financial sense; it also exists because only a few elements need be added to controlled trading to produce the functional equivalent of marketable permits. Once those elements are added, the only difference would be whether transferable requirements are created by reductions below a regulatory baseline or by allocations that start from some other point.

Here, as elsewhere, it is important to define the experiment to succeed rather than fail. Under either controlled trading or marketable permits, substantial government involvement will still be needed to assure accurate inventories and reduction assessments, define the commodity, prevent the same permits from being sold twice, deal with the nonlinear relation of emissions to environmental effects, and bring buyers together with sellers. Hence the short-term goal cannot be an active free market. Especially where the commodity is intangible, such markets do not spring up overnight; a hundred years ago the New York Stock Exchange consisted of men named Goldman and Loeb walking Wall Street with bid tickets in the bands of their stovepipe hats. But the large savings, flexibility, and increased predictability provided by the bubble, banking, and related steps are nothing to be ashamed of. Indeed, these steps are building blocks that create both a foundation for and a momentum towards marketable permits, while allowing participants to stop and regroup at any point if the system becomes too stressed.

Finally, it seems fair to say that the bubble experience provides a good model for implementing other "substantive," incentive-based reforms that cut across whole programs or groups of regulations and are meant to change how industry complies and how much compliance costs. Whatever the regulatory system, any major substantive reform:

- *must start as a supplement, not a replacement.* "Reform" threatens institutions that have reached an equilibrium and implies that the reformer knows their interests better. Existing attitudes and modes of doing business are supported by strongly felt beliefs that will not easily change, however inefficient they appear. The more ambitious the reform, the more skepticism and resistance it will meet. The point, it would seem, is to start small but structure the reform to create an internal dynamic that will broaden it once it starts being used;

- *must be easy to understand.* Because of the "not invented here" syndrome and the inevitable resistance to new approaches, any reform whose nature, purpose, and benefits cannot be clearly described in ten minutes is likely to be dismissed by key participants. Why change is needed and what it can do for each potential constituency must be plainly defined; sufficient safeguards to keep potential opponents neutral and allow implementation to begin must also be included;

- *must provide potential benefits large enough to outweigh its disruption costs to government entities and users.* "Habitat," the Montreal World's Fair modular housing exhibit, was supposed to revolutionize home building because it cut housing costs 90 percent. Unfortunately, it cut only *structural* costs 90 percent; since structural costs were only 10 percent of total house costs, this was insufficient to overcome local building codes and other inertiae. The Bubble Policy always offered large savings to industry, but it did not really start moving until removal of SIP revision burdens created both a large vocal constituency and large incentives for state agencies and EPA regional offices;

- *must provide regulated entities with more certainty than the current system.* Benefits include certainty; potentially large savings accompanied by sharp decreases in predictability will be shunned. The problem is difficult, since regulatory innovation, like other innovation, tends to increase uncertainty for both the innovator and the innovation's users. It was solved for the bubble because the "moving target" nature of the Clean Air Act created even more uncertainty, and controlled trading offered a way to reduce that uncertainty by using extra emission reductions to meet future compliance requirements;

- *must be gotten out on the street to be used.* As for individual regulations, optimality is a self-defeating goal. However imperfect, it is much more important to get the reform out so it can start being used and individual applications can provide concrete vehicles for later rationalization;

- *must be structured to produce quick real-world success stories.* Legislatures, regulatory agencies, and industry tend to act more on anecdotes than on analytic data. Nothing succeeds like success; business is imitative and will quickly join a bandwagon if it sees competing firms or industries profiting. On the other hand, no one wants to be the first to volunteer. The first question asked will be: "Who is doing it?" If the reform remains just a nice idea, it will fail;

- *must not be loaded down with constraints aimed at achieving other program goals.* Reforms that offer large benefits to regulated industry create large temptations to channel those benefits into mandatory correction of other program defects. Early proposals to use the bubble to secure mandatory state operating-permit programs or require bubble savings to be used for more stringent control or faster compliance are good examples. Though some compromise is inevitable, these restrictions must be resisted. They run counter to the whole purpose of an incentives approach and make potential users feel they are being asked to correct problems not of their making. If the program has defects, they should be faced directly; the reform must not be so burdensome that it cannot be easily used;

- *will inevitably evolve,* since problems and opportunities for further change cannot be foreseen. This implies that more and more resources will be needed to track individual applications, doument success stories, and make needed secondary changes as the reform moves from design through implementation and redesign towards institutionalization;

- *must be backed by organizational change.* Reorganization for its own sake is an exercise in turf-building. But limited organizational change can send strong signals to the agency and outside constituencies that the reform effort is serious, and can place reformers in decision-making centers that require other actors to respond;

• *must build a constituency within and outside an agency,* both by involving program staff, regulated firms, and interest groups in the reform's design, and by making sure their concerns are responded to so that they will develop a stake in the outcome once initial design work is done;

• *must be developed with and transferred to the relevant program offices if it is to be institutionalized.* Institutionalization means the reform becomes a normal part of program office thinking. Planning offices seldom have the resources for full-scale implementation of a major national reform, and the reform must become embedded in the reactions of midlevel program managers and GS−9 permit writers to survive. If the reform continues to be seen as a foreign body, a planning staff creature, over the long run it will wither and fail.

Because a meaningful incentives approach means decentralized decision making and more individual responsibility, it inevitably implies structural changes in the way regulations are applied and enforced. Successful reformers must develop an implementation strategy that deals with those threats, contingencies—and opportunities—too. If the bubble experience is any guide, major reforms are a combination of grass-roots organizing and trench warfare; to succeed, they require tenacity, expanding resources, constituency building, intimate knowledge of messy program details, and constant vigilance.

4

THOMAS P. GRUMBLY

Self-Regulation: Private Vice and Public Virtue Revisited

Three aspects of health and safety regulation. Voluntarism and consensus. Federal agencies and regulatory penalties. Willful noncompliance. Problems in deregulation. Carol Foreman and 1979 changes in mandatory quality control. Implementing voluntary and self-regulatory systems.

The search for alternatives to the command-and-control health and safety regulation of the 1970s will depend in part on the extent to which private arrangements can accomplish regulatory goals. This chapter examines experiments in "self-regulation" or "voluntarism" currently in progress in several federally regulated industries, mainly in the areas of food safety and quality.

AN ANATOMY OF CURRENT SELF-REGULATION

Few areas of commercial life remain in which the extreme definition of "voluntary" still exists, i.e., that "state of nature" in which the government has consciously or unconsciously decided to do nothing to achieve regulatory goals. Following implementation of the Medical Device Amendments of 1976, almost no consumer product industry now is regulated only by market pressures and moral suasion. Prior to implementation of these amendments by the Food and Drug Administration (FDA) in 1980, the highly innovative medical device manufacturers lived in a regulatory vacuum where the government only preached about doing good. Even as self-regulation begins to be examined seriously again, the regulatory juggernaut at FDA is advancing—because of congressional mandate—on the medical device industry.

Self-regulation can, however, keep formal regulation to a minimum when the goals of the regulated and the regulator roughly coincide, either through the practical necessities businesses face in protecting themselves from liability, or through a publicly encouraged recognition of what constitutes the public interest. The Bureau of Biologics of the FDA totally controls the regulation of vaccines, for example, but does so with relatively few pages of elaboration in the *Federal Register*. The process begins with the fact that most of the vaccine production in the United States is done at minimal profit by large pharmaceutical houses. In this case, the convergence of interests between companies and the government, and the general agreement on the science and safety factors that underlie vaccine development, have made it possible to minimize formal regulation.

Between the totally regulated environment of the biologics world and the shrinking entrepreneurial freedom of areas like medical devices lie a number of different kinds of "voluntarism" in current health and safety regulation.

Consensus facilitation in science, policy, and enforcement

Health and safety regulation traditionally has three discrete aspects: (1) the scientific and technical underpinnings that originally revealed the existence of problems; (2) the policies or standards derived from that science that appear (or fail to appear, as the case may be) in the *Federal Register* as the decisions of appropriate agency officials; and (3) the enforcement of these policies. Successful self-regulation requires a degree of consensus between government and industry in these three critical areas.

Scientific cooperation. In recent years most federal agencies have looked skeptically at the scientific evidence compiled by industries to support product safety claims. This skepticism has been particularly notable in areas where the government requires premarket approval for new products. The prevailing ethic in much of toxic substance and drug regulation can best be described as "gotcha!" Industry and government scientists spend inordinate amounts of time—often at the urging of politicians—looking for biases and elegant flimflams in each other's work and impugning each other's character. Fueled by adversarial legal processes, it might be said that the ideally cooperative framework for competition in science has fallen by the wayside, so that the scientific enterprise has looked more like a courtroom than a laboratory.

In significant ways, this adversarial atmosphere now seems to be changing and an important, if nascent, form of consensus building is emerging. In the chemical industry, a coalition of firms known as the American Industrial Health Council (AIHC) has offered to cooperate with health regulatory agencies to define scientific problems and begin searching for testing methodologies that government and industry can agree upon. For example, after almost two years of wrangling, AIHC and the five major health regulatory agencies have agreed on a process to identify certain chemicals, called teratogens, that may cause reproductive risks. Seminars between industrial and government scientists are making progress on the basic question of what constitutes a teratogen as well as the relative risk any of these chemicals imposes. This will not be a smooth process inasmuch as risk assessment depends mightily on the kind of dose-response curve that is drawn; this can be construed as both a scientific and a *policy* problem. It does, however, mark a significant voluntary reentry into the regulatory scientific process by industrial science. Much of this has been stimulated by the Reagan administration's obvious emphasis on "deregulation," and perhaps also by baser motives that resemble those of the fox in the chicken coop. However, other examples of scientific voluntarism were under way during the closing days of the Carter administration to demonstrate that this scientific consensus building is more than a partisan process.

The Health Effects Institute comes immediately to mind. Funded jointly by the Environmental Protection Agency (EPA) and the major automobile manufacturers in late 1980, its goal is to identify the major public health problems, if any, generated by automobile emissions and to structure a scientific process to address them that is jointly funded and operated by industry, government, and academia. To ensure credibility, the institute is governed by a board of directors that includes the presidents of major corporations and universities and is headed by Mr. Integrity, Archibald Cox. Its success is still in doubt, largely because of current instability in the EPA, but it marks an important milestone on the road to self-regulation for industries to be willing to participate in ventures that could ultimately mandate further regulation.

Standard setting and enforcement. Perhaps the most obvious form of self-regulation is standard setting. The regulation of microwave ovens is a good example. The Bureau of Radiological Health (BRH) in the Food and Drug Administration is responsible for the safety of these appliances, and when they began to enter the consumer market in the late 1960s and early 1970s the bureau, rather than issuing its own standards, made it clear to the microwave industry that private safety standards would have to be developed. In quick fashion, the organized industry convened with government officials to develop standards that met with BRH approval. Even more remarkable, from the perspective of hardened regulatory professionals, is the care with which the industry has in fact implemented and updated the standards. On only one occasion has the FDA found it necessary to intervene directly with a microwave manufacturer to force implementation of a standard.

Some of the reason for this activism doubtless lies in the inherent suspicion with which many people view a "new" technology like microwave ovens; on pure marketing grounds, it made sense for the industry to impress its concern with product safety upon the public. Scientific cooperation, however, definitely played a role in this policy success in standard setting. People in the radiation industry respect the professional competence of the Bureau of Radiological Health, and indeed consider the bureau on the edge of "the state of the art." Ironically, the willingness of an industry to regulate itself may depend not on dissatisfaction with government efforts so much as upon satisfaction with the high *quality* of the personnel in the government agency regulating or monitoring it.

A variation of the voluntary standard-setting process occurs when regulators make it clear that regulation will follow unless an industry is willing to take action itself. A recent example of this occurred with a safety standard proposed by the Consumer Product Safety Commission (CPSC) on miniature Christmas tree lights. CPSC proposed a standard in 1978, citing fire and shock hazards caused by defective lights. Since then industry groups, including Underwriters' Laboratory, have issued voluntary safety standards. This standard-setting one-upmanship led the commission to drop its own efforts, with the classic justification by Commissioner Samuel Zagoria: "This is a case of an industry, without compulsion, adopting standards which we can expect will reduce a household hazard to at least reasonable proportions" (*Washington Post*, 10 September 1981).

Dangers in excessive self-regulation.   If we want to encourage further voluntary standard setting in health and safety regulation, we need to guard against some of the obvious abuses that have accompanied voluntary standard setting in economic regulation. By permitting producers to restrict competition in the name of quality, voluntary standards for the size and quality of food items have had substantial adverse effects on price and quantity as well as on the distribution of benefits. For example, quality grading of oranges and tomatoes in California ensures that only parts of crops ever get to the marketplace and competition is restricted. Produce that is not "Grade A" or "U.S. Fancy" or some other determination is not delivered to city markets, even though it may be equally nutritious and would provide consumers with more choice at a variety of prices. While mandatory command-and-control regulation can no doubt have exactly the same kinds of pernicious economic effects, they may well be exacerbated when associations—inevitably dominated by larger members of industry—attempt to set policy and regulate themselves.

Voluntary and industry-supported regulation

In some cases, most notably in the food industry, fees are paid to the federal government in return for inspection. The government sets the standards and pays the inspectors.

Largely through historical accident in the development of legislation, fish and fish products are inspected for safety by the National Marine Fisheries Service in the Department of Commerce rather than by the Food and Drug Administration or the Department of Agriculture (USDA). Since the late 1950s, the health inspection of items like canned tuna or salmon has been conducted on a user-fee basis. Only firms that voluntarily pay for government inspection are inspected; a number of prominent food companies have used inspection—and the mark of approval placed on the product—as a marketing device to woo the public. The actual inspection is a relatively small part of production costs, and products bearing the mark of approval can command a higher price in the open market. There is little indication that these products differ in quality from those inspected by other agencies, although the Commerce Department is dealing with rather small quantities in a relatively narrow area. Whether user fees can be imposed successfully in larger sectors of the economy is open to question.

The very concept of user fees in regulation is deeply offensive to many liberals. How, they ask, can an industry be regulated in the public interest if it has direct economic control over the regulator? Indeed, it is hard to even justify the existence of a regulatory program if the benefits accrue to the party who pays. In response, it can be said that agencies have ample means to defend themselves against co-optation provided top managers are inclined to do so. And these managers do have the incentive, since any regulatory derelictions, whether real or apparent, would be harshly criticized in the media and in Congress.

It is one thing for a regulatory agency to go along with an industry's wishes to be placed in a user fee–style program such as the Fish Inspection Program at the Commerce Department. It is quite another for the agency and unwilling industry to be *told* that an industry will begin paying user fees where it has paid none before. Since at least 1976 the White House Office of Management and Budget (OMB) has been attempting to convince the USDA to transform its meat and poultry inspection at least partially into a user-fee program. Each time, the department has successfully argued that the political costs (i.e., an industry unhappy about having to pay such fees) are not worth the financial benefits of such a charge (a maximum of about $150 million could be obtained).

Self-regulation and the rejection of good manufacturing practices

A major ongoing debate in health and safety concerns the gradual intrusion of government into manufacturing practices. Behaving as though they were actually managers of businesses, health regulators began taking the position that end-product testing was insufficient to determine whether products met statutory definitions of safety, and began instead to regulate production facilities and processes. This approach seems perfectly reasonable, as is evident again in foods and drugs. The technology of food production requires that cans, for example, be processed at particular temperatures for specific lengths of time to ensure that deadly botulism toxin will not grow. Because the economics of both the industry and government preclude end-of-the-line examination of all products, and because the health outcome of a defective process is so serious, the justification for intrusion into the production process is reasonable as long as it is focused on critical variables. The regulator soon finds, however, that there are all too many critical variables; the consequent development of so-called "good manufacturing practices" becomes a flood tide of enormously detailed controls or production methods that easily become overinclusive and induce "nit-picking" enforcement.

Now that this tide seems to be turning, it is important for industry to develop flexibility of response by learning to distinguish the kinds of targets that can be met through alternative processes. Voluntarism at the process level works best where the desired *outcome* can be quantified or measured in some other reasonably precise way. Also, the goal must be well within existing technological capabilities, and must embody a result around which some social or scientific consensus exists.

The regulation of nitrosamines in meat and poultry products represents a good example of both the opportunities and the pitfalls in regulation where the outcome is specified but the means are left to the producer. For some time, there had been a *scientific* consensus that this class of chemicals caused cancerous tumors in laboratory animals. It also had become clear that frying bacon at high temperatures caused the development of nitrosamines in the prepared meat. Because of existing law, the Department of Agriculture had to find some way to eliminate or at least drastically reduce the presence of these chemicals. The department was left with the practical dilemma of telling many companies with different processes—each critical, of course, to the future of the company!—how to eliminate the substance. Because regulatory-reform fervor was already reaching a high pitch in the middle of the Carter years, the department decided to specify only the outcome it wanted—i.e., no confirmable nitrosamines in bacon as determined by certain departmentally specified tests—without specifying how to achieve that end. The department merely stated that it would have a group of consultants available to help companies comply.

The results were mixed. Nitrosamine levels in bacon dropped considerably over two years, and some firms made money because the regulation forced them to institute more rigorous process control. A number of firms also used the proffered consulting assistance. Ironically, however, many firms believed that the department's turn to results-oriented regulation was wrong, on the grounds that the department should have stipulated the outcome only after it knew that it was clearly possible to comply. Consequently, government's grant of private discretion over compliance processes was not interpreted by industry as a genuinely beneficent grant of discretion.*

On balance, the nitrosamine testing program was successful because the USDA enforced the new standards flexibly. Generally, however, self-regulation will work best where there is genuine choice among alternative technologies. This distinctly contradicts much of the ideology that drove the implementation of social regulation in the 1970s in both goals and process, and we shall have more to say about it later. Self-regulation that involves the rejection of government-specified "good manufacturing practices" must be more conservative in goals as well as process.

Voluntary compliance, quality assurance, and the threat of regulatory penalties

Thousands of pages of regulations in the *Federal Register* go unenforced. Even at the height of the regulatory fervor, federal compliance forces were never able even to approximate a tight compliance strategy with every business. At the heart of most federal compliance strategies lies the assumption that most businesses *will* comply with most of the regulations most of the time. For example, the average food or

---

*Perhaps as important as the frustrations of complying with the nitrosamine standard was the lack of consensus about what animal tests mean for people. Despite extensive scientific discussions between the industry and the Department of Agriculture about the validity of animal data on nitrosamines and cancer, much of the food processing community remained unconvinced.

drug establishment in the United States is visited no more than once a year by the FDA as a matter of course. Obvious factors can increase government surveillance, such as inadequate past compliance records or the manufacture of an exceedingly hazardous product. Nevertheless FDA and its overseers—the General Accounting Office (GAO), the OMB, two appropriations committees of the Congress, as well as its authorizing committees—believe that voluntary compliance works well for both production and labeling regulations, and that government does not need to put substantial additional resources into the system.

The source of this optimism lies primarily in confidence about the state of quality assurance in the food and drug industries. In the United States, the great majority of these firms spend substantial company resources on independent quality assurance departments or auditors to ensure adequate production processes. It is easy to see the reasons for this investment. Sales depend on the product; particularly in the food industry, customers may sample anything once because of advertising, but are unlikely to return if taste or consistency are unsatisfactory. Bacterial contamination and other serious health problems connected with a product can quickly eliminate a company. The food industry has not forgotten the fate of *Bon Vivant*, a major producer of gourmet foods that was destroyed as a direct result of bad publicity about two cases of botulism attributed to its vichyssoise. Many companies, at least in consumer products, have strong financial incentives to develop management mechanisms and technologies to prevent bad products from reaching the public.

Good quality assurance techniques are themselves strong weapons in the voluntary compliance arsenal, but the prospect of occasionally vigorous compliance actions by the government is also critical to their performance, because despite financial incentives, departures from those techniques can and do occur for three reasons: carelessness, willfulness, and ignorance. Even threatened or minor regulatory action will reduce the number of quality control lapses that fall into the first or third categories. No health and safety regulatory laws require "willfulness" as a standard for noncompliance; so most companies understand that carelessness can bring major regulatory and consequent financial troubles. Even if the government decides not to demand civil penalties, recalls, or condemnation of products, enormous damage to reputations can be done because of media interest in suspected noncompliance. In this age of the investigative press, often the mere presence of federal regulatory agents on company premises produces local media interest. Long before the government takes any action, a company may be tried and convicted in the press.

In the summer of 1980, for example, a Mississippi poultry firm was found by USDA inspectors to have illegally high pesticide levels in its product. No allegations of willfulness were involved; for economic reasons the company had decreased its quality assurance testing. At USDA's demand, the company undertook a recall that was rather quiet, since there was no evidence the product had reached consumers. The press learned about the situation and the local newspaper printed a front-page story about the problem with headlines larger than it had used on Pearl Harbor day. The company dramatically increased its surveillance. Its carelessness had been punished—severely.

With respect to regulatory ignorance, such as occasionally occurs in new or exceedingly small firms, polite but pointed letters can generally achieve compliance. The danger is that ignorant violators can be easily turned into willful ones if treated in a heavy-handed way by regulatory officials who are often cynical about cries of ignorance. In the FDA, at least, increasing attention is being paid to this problem by providing compliance officers with special training on the personal-relations problems that inevitably crop up with small businesses. Whether this important kind of training can be sustained through coming budget crises remains to be seen.

Businesses that *willfully* violate rules can, of course, spoil the whole self-regulatory effort, forcing the government to resort to detailed command-and-control regulation for well-intentioned firms as well. In order to tailor compliance strategies to this problem, it is important to explore the motivations involved. First, some people fundamentally disagree with certain regulations. Rather than take their complaints through the political process, they engage in a guerrilla warfare of noncompliance, and raise political and social arguments as defense only once they are caught. The illegal use of diethylstilbestrol (DES) in cattle is a good example. Banned by the FDA for promoting growth in cattle because it is a proven carcinogen in people, the drug continued to be sold because many farmers believed the levels at which it was used in animals were safe. This is a legitimate argument at the regulatory decision-making level, but it unquestionably influenced many cattle raisers to buy the substance on the black market. Until the widespread flouting of the ban was brought to the agency's attention by cowboy "informants" in April 1980, the FDA, counting on voluntary compliance, had no intention of mounting any enforcement program. When the problem became known, the secretary of health and human services threatened to put people in jail. Whether this will happen or not still remains to be seen, but the credible threat of criminal prosecution of individuals involved in this activity is critical if the public and the industry are to trust the government to enforce the law of the land.

This incident helps to demonstrate the importance of open scientific dialogue and consensus building if self-regulation is to be successfully employed.

Willful noncompliance also can result from a combination of historic precedents and the attitude that "I know best for my business." Contempt for bureaucratic procedures and enjoyment of the chase are also facets of the person who might

be called the true antiregulatory entrepreneur. There are not
many of these people left, and they live mostly in worlds like
meat inspection where there has traditionally been great
give-and-take between regulated and regulator. They can
make regulatory life a fascinating process because of the internal gamesmanship required to maintain some form of
control on their activities; but at the same time they can
make it exceedingly difficult politically to *deregulate* industries in which they flourish. One would think that industrial
colleagues would exert pressure through trade associations
to curb the activities of these entrepreneurs, but it more
often seems that they become folk heroes to their more timid
(or smarter but more cautious) brethren.

The third motive for willful noncompliance is simply economic. While the general motive is not surprising, it is a
surprising fact that some firms simply cannot comply with
regulations and stay in business. Particularly with the large
capital costs of start-up in many industries, the young company that complies with the letter of every single regulation
is not likely to survive. It is part of the lore among regulatory
professionals that even many of the best companies were initially outlaws.

To discourage these last two categories of willfulness, the
so-called "Park Doctrine" was developed. As a matter of law
and precedent under the drug laws, a chief executive officer
(CEO) can personally be held criminally and primarily responsible for any corporate violations of law to which criminal penalties attach. This rather draconian measure has all
but banished many violations in the drug industry, while at
the same time drawing understandable howls of protest from
the CEOs at risk. It may be the kind of ultimate trade-off
that can be made in return for increasing self-regulation. In
other words, the secret to controlling potential miscreant
companies is to attach personal responsibility in a way that
places the highest possible incentive on good corporate quality and regulatory control.

THE POLITICAL PROBLEMS OF DEREGULATION: A CASE STUDY IN ADVANCING SELF-REGULATION

Many current self-regulation practices have developed only through quirks in statutes or historic practice without much thought having been given to the planning of such enterprise. Now, however, agencies are beginning to turn consciously to regulation that depends greatly on the willingness of the regulated to police themselves.

To understand the problems and possibilities of increasing voluntary compliance and other forms of self-regulation, it is useful to examine a particular deregulation struggle. It is a tale of conflict and compromise, with some surprising results.

The problem

Since the passage of the Federal Meat Inspection Act of 1906, the U.S. Department of Agriculture has been responsible for ensuring the safety of all meat and meat products in interstate commerce in the United States. In 1957 that authority was extended to all poultry products.

Over the years the statutes were interpreted to mean that all meat and poultry products had to be carefully "inspected" before they could be literally "marked" fit for human consumption. By the mid-1970s this had led to a force of nearly 8,000 USDA and state inspectors distributed in about 7,000 meat and poultry plants around the United States. By contrast, the Food and Drug Administration had only 3,200 inspectors to cover well over 100,000 different production facilities in the United States. The budget for federal meat and poultry inspection alone was over $150 million and growing at the rate of 10 percent per year, as states began to exercise a statutory option to relinquish their own inspection programs and call upon the federal government to fill the void.

As this happened, the problems of meat inspection were also changing in the middle decades of this century. The American meat and poultry industry made enormous strides in cleaning up their facilities and modernizing their practices. From the farm to the slaughterhouse to the processing plant, new methods eliminated many of the potential health problems that had plagued the industry and necessitated intensive inspection. The main problems changed from health to aesthetics and economics; through the addition of water, fat, or other material, meat and poultry products can easily be cheapened without the consumer's knowledge.

The government's initial steps

Meanwhile, the practical science of "quality assurance" was making great strides in American industry. Not only were measurements of tolerances and production processes more precise, but American business management began to look upon quality control as integral to guaranteeing good reputations in the marketplace. Even before the cost of the meat and poultry inspection program was recognized as a serious problem, regulatory technocrats began to see quality assurance as a new weapon in their arsenal. In 1974 the Meat and Poultry Inspection Program proposed a regulation that would have mandated quality control programs in meat and poultry processing establishments. However, no *quid pro quo*s were proposed in the way of lessened inspection, and the industry successfully pressured senior department officials to kill the proposal.

During the fall 1976 federal budget preparation for fiscal year 1977, the Office of Management and Budget began questioning the prospect of continued increased costs for this program. While a minor issue in the total budgetary context, the first stirrings of regulatory reform were already being felt in the Ford White House. A number of senior administration officials, including Budget Director James T. Lynn, could see no reason for the government to continue "to inspect every damn chicken," and OMB directed the department to conduct an external review of this program. The consulting firm of Booz, Allen, and Hamilton was retained and, working into the early days of the Carter administration, it concluded that quality control programs as a substitute for government inspection were both feasible and desirable tools for controlling costs.

Completed in June 1977, the Booz, Allen, and Hamilton study also accurately forecast many of the problems of implementing reduced inspection in return for enhanced quality control:

(a) consumer groups and labor groups would be wary of any program that placed more compliance responsibility on business and less on the federal government;

(b) small businesses would resist any cost increases, *even if regulation were decreasing;* and

(c) existing law and legal precedents would make it difficult to remove the regulatory burden from the federal government.

Carol Tucker Foreman and the 1979 proposal

In March 1977 the president of the Consumer Federation of America, Carol Tucker Foreman, became assistant secretary of agriculture responsible for food regulation and nutrition programs. Foreman had such a vigorously pro-consumer reputation that for a time within the industry-oriented Senate Agriculture Committee her nomination appeared threatened. Soon after her confirmation, she was presented with the Booz, Allen, and Hamilton report. Because the initial reaction of consumer, industry, and labor groups was predictably unfavorable to deregulation of this area, and also because her priorities were in other areas such as food additives and environmental contaminants, the recommendations were permitted to languish. In the meantime, however, the General Accounting Office also produced a report calling for mandatory quality control in the meat and poultry industry as a substitute for the USDA's labor-intensive program. And perhaps most important, it became abundantly clear that federal funds for inspection were not going to be expanded by the Office of Management and Budget or the Congress. Foreman and the agency found themselves having to reduce spending: self-regulation in the form of quality control beckoned.

Besides the argument of necessity, the proposal for a mandatory quality control program in meat and poultry inspection rested on the fundamental argument that an objective assessment of critical production points carried out by industry personnel could provide *better* consumer protection than a program in which inspectors, most of whom are not professionally trained in the sciences, made subjective determinations. This was partly because the major problems in meat inspection, such as residues of pesticides or the percentage of fat in a product, are more amenable to scientific sampling than to continuous eyeballing.

Also, it was argued that depending on objective tests (i.e., quantified reports of time and temperature, specified checklists of things that need to be done, written compliance procedures) could help eliminate human error, reduce the amount of bargaining between inspectors and businessmen, and give each protection against coercion from the other.

While Foreman found herself constantly in hot water with the industry because of her tough views on food additives, environmental contaminants, and nutrition issues, she was also an extremely skillful political operator. Faced with a very difficult budget situation in late 1978, she gave the initial go-ahead to developing a quality control proposal by the department, while still reserving the right to back out if the technocrats could not demonstrate the validity of their case, or if the political environment proved too unfavorable.

In practically every forum from early 1979 on, she talked tough about the budget—indeed, tougher than the messages she was actually getting from the department and from OMB—to create an environment in which she could forge a coalition around quality control or at least neutralize potential opponents. She had some great political advantages. Only someone with her impeccable consumer background could convince consumer activists that a move to self-regulation via mandatory private quality control systems might be in the larger interests of the American people. Only someone with ties to the labor movement, which Foreman had through the consumer/labor coalition, could have convinced the American Federation of Government Employees to keep still at the national level on an issue that in the long run would inevitably mean the erosion of union jobs.

The costs of introducing quality control programs are proportionately higher for small firms than for others. In order to satisfy the vocal and politically powerful small packing industry, Foreman made the critical decision to go forward only with an entirely voluntary program. Unlike many larger companies, like Campbell's Soup or Oscar Mayer, which had long ago begun to develop quality control departments, small packers remained totally dependent upon government inspectors for quality control and upon a government seal of inspection for consumer quality judgments. In order to increase the incentive for these companies to switch to a less labor-intensive inspection program, Foreman also offered less "overtime" inspection. Under the old system, the government paid for federal inspection that was carried out during regular business hours, but companies paid, through a user-fee system, in other circumstances. Foreman essentially promised that overtime expenses for inspection would substantially decrease if the industry would go along with quality control.

Finally, Foreman encountered the intractability of legal bureaucrats within the USDA. For years the inspection program had grown rather uncontrollably, largely because the department's lawyers, reinforced by those from industry, had insisted that a federal inspector be present whenever meat products were being made, that inspectors could apply the identifying "mark of inspection" only to meat products they had actually seen being produced, and that they must respond immediately to industry demands for inspection at any time of the day or night. These requirements grew from a statute clause mandating continuous inspection. After months of resistance, attorneys for the department finally agreed that companies' use of quality assurance programs could permit a reduction in the amount of time spent by an inspector at the plant. Every plant would still have to be visited every day under the voluntary program in order to satisfy—in some vague way—the "continuous" demands of an outmoded law, but the attendance could be minimal.

Foreman did not simply go to Congress for a change in the law to end the so-called "continuous inspection" requirements, because a department analysis made in mid-1979 indicated that very liberal and very conservative members would join ranks to defeat such a bill. Because both public health and economic interests were perceived to be at stake, any position that encouraged self-regulation—without proof that it could actually be done—was unacceptable.

What emerged from these competing interests and intensive negotiations? In essence, the USDA accepted the old 1974 proposal for a mandatory quality control program as an additional regulatory tool, with the following changes:

The program was repackaged to make compliance totally voluntary, and it was sold to the Congress as a *pilot* program, the evaluation of which would determine its continuance.

The department promised to retain all current employees, and not to hire more when people retired. This dampened labor union opposition.

In addition to offering the positive incentive of less overtime to small industry, the agency proposed a new labeling logo to indicate a confirmed level of public protection. This was designed to encourage participation through competition.

To allay consumer fears, the USDA promised—and ultimately delivered, but not until very late—to introduce legislation substantially increasing the penalties for violation of the law, and promised a vigorous independent compliance program.

To further cement the political acceptability of these changes, Foreman secured the support of both the White House Office of Consumer Affairs and the newly formed regulatory watchdog, the U.S. Regulatory Council. Armed with a package that seemed to save money, was acceptable from a number of political perspectives, was legal under existing law, and was wrapped in praise from the executive branch "interest groups," Foreman then approached the Hill with extensive personal and telephone briefings of key members of the health, agriculture, and appropriations committees. No one objected, and on 14 September 1979 a modest proposal to introduce voluntarism into a staid, old-line, federal regulatory program was made.

It is obvious, then, that the conversion of regulation into self-regulation is no easy task. Not only is the "fox in the chicken coop" argument inevitably raised by health and safety advocates, but industries become attuned to regulation that cements them into a particular economic position. Much industry opposition, both before and during the proposal period on quality control, stemmed from a personal distrust of Carol Foreman, although some also grew naturally from the old argument that it is better to deal with the devil you know. At any rate, it required a substantial political effort to introduce quality assurance, which had been used for many years in American industry, into this new industrial setting.

Finalizing the regulation and initial implementation

Even after such extensive spadework, the deep antagonism of the meat and poultry industry toward Assistant Secretary Foreman guaranteed that implementation would not be easy. The relevant industry associations decided to throw down the gauntlet on the relatively minor issue of the logo. The logo was perceived as a strong incentive to participate because the competitive nature of the industry would drive firms to the same accomplishments as their rivals. The industry lobbyists decided to take the position that no incentives to voluntarism should be included lest initial momentum encourage the government to make further movement mandatory and perhaps even force user fees on those firms continuing to use the department's services. Foreman simply overrode this criticism as well as one that objected to the use of the term "quality control." While the words are actually a "term of art" in the industry, some people argued that they implied improved product quality under this new system. The department insisted that this was not the case and refused to yield. Some minor changes were made, but in August 1980 the regulation was finalized. Two months later, amidst great fanfare, a company supplying meat to the McDonald's Corporation and (somewhat strangely) two small packing companies in Pennsylvania began a new adventure in regulatory voluntarism. They introduced total quality control programs into their plants, and began to do away with the constant presence of federal inspectors.

At about this point the administration changed, and pressure for increased efficiency heightened. At the beginning of the Reagan administration, a proposal was seriously considered to convert the entire meat and poultry inspection program to user fees—the ultimate voluntary approach. Given the difficulties that USDA had in proposing the voluntary quality assurance program, one can imagine how negatively both the industry and health interests responded to this user-fee idea. The result was to increase the legitimacy of the quality control program, and to further the objective of ultimately giving the secretary of agriculture the discretion to carry out the law however he or she sees fit. USDA made substantial additional concessions on overtime charges to encourage participation, and began drafting legislation to make "voluntarism"—i.e., self-regulated compliance—mandatory. This, too, will undoubtedly be opposed by competing interests. Consumer groups will see the proposals as attempts to decrease the amount of public protection, while producer interests are unlikely to support policies that may eliminate their taxpayer-paid quality assurance programs before they feel ready to assume additional financial burdens.

LESSONS FOR THE FUTURE

What lessons can be drawn from the meat and poultry case and from the discussion that preceded it? Several conditions appear to favor the implementation of voluntary and self-regulatory systems; if these conditions do not exist, it may be necessary to create them before implementation is attempted.

1. *Broad social consensus on programmatic goals.* Of course, consensus is equally necessary in the command-and-control systems currently at hand. However, it is not by accident that voluntarism seems to have made the greatest strides in areas like food and drug regulation, where statutes have been on the books for decades, and in which there seems to be little doubt concerning the necessity of action. Consensus must consist of more than the usual compromises that result in legislation; it must come through the more difficult but ultimately more helpful process of having these groups work with each other, in scientific and other forums, before approaching Congress for solutions. Congressmen can mediate minor differences; they cannot create consensus.

2. *Administrative and technical skill in monitoring self-regulatory arrangements.* In areas like vaccine development and radiation protection, industries look to the government for guidance on technical matters and react positively to suggestions for change. In attempting to secure greater consensus on regulatory issues, government may frequently be called upon to mediate technical disputes and facilitate scientific consensus. At present, agencies like the Consumer Product Safety Commission and the Occupational Safety and Health Administration are not held in high technical regard, which contributes to their political difficulties. Even within the relatively stable Food and Drug Administration, conflict between agency and industry officials is high on the drug side because industry has developed little or no respect for the quality of the agency scientists involved. Thus any move toward self-regulation may have to be accompanied by substantial efforts to upgrade the regulators' technical and scientific proficiency.

3. *Availability of technical knowledge and skills in the firms and industries at issue.* The nitrosamine testing program showed that industries should be left to their own devices only when alternative technologies are readily available, or at least within easy reach.

4. *Willingness and ability of regulatory agencies to crack down harder on the "bad apples" even while letting up on the "good apples."* It needs to be emphasized that both the current public mood and the incentive structures presented to industry require penalties for breaking the law to be sufficiently strong. While practically all polls indicate that the American people believe they are overregulated in general, those same polls reflect a rather strong consensus that the public wants to be protected from a variety of harms. Unfortunately, the penalty structures of many current regulatory statutes have been destroyed by inflation. Few agencies have the authority to collect money penalties, and even when collected these are usually paltry sums; only the Food and Drug

Act makes chief executive officers criminally responsible for the willful acts of their subordinates. Willful noncompliance cannot simply result in fines that can be seen as the "cost of doing business" if the public is to permit regulatory agencies and the Congress to withdraw from paternalistic oversight.

5. *Climate of change bordering on turbulence.* The case of meat and poultry inspection drives home again the truth that frugality often breeds creativity. In addition, today's juggernaut politics destroy some of the usual obstacles that face change. In particular, the protests of government employee unions that would resist this kind of regulatory change are crushed in the general mood of "improving governmental efficiency."

6. *Readiness to cope with political opposition from industries and firms that benefit from the regulatory status quo.* It needs to be said again that most business does not really like the free market. Either past investments have been made to build upon a system that has mandatory compliance aspects, or else—as in the case of meat inspection—businesses like certain costs of doing business, like quality assurance, to be performed by government and borne by the taxpayers at large. The politics of regulatory reform, therefore, require that reformers be prepared either to buy off the economic interests that would oppose them or else trounce them in a straight field. A mix of these two strategies was adopted in the meat and poultry case.

7. *Readiness on the part of consumer organizations and sympathetic legislators to give the idea of voluntarism a fair hearing.* Even though we have demonstrated here that a number of "voluntary" health and safety regulatory programs are already in place, this is not widely known in legislative circles. Because voluntarism often seems to work against a variety of interests, the skillful executive branch proponent of self-regulation will take great pains to enhance legislative receptivity and understanding before attempting implementation.

CONCLUSION

There is no reason to expect that self-regulation and governmental oversight will work smoothly or happily. At the very
least, the heightened threat of enforcement and heavy penalties guarantees some trouble. Further, we cannot simply
disavow the culture in which the regulation of the last fifty
years was spawned. America is not the homogeneous society
that permits the government and the governed to exist in
happy alliance. To the contrary—we live in a society where
the tension between power and liberty is evident, a society in
which that tension was deliberately created. Distrust and
litigation form a powerful dynamic in our political culture
that will not easily be overcome by bureaucrats or legislators
desiring to deed over political power. Initially, at least, many
people will simply not believe in the possibility of
cooperation.

The Founding Fathers created a system in which private
vice would be transformed into public virtue. Two hundred
years later, we face the challenge of modifying that prescription in the hope that U.S. businesses will do unto themselves
in lieu of the government doing unto them.

5

TIMOTHY J. SULLIVAN

Tailoring Government Response to Diversity*

Regulatory classes and tiered regulations. Exemption procedures. Class-by-class programs. Costs of compliance. Information needed for program development, design, and administration. The problems of a tiered regulatory program. The need for change.

This chapter explores the potential of targeting regulations to classes of activities or substances for improving the efficiency of government regulations. Although the use of such a

*The author would like to thank Eugene Bardach, A. Lawrence Chickering, Curtis Haymore, Robert Kagan, Arnold Meltsner, and John Quigley for their comments on earlier drafts. A special thanks to Andrea Altschuler for her assistance in investigating the intricacies of the Medical Devices Act.

119

regulatory program cannot achieve the theoretical efficiencies of a tax program (see Bardach and Kagan's chapter 1), it can offer a practical tool to help lower the costs of achieving a regulatory goal.

A regulatory program that relies on classifications can either group practices or substances into classes for similar treatment, or create tiers that make fine distinctions between similar practices or substances. These regulatory classes and tiered regulations can reflect the differential costs of producing a desired outcome or the different consequences of a particular activity or product. In some situations, this flexibility can offer substantially more efficient regulation than programs that treat uniformly all regulated activities or substances. In other situations, classification imposes costs on both the regulatory agency and the regulated firms that offset any potential benefits.

Government experiences with classification raise a series of questions. What factors should be most important in deciding to develop regulatory classifications? How can regulators reduce the costs of designing these programs? What can government do to encourage wider consideration of regulatory alternatives?

TAILORING REGULATIONS—EXEMPTIONS, CASE-BY-CASE REVIEW, TIERING, AND CLASS-BY-CLASS REGULATION

One response to the inherent diversity of industrial practices and geography is to tailor regulatory requirements to specific situations. This can be done by uniform regulatory requirements with procedures for granting exemptions, case-by-case regulatory decision making, and requirements designed for specific classes of activities or substances. Conceptually, these programs are similar—each offers a flexible response to varied situations. In operation, they differ greatly in administrative and procedural consequences for the regulatory agencies and the public alike. Although they could all produce identical controls for a particular practice or substance, the regulatory costs of each will vary with the procedures used for tailoring requirements to exceptional cases, as well as with the number and diversity of the exceptions.

In general, exemption procedures work best when only a few practices or substances require special treatment. For example, all used cars brought to California must meet emissions control standards before owners can obtain a California license plate. Most cars are alike, and those that fail generally can pass after an adjustment of the carburetor, replacement of cracked hoses, or a tune-up. If these procedures fail and only expensive repairs can make a car passable, the owner may petition for an exception. This procedure aims to avoid imposing costs on individuals that greatly exceed social benefits.

Case-by-case review may prove necessary when the factors affecting a regulatory decision are specific to a situation. For example, the Environmental Protection Agency (EPA) sets emissions standards for power plants based on the location of each plant, current ambient concentrations of air pollutants, a computer model of the plant's impacts on local air quality, and a consideration of the available technology for controlling pollutants. These case-by-case decisions require major commitments of time and resources by both the regulated utility and the regulatory agency. Once again, if the total number of cases requiring review is small, this may prove highly efficient.

These two alternatives—establishing a uniform regulatory practice with an exception procedure, and designing a review to establish case-by-case regulations—constitute the ends of a spectrum of regulatory responses to divergent situations. A program that aims to regulate a firm's practices

and products by targeting different classes offers an intermediate regulatory response. Sometimes these regulations
are tiered, i.e., products or practices are subject to different
levels of regulation and control depending on their class.
Medical devices, for example, must fulfill regulatory requirements that become more stringent to reflect the degree of
risk that the failure of the device poses to a patient's health.
At other times, categories may subdivide a large class into
different subclasses requiring quite different treatments.
The EPA divides the treatment technologies for hazardous
wastes into landfills, incinerators, chemical treatment, land
treatment, and deep-well injection, and regulates each type
of disposal technology separately. Other regulatory programs, such as the Clean Air Act, distinguish between old
and new facilities and place less stringent controls on existing plants. Many programs distinguish between small and
large producers, and exempt smaller producers from requirements. These practices seek to tailor regulations to the diversity that often underlies a surface uniformity.

Despite the arguments of common sense and the potential
economic benefits from more efficient regulation that support a wider use of regulatory classes, tiered regulations and
regulation by class are less widely used than we might expect. This results in part because many practical problems
combine to limit the development of classification schemes.
For a regulatory agency, determining when things are similar and when they are different raises both political and
practical problems. Efficiency considerations suggest that
society achieve a regulatory goal by requiring firms with the
lowest abatement costs to do the most. However, forcing
these firms to bear the major share of abatement or compliance costs raises political questions of fairness that limit a
regulatory agency's ability to adopt this strategy. Developing
regulatory classifications also requires a lot of work. For distinctions to have practical significance, an agency must
determine appropriate and different regulations for each

class or category that it creates. Next, the agency must assign the regulated activities, products, or procedures to each of the different categories in a way that can withstand legal challenges. Finally, an agency must enforce the regulations for each of its classifications. Thus, the decision to use this regulatory technique requires careful consideration of the many benefits and costs in specific settings.

BENEFITS PRODUCED BY TIERING OR CLASS-BY-CLASS REGULATORY PROGRAMS

The use of tiered regulations or class-by-class regulatory programs offers potential benefits, both from the protection the regulatory program offers the public, and from the efficiency advantages of tiered regulations and categorical schemes over other forms of regulation. Class-by-class regulatory programs can allow a government agency to reduce an industry's costs of meeting a regulatory goal or, alternatively, to produce a better performance for a required outlay than a uniform regulatory program. Furthermore, categorical schemes can also enhance government's ability to manage regulatory programs.

The development of the Occupational Safety and Health Administration's (OSHA) cotton dust control program illustrates how targeting regulations to classes of textile processes can substantially increase the benefits of imposed regulatory costs. In 1976 OSHA proposed a regulatory program to control exposure to cotton dust in workplaces throughout the cotton industry (41 *Federal Register* 56498–527). The proposed regulation set a uniform exposure standard of 200 micrograms per cubic meter as an ambient concentration for cotton dust particles in the workplace and applied this standard to the entire cotton industry. The agency commissioned

a study that estimated the costs of complying with this proposed uniform cotton dust standard at $808 million a year on
an annualized basis. The magnitude of these costs led to demands by management that OSHA develop an alternative
approach (DeMuth 1980, p. 18).

Data that were received during the public comment period
following the proposed regulatory standard demonstrated
that the health consequences of exposure to cotton dust
varied by job within the cotton industry (43 *Federal Register*
27350–418). In response, OSHA separated cotton ginning —
which is generally done for about eight weeks following the
cotton harvest and does not appear to induce brown lung disease — from the year-round cotton textile industry. OSHA
then eliminated exposure standards for cotton dust in cotton
ginning, but required the cotton ginners to keep health records on workers and to provide workers with respirators.

Additional information showed that the incidence of
brown lung disease varied by textile process, so OSHA set an
exposure standard of 200 micrograms per cubic meter for
yarn manufacturing, 750 micrograms per cubic meter for
slashing and weaving, and 500 micrograms per cubic meter
for all other textile processes. OSHA argued that these class-
specific standards would provide workers within a plant with
equal health protection and produce a better use of the industry's resources. OSHA stated (43 *Federal Register* 27360),
"Optimal worker protection would be served by concentrating
the textile industry's technical and economic resources on
achieving 200 micrograms per cubic meter in yarn manufacturing as rapidly as feasible, rather than directing substantial resources to eliminating dust exposure in weaving."
These final regulations targeting standards to textile
processes have an estimated cost only one-quarter of the
original uniform standard (DeMuth 1980, p. 19).

In many situations, regulatory classes and tiered regulations can reflect the differential costs or benefits of taking steps towards a regulatory goal (although perhaps not as

subtly as a tax program). The most common use of regulatory classifications is to distinguish between small and large firms and to regulate the smaller less strictly (U.S. Regulatory Council 1980*b*, p. 5). The Federal Energy Regulatory Commission, for example, has exempted small hydroelectric power facilities (up to 5 megawatts capacity) from licensing requirements (U.S. Regulatory Council 1980*b*, p. 6). The Civil Aeronautics Board has reduced the scope of reporting requirements for small airlines (U.S. Regulatory Council 1980*a*, p. 14). The Clean Air Act amendments of 1977 and their implementing regulations exempt power plants that consume less than 73 megawatts of fossil fuel from regulations that control sulfur dioxide emissions (40 Code of Federal Regulations 40a[b]). These examples are typical of a wide variety of tiered regulations (U.S. Regulatory Council 1980*a*, pp. 13–14).

When the costs of compliance decrease with facility size, subjecting large facilities to stricter regulation than small ones can offer efficiency gains over programs that treat everything alike. However, this practice raises a question of fairness. Why should those who can abate pollution most efficiently be forced to do it? This question has no simple answer, and illustrates the political dimension of attempts to improve the efficiency of regulatory programs. Furthermore, when a regulatory agency is not allocating a scarce resource but providing a service, such as worker or consumer safety, there are fewer compelling reasons for distinguishing between firms by their size, the size of their production runs, or their compliance costs. Many would argue that all workers in a particular industry should enjoy the same level of safety, no matter what the size of the workplace. In addition, expenditures by small firms for safety improvements may provide more benefits than those by large firms. Thus we are led to a note of caution: in establishing classes for regulation, one must consider the forgone benefits of looser regulation as well as the costs saved.

Old plants are commonly required to meet less strict regulations than plants at the design or planning stage. Since existing facilities are often unable to change their operations to incorporate the latest devices for reducing the harms their operations produce, regulatory requirements can impose high costs on them. Many older power plants, for example, lack the physical space necessary to install pollution abatement devices, such as scrubbers, on their plants. Strict regulatory requirements can force these plants to close down.

Reducing requirements for older plants can help an agency avoid the high political costs incurred when its actions are linked to plant closures and concentrated job losses. Although almost none of the many steel mills slated for closure in 1980 failed to meet *interim* pollution standards, industry officials argued that their regulatory expenditures consumed resources needed to modernize plants. Meeting stricter *future* standards would, in their view, require expenditures on pollution equipment that would make older plants unprofitable. EPA's regulatory program became an issue in the presidential campaign of 1980, and led to amendments of the Clean Air Act (the Steel Industry Compliance Act of 1981) to allow compliance with air pollution standards for older steel plants to be deferred.

Tailoring regulations to classes may not only increase the efficiency of an industry's expenditures, but also provide a regulatory agency with an efficient way to manage its programs. A government agency can target its resources on those classes of substances and practices where regulatory action can prove most effective. Exempting small firms from regulation can dramatically reduce an agency's administrative burden and permit it to use its own resources more productively. In implementing a regulatory program to control hazardous waste, EPA initially exempted firms that produce less than 1,000 kilograms per month (45 *Federal Register* 33104). EPA argued that it could not regulate all 760,000 generators of hazardous waste with its current staff. An exclusion standard of 1,000 kilograms per month would exempt 91.2 percent of the generators from regulations, yet regulate 99.0 percent of the total wastes generated. EPA judged that this approach would best serve its objective of insuring environmental quality until it gained resources to regulate generators of small quantities of wastes.

Despite the examples discussed so far, regulatory programs use tiered regulations or regulatory classification schemes less frequently than they could. Sometimes Congress forces a regulatory agency to adopt a uniform standard. At other times, an agency can lack the information, resources, or initiative to develop these relatively complex programs.

The regulatory program to control automobile emissions illustrates how simple distinctions could dramatically lower regulatory costs without seriously affecting health benefits. The Clean Air Act of 1970 and its amendments of 1977 mandate the control of automobile emissions throughout the country. Under the 1970 provisions (modified slightly in 1977), all cars sold in the United States must eventually achieve a 90 percent reduction in carbon monoxide, hydrocarbons, and nitrous oxide emissions from the level of the 1970 controls. In an analysis of the Clean Air Act of 1970, David Harrison (1977, p. 530) estimated that these mandated standards will cost about $4 billion a year (in 1972 dollars) by 1990. Harrison then proposed a two-class regulatory program that exploits the variations in air quality between urban and rural areas. He estimated that a two-tier strategy applying the 1970 standards to the forty-three most polluted areas of the country while retaining 1968 emission standards for all other areas would save American households about $1.4 billion per year by 1990 with "virtually no sacrifice in air quality" (Harrison 1977, p. 543). In addition, Harrison's analysis indicated that this two-tier strategy would reduce the regulatory program's burden on the poor. Thus, the failure of Congress to exploit these geographic distinctions

threw away an opportunity to save over $1 billion per year in
regulatory costs that provide almost no benefits.

COSTS OF DESIGN, IMPLEMENTATION, AND ADMINISTRATION OF CLASS-BY-CLASS REGULATORY PROGRAMS

The costs of classification schemes increase with their complexity and fall on both industry and the government. Unlike
expenditures on new equipment for safety or emission controls, the costs generated by regulatory procedures provide
no benefits in themselves. Complex classification schemes
increase the information, labor, and time needed to develop a
regulatory program, require more administrative resources,
and increase the potential for costly litigation. Industry
needs more information to comply with a complex program,
and may face a regulatory process that introduces costly uncertainty into business decisions. In addition, the very process of creating multiple regulatory classes runs the risk of
intervention by politicians to create additional classes —
unrelated to risks, benefits, or costs — to reward special interest constituencies.

Obtaining information for the design of regulations

In areas of new regulation, such as environmental or health
and safety programs, the implementing agency inevitably
proceeds from a state of ignorance. Although aware of the
harms associated with a business process or product in a
general way, it will possess little information detailing how
the harm arises, what alternative measures could correct or
reduce it, how much required measures would cost, or how
many firms would pay. OSHA learned how health risks vary

within the cotton industry only after it publicly proposed a strict uniform standard. EPA had only crude estimates of the number of firms generating hazardous wastes before initiating its regulatory program, and placed ads in the *Wall Street Journal* reminding businesses to notify EPA if they produced hazardous wastes.

Initially, industry will possess more of the information and expertise necessary to address the problems that generated the demand for government regulation. The fact that regulatory agencies must often adopt an adversarial stance towards the industry limits the government's ability to acquire that information. Businesses seldom share information concerning manufacturing or trade practices with anyone. Although some firms will cooperate with government regulatory agencies, sharing information often leads only to requirements that impose further costs and restrictions on their operations.

Government agencies, for good political reasons, cannot easily hire technical experts away from business. Such practices create the risk that the regulatory agency will be captured by the regulated industry, and they almost always generate attacks by agency critics that erode public confidence in government action. Consequently, an agency often can gain the information necessary to design an effective regulatory program only through the formal regulatory process. Thus, an agency must propose a regulatory strategy, wait for public comments and criticisms, and then promulgate final regulations. When government agencies lack information, this process can lead to embarrassing mistakes and inappropriate regulation.

Classification schemes increase the amount of information a regulatory agency requires. The agency must obtain enough data to discriminate between different classes of substances or practices and to develop regulatory criteria. Classification schemes that have relied on obvious distinctions—such as the difference between an old or new

plant, or a large or small firm—or on different technological
processes, have proved the easiest to implement. When
classifications are based on something difficult to measure,
such as risk, the amount of information needed can become
prohibitively large.

The Medical Devices Act offers an example in which the
use of a flexible regulatory scheme led to the extension of
regulations to inappropriate areas and produced an endless
bureaucratic exercise of obtaining information for classifying medical devices. The act calls for the regulation in three
risk categories of all medical devices whose failure may harm
patients. Class I medical devices, which are subject to only
general controls (such as the registration of manufacturers,
labeling, and record-keeping requirements), include tongue
depressors, arm slings, bedpans, and even autopsy tables.
Class II contains devices that the Food and Drug Administration (FDA) believes require more controls to assure safety
and effectiveness, but for which performance standards,
once established, can promote safety; this class includes
blood pressure machines and hearing aids. Class III contains
implanted, life-sustaining, or new medical devices; these require a premarket review by FDA to determine whether they
are safe and effective. This class includes heart pacemakers
and intrauterine contraceptive devices.

This program, although possessing a flexible structure,
has led to unnecessary regulation and to a prolonged bureaucratic exercise in classifying medical devices. It is hard to imagine who benefits from the regulation of bedpans or autopsy
tables. In response to this ambitious program, the FDA spent
over five years in classifying devices; so far, no standards
have been promulgated for those in Class II. Despite the
nobility of this desire to promote safety, it is unclear what
protections the regulations provide beyond those offered by
existing liability laws, medical-products testing services, and
the scrutiny of hospitals and doctors. Basing a regulatory
classification scheme on the abstract notion of risk imposed
insurmountable information burdens on the FDA.

Implementing and administering
a regulatory program

After the information required for developing a regulatory program has been gained, its actual design, implementation, and administration will require much time and effort. A two-class regulatory scheme, for example, will require almost twice as much regulation writing as a one-class structure. The actual tasks of writing and obtaining agency and Office of Management and Budget (OMB) approvals can consume incredible amounts of administrative time and resources. The EPA regulatory process, for example, requires many reviews at several levels of the organization before the proposed regulations pass to OMB for final approval. Nothing is easy.

Running a program with more classes and categories also requires more administrative resources. Classifying substances and activities will likely necessitate more refined tests and procedures. In addition, if the regulations are tailored to a particular class, then enforcement personnel may need special training. Under the Medical Devices Act, for example, manufacturers of the most-controlled devices, those used in the body (*in vivo*) and new devices (Class III), must submit data demonstrating the effectiveness and reliability of their products before they are certified for use. In the least risk-imposing class (I), the manufacturers must insure that the devices fulfill their manufacturing claims. Personnel evaluating the safety of Class III devices will require more training and expertise than those who seek to guarantee compliance with the truthful advertising requirements of Class I.

The design and implementation of a regulatory program requires time, and the time needed grows with the program's sophistication. Government agencies, however, rarely have much leeway. When legislation seeks to solve a pressing national problem, Congress and the country want to see quick action; recent Congresses have attempted to force agency action through statutorily mandated deadlines. Despite the complexity and dearth of information on hazardous wastes, the Resource Conservation and Recovery Act of 1976 required the publication of regulations within one and a half years. In fact, EPA did not publish its major regulations until more than three and a half years later. Similar short deadlines were set in legislation to produce clean air and control toxic substances. Although these deadlines spur regulatory progress and give the program priority on an agency's working agenda, they limit the time that an agency has for considering regulatory alternatives.

Political costs, too, can rise when a certain class of practices or substances is exempted from the most stringent regulatory requirements. Critics of an agency may ask why a risk-producing activity should not be held to all possible safety requirements. As long as an agency can argue that it is doing everything it can to assure safety, the troublesome issue of deciding when enough has been done need not be faced. A classification scheme that permits a regulatory agency to separate industrial practices and substances on the basis of health or safety risks may give the agency more flexibility than it might wish to have. For just this reason, the FDA has never liked the National Academy of Science's recommendation to group food additives by risk.

The potential for costly litigation increases with regulatory complexity. An agency can face particularly large litigation costs when firms challenge its classification of their products or procedures as arbitrary or capricious. Other firms may claim that the applicable regulations are too strict compared to other classes or tiers. Regulators designing a flexible classification scheme often find that their agency's lawyers favor simpler programs without high risks of litigation.

Industry requires regulatory information and faces added uncertainty

A complex program will increase the costs to a firm in acquiring the information needed to understand it. These costs offset some of the savings that targeted regulations produce. Firms often must hire experts to chart their course through a sea of regulations. In the 1977 Clean Air Act amendments, which subject all existing plants to less-strict regulations than new ones, a dispute arose between the Montana Power Company and the EPA over interpretation of the legislative language defining which regulations a plant under construction had to meet. This led to prolonged and costly litigation. It is important to remember that the costs of understanding a program or resolving ambiguities in legislation and regulation provide no benefits—environmental quality is only improved by expenditures on actual pollution control measures.

Complexity can create uncertainties that reduce management's ability to plan ahead. This can impose costs on firms such as construction companies that unexpected decisions or delays affect most seriously. These costs offset the savings of targeted regulations. Although complexity does not necessitate unpredictability, complex programs will likely generate ambiguous regulatory situations that require administrative or judicial resolution.

INCENTIVES AFFECTING THE DESIGN OF REGULATIONS

In considering the costs or benefits of developing a system of regulatory classes, an agency will likely prove more sensitive to the costs and benefits for itself rather than to the costs and benefits for the regulated industry and the public. Not surprisingly, the most common use of tiered regulations is to reduce the compliance burdens regulatory programs place on old plants and small businesses. These distinctions help an agency to target its regulations to firms best able to comply and to reduce its administrative tasks, which can prove especially important in preserving political acceptance and in allowing program implementation with limited staff. In particular, the distinction between old and new plants provides a way for an administrative agency or Congress to avoid the visible costs—especially workers' jobs—associated with taking regulatory action against existing plants, even where regulatory controls may provide benefits to society far exceeding costs.

The government has a poorer record in making regulatory distinctions when targeted regulations could produce benefits for the consuming public but impose costs on the agency or congressional decision making. As already mentioned, Congress's failure to distinguish between the effects of reducing emissions from automobiles driven in the country from those driven in the city has added over $1 billion per year to the costs of regulation. Similarly, EPA's program to regulate power plant emissions uses a regulatory scheme that is only partially sensitive to the regional variations of the concentrations of pollutants in coal. Ackerman and Hassler (1981, pp. 79–104) in *Clean Coal, Dirty Air* argue that in designing its air pollution regulations, EPA used ambiguous legislative language to accede to the lobbying efforts of a coalition of Eastern coal producers and environmental interests. They charge that to avoid the political costs of antagonizing these interests, EPA adopted an across-the-board scrubber requirement that fosters the use of dirty coal. This leads to both higher concentrations of sulfur pollutants east of the Mississippi and higher levels of expenditure on pollution control equipment than do other programs developed by EPA's own staff. In both these programs, government failed to exploit opportunities to provide benefits to society at lower cost to the public.

Even when government is particularly sensitive to the costs it is imposing, the development of a tiered regulatory program can prove a thankless task. In moving from a uniform standard to control cotton dust to separate standards for different cotton processes, OSHA did not win acclaim. Industry groups sued, claiming that even the final modified standards were too high. Labor unions and special interest groups called for stricter regulations.

When regulatory reformers measure the regulatory burden by number of pages, tiered regulations will look bad. Although the final cotton dust standards should reduce compliance costs by 75 percent over the initial uniform standard, the increased consumption of *Federal Register* pages by these tiered standards is dramatic. The original proposed uniform standard required 29 *Federal Register* pages—12 pages to describe, and 17 pages to discuss (41 *Federal Register* 56498–527). The final tiered regulations (including those regulating cotton ginning) were almost twice as long, covering 113 *Federal Register* pages—52 pages to describe, and 61 pages to discuss (43 *Federal Register* 27350–463).

It is hard to generate enthusiasm for regulatory programs that, while efficient, incur higher administration and implementation costs. Neither the press, public scrutiny, nor congressional review will consistently encourage the search for flexibility. Although the textile industry effectively presented its case to OSHA to win modification of the cotton dust standards, no group forcefully lobbied for a two-tier automobile regulatory strategy. Although the regulatory compliance costs for automobiles will total more per year than those resulting from cotton dust, the lack of an organized group to represent the interests of nonurban car drivers left their cause unchampioned.

DEVELOPING AND USING REGULATORY PROGRAMS WITH CLASSES

Congress and regulatory agencies have missed numerous opportunities, as in auto regulation, to modify regulatory programs in simple ways and produce savings to the regulated community without causing a drop in benefits. At other times, such as in the regulation of medical devices, classification programs have consumed larger amounts of administrative resources than expected.

The availability of information needed for sensible regulation is crucial to the development of a successful regulatory program. When industry and agency adopt an adversarial stance, government will have great difficulty gaining useful information. Only the passage of time will likely allow a regulatory agency to acquire information and the ability to use it. In the interim, a classification scheme may allow an agency to act immediately to fulfill congressional commands, while creating categories for practices and substances that will be regulated only after the agency gains experience.

The common uses of tiering, making simple distinctions between old and new plants and small and large businesses, offer practical and simple ways of sorting firms for separate treatment. OSHA's reliance on existing distinctions within the cotton industry—ginning, yarn making, thrashing and weaving, and all others—offered it classes where different risks justified different standards. The Medical Devices Act's Classes I and II, differing as we have seen by degree of risk, offer no obvious way to sort devices. These experiences suggest that agencies should look for and exploit natural classes when specialized treatment offers opportunities for efficiency gains, but avoid attempts to classify practices and substances that differ only in degree.

To encourage the wider use of tiering or programs that regulate by class, changes must be made in the incentives and constraints on regulatory agencies. When no organized interests force consideration of a classification program, an agency's time and resources may be too limited for the added efforts needed to develop flexible regulatory alternatives. Congress must allow more time for the agency to explore regulatory strategies, or else conduct its own analysis prior to passing legislation. Beyond this, efforts to educate agency personnel, such as the FDA's handbook *Flexible Regulatory Alternatives*, are an obvious first step in encouraging personnel to consider options beyond traditional command-and-control forms of regulation. The Regulatory Council's efforts to catalogue and publicize the uses of flexible regulatory programs also fill a real information need. Other institutional changes, such as Executive Order 12291 to require cost-benefit analysis, may promote a more thorough consideration of all regulatory alternatives, including tiering.

There is no question that tiered regulations targeting requirements to different classes offer a potentially efficient regulatory technique. Although implementing this suggestion seems simple conceptually, in practice implementation can be extremely complex. Unfortunately, just as the failure to target regulations can impose needless costs on industry while providing few benefits, the attempt to create classification schemes can sometimes lead to expensive bureaucratic exercises with no tangible benefits. No one strategy offers a panacea for all regulatory problems. The trick is to find appropriate remedies in specific situations—a matter, ultimately, not of theoretical program design, but of judgment tempered by experience.

6

PAUL DANACEAU

Developing Successful Enforcement Programs

On-site inspection programs. Regulatory variations. The adversary relationship between inspectors, business, and industry. Standards, procedures, and company problems. Violations, citations, and fines. Preventive measures. The USDA, OSHA, and OSM programs. The potential role for on-site inspectors.

Robert C. Limpert, a 35-year-old veterinarian, has for the past several years directed a meat and poultry inspection program in the Green Bay, Wisconsin, area that U.S. Department of Agriculture (USDA) officials would like others to emulate. Green Bay meat industry people evidently agree. They not only are satisfied with the way the federal Meat

and Poultry Inspection Program (MPIP) works in their nine-
teen plants, but some executives even prefer it to a system of
self-regulation or self-certification in which USDA agents,
who now inspect plants during every shift of every day,
would leave the daily inspection process to the companies
and limit their role to monitoring the companies' performance from time to time.

Some self-interest is at work here. If USDA inspectors
were not available, the plants would have to hire their own
quality assurance people. That would be a much more expensive proposition than the current practice of having companies reimburse the USDA only for overtime hours the inspectors work. In addition, several executives fear the absence of federal inspectors might lead consumers to wonder
if the companies were cutting corners on the quality of their
products, if the steak or sausage they bought in the super-
market today was as wholesome as what they bought yester-
day. But the main reason the Green Bay meat industry did
not join the nationwide cry for an end to government regulation, inspection, and enforcement was that they were
satisfied with the way the meat and poultry inspection program worked in their plants. "What can I tell you?" asked
the vice-president of a company that owns a slaughterhouse
and some meat processing plants.

This is regulation that works. The inspectors are tough, but they
are fair. I can remember a time when I was ready to go to Washington once a week to complain. Now I can't even remember the last
time I wanted to argue with an inspector.

Inspectors handpicked by their agencies to represent programs in a favorable light hardly constitute a representative
sample of the enforcement process at work, either in terms
of the individual agency or the regulatory process as a whole.
Model inspectors, after all, rarely are accused of such sins as
focusing on "nit-picking details," being unsympathetic to the
problems of the business or industry they regulate, or hiding
behind their authority and rulebooks instead of regarding

business as an equal and respected partner in the regulatory process. But the work of Limpert and other model inspectors—David Hollenbeck of the Department of the Interior's Office of Surface Mining (OSM) and Matt Finucane of the Occupational Safety and Health Administration (OSHA) in the Department of Labor were two others accorded this status[1]—can be used as a standard by companies inspected on a regular basis to measure their own experience, and by regulatory agencies to measure their own on-site inspection and enforcement programs.

Regulatory programs, however, do not succeed just because the on-site inspector is good at his job. They also succeed because individual businessmen and regulatory agency policymakers are equally good at their jobs, even though most discussions of the strengths and weaknesses of regulatory programs focus almost exclusively on the activities of on-site inspectors—what they look for, what they find, what kinds of citations they issue, how they resolve problems that arise. Efforts to develop successful enforcement programs, therefore, need to focus on the roles and responsibilities of all three actors in the process: the on-site inspector, the businessman, and the policymaker.

WHAT INSPECTORS CAN DO

Differences in regulatory programs and variations in local conditions make it virtually impossible to develop detailed blueprints for effective enforcement programs. A program that has on-site inspections every day is going to function differently from one that conducts on-site inspections every six months. And a program in which federal and state regulators share responsibility and authority has different constraints from one in which federal regulators have sole responsibility and authority. Inspectors, though, are the most visible actors in the enforcement process and, in policy terms, they can contribute to successful and effective programs in three ways.

First, inspectors can develop working styles that allow them to accommodate the concerns of the business or industry they inspect without compromising the objectives or the integrity of the programs they represent.

Second, they can follow organized, consistent, and uniform patterns that, for the most part, are as familiar to the people being inspected as to those conducting the inspections.

Third, they can define their goals in terms of preventing — rather than finding — violations.

Supporters and critics of regulation alike often complain that the regulatory process does not work the way it should. What both groups want, they say, is a spirit of accommodation in which the regulator and the regulated work out a mutually acceptable solution to a common problem. What they get, they say, is an adversary relationship in which regulators more often than not try to force something down someone's throat because it was written down in a manual, not because it was a better solution. "The thing that bothers me more than anything," Philip L. Deaton, the city manager of Janesville, Wisconsin, once said,

is when someone from the government comes down here to talk with us about regulations and the first thing they do is pull out a document and point to the section that says they have the authority to tell us what to do. In a legal proceeding, the theory is that you are innocent until someone proves you guilty. In a regulatory proceeding, you are made to feel you are guilty until you can prove your own innocence.[2]

Inspectors obviously must be knowledgeable about the underlying social goals of the programs they work for. They also must possess a clear understanding, which they should pass on to the regulated businesses, about how the regulations they enforce contribute to those objectives. And they must be secure enough in their convictions not to retreat from confrontation if the safety of an individual, the wholesomeness of meat, or the quality of the environment are at stake. No competent inspector is going to tolerate procedures, activities, or omissions on the part of business or industry that directly threaten these fundamental social objectives of regulatory programs.

On the other hand, it is both desirable and possible for inspectors to respond to the concerns and anxieties of business and industry without jeopardizing either the goals of the programs they represent or their own positions as enforcement officers. For instance, they sometimes can allow plants in shaky financial condition to develop temporary and less costly ways of complying with regulations. Companies still must comply with regulations but, by granting an extension on the deadline, inspectors can ease the financial burden provided an alternative measure is adopted that satisfies the basic objective of the regulation. USDA regulations, for example, require that loading and parking areas be black-topped to reduce the possibility of dust and dirt contaminating fresh meat being shipped into or out of a plant. However, the inspector granted one company, which had built a new plant but which also had been the victim of high interest rates and declining sales, a four-month extension in meeting that requirement. The company in turn agreed to treat the unsurfaced area regularly with a bonding or wetting agent to keep dirt from blowing around.

Considering a company's financial position and developing an alternative that allows it to meet the intent if not the letter of the regulation is one way enforcement officers can be responsive to the businesses they regulate. Another way is to organize their inspections so the work under way at each plant or work site is subjected to as little disruption as possible. Although there is a genuine need for unscheduled and unannounced visits when verifying records, many on-site inspectors have proved to be unnecessarily rude and high-handed—walking in unannounced to regulated businesses

144 PAUL DANACEAU

and expecting everything to be dropped, going through files when the proprietors are out, etc. An atmosphere of mutual courtesy is far more productive of good regulation.

Inspectors also can avoid conducting tests for laboratory analysis samples when that clearly is not necessary, such as when plants do not use enough of any one material or substance, or do not engage in any single operation long enough, to result in overexposure to a health or safety hazard. They can take whatever extra time is needed to answer employers' questions about the enforcement process as a whole, any particular aspect of it, or a certain standard or violation. And they can point out situations that, if left unattended, could result in violations, citations, or monetary fines the next time an inspection occurred.

Doing the job well, however, means more than being responsive to problems an individual company might be having. It also means developing standards and procedures for conducting inspections and then making sure they are known by the people whose plants and businesses are inspected. If an enforcement officer does his job correctly, nobody should be surprised by what he looks for or how he reacts to a particular situation.

Injecting this kind of consistency into the inspections makes the inspectors' jobs easier because it can create systematic, efficient, and stable working routines for inspecting a plant or work site. Consistency is an important issue in its own right, because all plants must be treated fairly and equitably, with respect both to the way inspections are conducted and to how regulations are interpreted and enforced. Few mistakes are as serious as interpreting a regulation one way in one plant and another way in a second, or conducting inspections differently in different plants when there is no logical reason for doing so. Company representatives invariably concur. They do not object to an inspector's being thorough or vigorous; they object to an inspector's being arbitrary, requiring one plant to go through its paces without requiring the same of others, or to an inspector's making a decision that seems to be based on nothing stronger or more reliable than personal whim.

While all inspectors should guard against these problems, the overall issue of consistency—or the lack of it—can have a more profound impact in programs where inspections occur every day or where inspectors are rotated among plants within a certain geographic area. A person in Robert Limpert's position, for example, not only has to decide how he will conduct himself, but he also has to set and maintain a standard for the thirty-five other inspectors whose activities he supervises. The USDA manual often provides little help. How do you interpret a regulation that says, "All wall and floor surfaces must be clean"? Or one that says, "Driveways and vehicular loading areas must be paved and properly drained"? How do you define the terms "clean" and "properly drained"? A supervisor clearly would not want a plant inspector making a major case out of a few puddles in the parking lot or a small grease smudge underneath the corner of a cutting table.

Limpert's solution was to meet with his inspectors on a regular basis and show them, in person, those conditions in a plant he felt were acceptable, those he felt were not acceptable, and those he felt were borderline. "You can't describe any of this in writing," he explained.

You can't describe it on the phone. You can't even describe it in a face-to-face conversation. You have to actually walk them through a plant and point out what you mean by a "clean" table, a "clean" wall, or a "clean" outside area. And then you have to spend some time with the plant personnel to make sure they understand these standards and the reasons for them.

If the system works, says Limpert, companies should see no dramatic changes or differences in inspectors' attitudes or behaviors when assignments are rotated. There also should be no dramatic changes or differences in the way various in-plant inspectors respond to given situations or between the way an inspector responds and the way the supervisor responds.

Part of the enforcement officer's job is to issue or recommend citations that can result in fines and other penalties. Enforcement officers cannot avoid looking at their jobs, at least partially, in terms of the number of violations they find. But the regulatory environment can be improved substantially when enforcement officers also see their job in terms of prevention—identifying situations and circumstances that could lead to violations, citations, and fines, and encouraging companies to take steps to reduce these possibilities.

Limpert looked at the meat inspection program he directed in the following way. "The goal of this program," he said,

isn't to see how many people or plants we can catch who are not complying with regulations in some way, or how often we can catch them. We are not trying to surprise people or catch them off guard or interfere with the work they are doing. The goal of this program is to prevent problems from occurring in the first place.

Success, in other words, should not be measured in terms of how many problems an enforcement officer encounters and how often he encounters them. It should be measured in terms of how few problems he finds and how minor these turn out to be. In fact, some inspectors who visit plants on a daily basis believe frequent and serious violations are an indication that the inspector may not be doing his job well.

Violations still occur in the best of plants, and some plants are harder to work with than others. Some inspectors, such as those who work for OSHA, frequently function more as enforcement agents than as informal consultants simply because area office work loads are so heavy that compliance officers inspect a plant only after someone has filed a specific complaint alleging a serious hazard. In addition, company officials sympathetic to the idea of prevention in other plants may find it difficult to accept it in their own. Many items the enforcement officer looks for or wants to discuss to make sure the plant has an effective surveillance program may seem unimportant or insignificant to them.

Prevention means more than an enforcement officer's commanding a company to comply in a prescribed manner with everything that is noted in an inspection manual. That is nit-picking, and often borders on harassment. Inspectors reportedly have worn white gloves in a fastidious, and totally unnecessary, search for dirt or grease. Such vindictive acts toward management naturally poison the atmosphere, making the victims start to think of ways to retaliate.

Prevention means having a sense of priorities, knowing what is important and what is of minor consequence. It means making sure the small details an enforcement officer is concerned about are relevant to both the broad social goals of the regulatory program and the company's own purposes. "There is a tremendous amount of detail you are looking for in each inspection," Robert Limpert explained.

Your mind takes in a lot, and if something seems abnormal, it's like a light going on inside a computer. But it all should be designed to enhance the wholesomeness of the product. The problems come when you start getting too picayune about the level of detail you are interested in.

Thus, while Limpert is concerned about the condition of the walls inside a meat plant, he is not concerned about whether the exterior walls are painted. Exterior paint, he said, is largely cosmetic and "just doesn't have anything to do with the wholesomeness of the product," particularly when most plants are made of bricks or stone. By the same token, when Matt Finucane encounters radio-frequency ovens in the plants he inspects, he doesn't really care whether warning signs the companies are required to post conform to OSHA regulations regarding size, shape, and color. It matters only that the signs clearly inform employees that the ovens can be hazardous.

WHAT BUSINESS CAN DO

One meat company executive welcomed federal regulation because he felt his company was better off when inspectors found paint flakes on the walls than when wholesalers or customers found them in the product. This person also said that people who complained about nit-picking inspectors usually were marginal operators, the same people who "would be making fat balls instead of hot dogs if there weren't any regulations." The superintendent at another plant said he never argued when an inspector pointed out rust. "Condensation, rust, and paint," he said, "are not problems because the government says they are. They are problems because they lead to contamination."

These views underscore the responsibility of business and industry in developing effective enforcement programs based on mutual trust rather than suspicion, in which disputes are settled amicably even though disagreements may be fundamental and strenuously argued, and in which both sides see themselves as participants instead of as winners or losers. That kind of regulatory climate requires time and effort, but there are two ways a business can facilitate the process.

First, a business can become better informed about the regulatory process and the specific requirements individual regulatory programs place on it.

Second, it can avoid overreacting when faced with a compliance problem or enforcement action.

Businesses and industries that have successful regulatory experiences usually accord enforcement officers the same courtesies and privileges they want the regulators to accord them. They take the time to learn the history of the program in which they are involved, the ideas behind it, its goals, and how on-site inspection actually works. In some cases, en-

forcement officers have taken the initiative to make this information available. In most instances, the company takes
the initiative. Furthermore, companies in this position have
executives who tend to look at the enforcement process as a
problem to be solved, not resisted. They know regulation is
not going to disappear. They know problems will crop up. But
they also know that business can create its own problems by
adopting an obstructionist attitude, and that many potential
points of regulatory conflict and tension can be eased or
eliminated in a climate of cooperation.

"Everything we do in construction is inspected," said the
chief engineer of a commercial construction firm in
Janesville, Wisconsin.

We have found that you never win the battle by fighting the
system. You have to work with it. There is no way you are going to
eliminate inspections and regulation. So rather than cause a big
stink, we see if regulations can give us an advantage. If we can improve the quality of our work and be better builders because of
regulations, then we are ahead of the game.

Another member of the Janesville business community
contended that many businessmen who criticized regulations and on-site inspectors, although eager to receive
federal funds and contracts, adamantly opposed the conditions often attached to those advantages. Most criticisms he
heard, he said, were narrowly focused grievances made by
people who refused to accept that the world and their own
community had changed in the last twenty years.

Just because a regulation doesn't benefit Janesville (or your plant)
directly [he said] doesn't mean it isn't a good regulation. People
complain because they don't know how to function under regulations, and they don't want to take the time to learn. It's a lot easier
to have a knee-jerk reaction than it is to study an issue and find out
what it really means.

Learning how a regulatory program actually works may
force a company to give up some of its cherished stereotypes.
OSHA, for example, received so much negative publicity dur-

ing its early days—some of it justified—that the agency and
its enforcement agents ended up convenient and fashionable
targets for grievances, both real and imagined. As a result,
OSHA became known as a program where inspectors were
ready to close plants down for the slightest reason and in
which employers were denied due process. Due process,
however, is required at every step of every OSHA inspection,
from the time the compliance officer asks the employer's
permission to conduct the inspection—employers can refuse
OSHA compliance officers entrance into their plants or ask
them to obtain warrants, although the majority do not do
so—to the moment the employer might want to request a
formal hearing before an administrative law judge in order
to challenge the result of an inspection. Moreover, not even
the agency, let alone a single compliance officer, has the
power to close down a plant. The most a compliance officer
can do is post an "imminent danger" sign at a particularly
hazardous place at the work site. And then it takes a court
order to require the employer to remove the hazard.

OSHA also became known as a program in which it was extremely difficult for an employer to establish a good working
relationship with an inspector. But the employer is often to
blame. Sometimes, for example, employers flatly refuse to
correct blatant violations. Finucane recently encountered an
employer who would not agree to provide additional protective clothing for an employee who was lubricating a hot
metal mold; flames were coming out both ends of the mold
and, said Finucane, the employee's protective clothing was
covered with oil from his neck down to his shoes. The
employer relented only after OSHA threatened court action.

Even companies that are conscientious about protecting
their workers from illness or injury are nervous and ap-
prehensive when the OSHA inspector knocks at the door.
They rarely have advance notice of his visit and they have no
idea what he will find. For that reason, companies often do
not reveal any information not specifically requested. And, of

course, the fact that a given OSHA inspector rarely visits the same plant twice makes it difficult for employers and inspectors to develop the rapport that exists in other regulatory programs. Nevertheless, according to Finucane and his colleagues at the Harrisburg, Pennsylvania, area office of OSHA, companies that want to establish good working relationships with OSHA inspectors are now more the rule than the exception. "Most companies we inspect," Finucane said,

understand why we are there, even if they are nervous about our presence. They listen to what we have to say and try to correct the violations we find. And we try to go along with them when we can. If they cannot solve a problem one way, we will work with them to find another way. The important thing a company needs to understand is that being cooperative doesn't mean you have to roll over and play dead. They don't and they shouldn't. Companies often disagree with us, and sometimes those disagreements are significant and prolonged. But they rarely result in open hostility or acrimony.

Meanwhile, the information a company needs to improve its regulatory climate may be just a file drawer away. During the early days of the OSM program, strip-mine operators were upset about the number of violations they received. Many, though, were being cited largely because they had not read their permit packages. Before OSM, the permit most companies received from state regulatory authorities to conduct strip-mining operations was just a piece of paper with a number on it. The states still grant permits, but companies now must prepare applications containing specific information about their plans to comply with OSM regulations: how many silt basins and groundwater monitoring wells they will put in, where they will be located, how often the wells will be tested, how the topsoil will be removed, how reclamation work will be performed, and what vegetative growth will be put down after the coal has been removed and the land restored to its original contours. Since this was much more detail than companies were used to providing, many (quite sensibly) hired consultants to prepare permit applications.

The problem was that the companies sometimes failed to read carefully either the application or the new permit. No cover-up or deliberate misrepresentation was involved; the operators were simply not paying enough attention to their own descriptions of the work they had agreed to perform.

No matter how effective the enforcement program or how skilled the enforcement agent, regulation is essentially unpopular. It requires companies to alter traditional ways of doing business and places additional constraints on them. It costs them money, adds to their paperwork, and increases the amount of time they spend handling problems that did not exist before regulation. So there always are complaints. Small meat companies complain that USDA regulations requiring plants to pay overtime to inspectors who must spend more than eight hours at a plant discriminate against the small company, because larger operations work more than one shift and can avoid paying their own people time and a half. Manufacturers criticize OSHA for imposing a double financial penalty on companies—paying the fines assessed when violations are issued, and then financing changes in design or operation necessary to put a plant and its equipment in compliance. Companies also resent being fined for "unimportant" violations, and many feel no fine should be assessed if they make a good-faith effort to correct violations. Strip-mine operators, in the meantime, complain that the presence of both federal and state regulatory agencies causes duplication and confusion, and that through no fault of their own they frequently are caught in the middle when the two levels of government either interpret regulations differently or experience a breakdown in communications.

The complaints are valid. But business needs to distinguish between problems that enforcement agents can control and those they cannot. Business also must understand that even model inspectors have their bad moments and off days, just like everyone else, and must not allow one unsettling experience to become the basis for discrediting an entire process or for negating their own considerable effort in helping to develop enforcement programs relatively free of conflict and resentment. This perspective is easier to come by when a business is dealing with a well-established regulatory program. Meat inspection, for instance, is one of the oldest federal regulatory activities. Although regulations change as new information and technology are developed, the basic philosophy of the program—to make sure meat sold in interstate and foreign commerce is clean and wholesome—has existed in one form or another since 1906. Disagreements occur at the local level, but by and large this is not a program where the basic legitimacy of the federal role is constantly challenged or where the people being inspected do not understand the regulations or the inspection process.

Developing a conciliatory attitude is more difficult when a business is regulated by a program that is experiencing growing pains. The OSM program has had a particularly difficult development, caused in no small part by the fact that there never was a long enough grace period to explain the new law and the federal regulations. This problem was exacerbated when case after case had to be taken to court because regulations were worded so vaguely. The crowning touch was an OSM policy requiring inspectors to issue citations for all violations that affected the environment, no matter how minor or how easy to correct, before they left the permit area. The theory was that if OSM allowed operators the same kinds of exceptions state inspectors granted, the job might never be accomplished.

The temptation to lose patience with regulators is powerful, particularly when agency behavior is rigid or bizarre. City officials in Janesville, Wisconsin, recall an incident when the federal Urban Mass Transit Administration (UMTA) told the city that its public hearing on bus garage improvements was invalid because the city's announcement notices did not specify the exact address where the hearing would be held, although they did clearly identify the location. A second hearing was scheduled; notices went out; nobody attended. And a grant application was delayed another two months.

Some executives, though, feel that their goal is to make the regulatory system work for them, not to let it control their actions. That attitude sometimes pays off. The OSHA area office in Harrisburg, Pennsylvania, agreed to reduce by more than one-half the $3,340 fine assessed a company inspected by Matt Finucane. The reduction occurred because the company described actions it already had taken to correct some violations and its plans to correct others. The reduction was also granted because, in the opinion of the area supervisor and the compliance officers, the company demonstrated good faith when it allowed Finucane to inspect the entire plant instead of restricting him to an item stated in the complaint that prompted the investigation, and it demonstrated good faith in its willingness to correct violations. (The reduction was not a lump sum; it represented the total of various reductions granted on individual items.)

OSHA area offices also have authority to grant companies an overall reduction of up to 30 percent for making a good-faith effort to abate violations promptly, and an additional 10 percent reduction if the company has not received any previous citations. This bonus can also be accorded to companies that have not been inspected before. Another 40 percent reduction can occur if companies have 10 or fewer employees, and smaller reductions are available for companies employing between 10 and 100 people. Thus, a company with fewer than 10 employees could have its financial penalty reduced by as much as 80 percent.

WHAT POLICYMAKERS CAN DO

While a skilled inspector can find ways of easing the tension, friction, and conflict inherent in the regulatory process, he cannot overcome major shortcomings in agency policy and program management. Enforcement officers can do only what their agencies permit and, in the last analysis, the agency—not the inspector—is the central actor. The agency sets the tone for both the regulatory process and the on-site enforcement program. The agency establishes the framework within which enforcement agents will function. The agency sets the ground rules inspectors are required to follow in carrying out their duties and responsibilities. The agency also decides two other important issues: how enforcement officers will be selected and trained, and how much discretionary authority will be granted to people in the field.

Salary, the availability of other jobs, the duties and responsibilities that comprise the compliance officer's job, and the prospect of working in a government bureaucracy invariably affect the ability of regulatory agencies to attract large enough numbers of well-qualified candidates. Still, agencies can make special efforts to find employees who combine a strong sense of social responsibility with an instinct for handling the sensitive personal relationships that frequently determine program success or failure.

The comments a company executive made about two compliance officers who inspected his plant capture the essence of this combination: "We never had anyone go over this plant in as much detail and depth as these guys did," the executive reported.

But what impressed me most about them was that they were good listeners. They were willing to hear us out. I don't think they gave an inch when they didn't want to, but I also don't think this was a one-sided inspection. We had a few more citations than I thought we would receive, but all in all I came away with a feeling that we were inspected fairly, that we had our day in court, and that we were listened to.

Agencies also can provide recruits with training experiences similar to situations they are likely to encounter in the field. Spending time with model inspectors is a good way to achieve this objective. There are limits, though, to what recruitment and training can accomplish. In general, enforcement programs with the widest acceptance tend to be those in which on-site inspectors are granted the broadest discretionary authority, while programs with the least acceptance tend to be those in which the agency keeps its inspectors on a short rein.

Some argue that discretionary authority is not necessary, that from an administrative standpoint it makes more sense if on-site inspectors function as extensions of national and regional offices. Others contend it is impractical to give on-site inspectors additional responsibilities, that many offices are so understaffed and the individual work loads so heavy that no inspector should be asked to undertake new duties such as working with businesses to develop alternative methods of accomplishing regulatory goals. However, on-site inspectors occupy a unique position within the regulatory system simply because they are in direct contact with the regulated parties. They therefore are likely to be better informed than regional or national officials about problems a local business is facing, more sensitive about the need to find solutions, and more inventive about devising alternative ways of meeting regulatory objectives.

This potential role for on-site inspectors provides a strong argument in favor of regulatory programs based on performance standards and against those that are rigid and restrictive. Advocates of regulatory reform have sought performance standards for years, mostly because they feel it makes more sense to judge in terms of achieving regulatory goals than in terms of following various technical requirements. The extent to which performance standards represent a way out of the present regulatory dilemma remains to be seen. But there is no doubt that rigid and overly restrictive programs anger the people who must comply with them and place severe handicaps on the ability of the on-site enforcement officer to develop the cooperative working relationships with business, industry, and local communities that a regulatory program must have in order to succeed.

Once again, the regulatory agency holds the trump card. The agency must establish a framework and ground rules broad enough to allow the inspector enough flexibility to develop an on-site enforcement program in which he can make decisions that respond to both the concerns of the company he is inspecting and the program he represents. If, however, the regulatory program is organized along such rigid lines that the inspector has no room to maneuver and no authority to decide how a particular situation should be handled, then his talents and skills are going to be wasted and the inspector eventually will become as much a victim of the regulatory process as the businessman whose plants he inspects.

CONCLUSION

The ideas presented here are only preliminary suggestions for improving enforcement programs. They are general. They tend toward the ideal and cannot apply to all enforcement programs. But they are based on practical experience. They can work; that much has been demonstrated. Nevertheless, regulatory agencies, as well as other advocates of regulation, often are inclined to resist change because they fear that enforcement officers will be co-opted, that if the enforcement officer is not given strict marching orders and placed under close supervision the regulatory goals of the program may be subverted. Clearly, there is merit to this argument in some situations. Enforcement officers, like every other group in society, are going to be susceptible to pressures and influences militating against the social goals of a program.

The counterargument, though, is that the existing situation in which mistrust, anger, and resentment often define the regulatory system does not seem to be a better alternative; no enforcement program can succeed if the regulatory agency cannot trust the judgment and integrity of the people it sends into the field. A regulatory program also cannot succeed if its unstated premise—as the Janesville, Wisconsin, city manager suggested—is that people are guilty until the regulatory agency proves them innocent, an idea as out of place in regulation as it is in law.

7

Legislative Issues in Food Safety Regulation

Technology-based grouping of food constituents. Food additives. Tolerance criteria and contaminants. Pesticides. Color additives. GRAS status and grandfather exemptions. Animal drugs. The Delaney clause of the FDC Act.

Few laws routinely affect the lives of as many American consumers as the federal Food, Drug, and Cosmetic Act (FDC Act), under which a multitude of food labeling, standards, tolerance, and safety requirements are imposed by the federal Food and Drug Administration (FDA). For example, under the FDC Act, the FDA decides what ingredients may be used in food and at what levels, what level of contaminants, if any, may be tolerated, what information must be placed on labels, and what tests food processors must conduct to establish the safety of the ingredients they use. Also, through the control it exercises over ingredients, packaging, testing requirements, tolerances for contaminants, and other factors, the agency's actions directly and substantially affect the cost and availability of food.

The food safety portions of the FDC Act have become increasingly controversial. Extraordinary developments in food technology, the sensitivity of analytical techniques, tests for assessing the toxicity of food constituents, and our understanding of the causes and mechanisms of cancer have raised considerable doubt about the viability of many of the public policies reflected in the law. Proposals to revise the food safety laws abound. Of late, these efforts have been fueled by the controversies over the FDA's efforts to ban the artificial sweetener saccharin and the preservative sodium nitrite.

Reformers focus on two main issues. One is the seemingly byzantine and irrational structure of categories into which the law organizes various food substances for regulatory purposes. The second is the absolutism of the prohibition against any carcinogenic additive, no matter how weak or otherwise beneficial it might be, embodied in the famous "Delaney clause." I will argue in this chapter that the category structure is in fact more practical and reasonable than appearances would have it. I will also argue that the deleterious effects of the Delaney clause can be mitigated without incurring the political costs of a frontal attack on the clause itself.

CURRENT FOOD SAFETY LAW AND POLICY

Unlike federal health and safety regulation in the environmental, occupational, and consumer product areas, largely based on laws enacted in the first part of the 1970s, the food safety portions of the FDC Act have their origins in federal law first enacted in 1906. The origins of national food safety regulation extend much further back than 1906. References to laws governing food adulteration can be found in the Bible and in documents from medieval England and colonial America. Remarkably, those early laws embodied concepts that have remained central features of current law and policy.

Current food safety law and policy, developed and refined by the FDA over the last seventy-five years, is a complex and confusing amalgam drawn from the basic law, the federal Food, Drug, and Cosmetic Act of 1938, and four major amendments: the Miller pesticide amendments of 1954, which established a comprehensive scheme for regulating pesticides and their residues; the food additives amendment of 1958, which established a premarket approval-for-safety requirement for food additives; the color additive amendments of 1960, which did the same for color additives; and the animal drug amendments of 1962, which consolidated the disparate requirements for animal drugs and their residues in the edible tissue of food-producing animals.

Current law and policy is complex, largely because the 1938 act and each of the successive amendments to it established different categories of substances that may be found in food and separate regulatory criteria and procedures for each. Consistency is not the hallmark of current law and policy; similar substances or comparable risks are not always regulated in the same way. Since the different categories involve different policy orientations that often determine the FDA's decisions on specific food constituents, regulatory policy is commonly driven by competing efforts among the

FDA, the food industry, and consumer interest groups to place a substance in one category or another.

The FDC Act creates at least ten statutory categories of food constituents: food, including naturally occurring substances in food; unavoidable food contaminants; avoidable food contaminants; food additives; substances generally recognized as safe (GRAS); substances with prior-sanctioned status; provisionally listed color additives; permanently listed color additives; animal drug residues; and pesticide residues. These statutory categories may be grouped roughly according to the way in which substances in each category get into food. Such a "technology-based" grouping would look as follows:

1. *Food, including its inherent constituents,* such as potatoes (which contain solanine), rhubarb (which contains oxalic acid), and coffee (which contains caffeine).

2. *Food contaminants,* such as polychlorinated biphenyls (PCBs) in fish and aflatoxin in peanuts.

3. *Intentional food ingredients,* such as saccharin, nitrites, FD&C Red No. 40 (a widely used color additive), salt, and sugar.

4. *Unintentional food ingredients,* such as residues of DES administered to promote growth in cattle (animal drug residues), food packaging migrants (indirect food additives), and pesticide residues.

Under technology-based grouping, the degree of regulatory control exercised by the FDA over each category increases as one moves from inherent constituents to substances used in food production, processing, or packaging to achieve certain desired technical or physical effects (e.g., growth promotion, preservation, sweetening, pest control). The progression from moderate to stringent regulatory control is not, however, nearly as consistent as the grouping suggests: under the unintentional and intentional food ingredient categories is a panoply of subcategories with different regulatory approaches and control. A brief review of the statutory categories and regulatory controls imposed on them will expose the complexity of the current statutory scheme, the inconsistency in outcome that the different categories sometimes cause, and the opportunities for "creative regulation" that the categories afford the ingenious regulator.

CATEGORIES AND CONTROLS

The litany of categories and different regulatory approaches embodied in them may tempt one to conclude that a single standard should be applied to all food constituents regardless of origin. This, in fact, was the view of a National Academy of Sciences (NAS) committee that examined federal food safety policy in the aftermath of the controversy over the FDA's announced intention to ban saccharin (Institute of Medicine 1979). Such a standard might, for example, direct the FDA to rank all food constituents in order of risk, with progressively wider and more restrictive regulatory options as the risks increase.

This straightforward, simple, and understandable approach is not without appeal. If food safety laws are supposed to protect consumers from foodborne risk and the potato is found to be more risky than saccharin, why should the law ban saccharin while simultaneously shielding the potato from the FDA's action?

The answer, at least in part, is that the goals of food safety laws go beyond safety to ensuring an abundant, varied, nutritious, and affordable food supply. Therefore, the current statutory categories often, but not always, reflect a sensible balancing of the risks and benefits of substances in a particular category. For example, to protect the obvious benefits of food, the most general category, Congress provided that only in the case of extraordinary risks from a dangerous inherent

164   STUART M. PAPE

constituent will regulatory action be authorized. However, in the case of food additives—which may be important but which, as a group, usually contain fungible alternatives—a far stricter regulatory scheme is imposed. Without the generic risk-benefit judgments reflected in the categories, the FDA might find itself spending resources chasing risks inherent in foods it could never expect to ban, such as coffee, tea, or milk. Other important features of a categorical system, as well as opportunities for revising it, will become apparent in the following discussion of the current statutory scheme.

Contaminants

The oldest and largest category of food constituents—and from 1906 to 1938 the *only* category—is called "added poisonous or deleterious substances." Since 1906 the law has provided that an added substance adulterates food if it might cause the food to be "injurious to health." The definitive interpretation of this standard was given by the Supreme Court in 1914 when it held that a "reasonable possibility of harm" to consumers must be shown by the FDA before it meets its burden to demonstrate that a food is adulterated to that point.

In the federal Food, Drug, and Cosmetic Act enacted in 1938, Congress established several new categories. First, it recognized the reverse of added substances by providing that "naturally occurring" poisonous or deleterious substances, such as solanine in potatoes, oxalic acid in rhubarb, or caffeine in coffee, would adulterate food if their presence made the food "ordinarily injurious to health." This standard is clearly less stringent than that which applies to added substances, because to satisfy it the FDA is required to demonstrate a greater probability of serious harm from consumption of a food containing the nonadded substance than is the case for added substances. It is difficult to demonstrate such a strong probability of harm, and this provision has rarely been invoked—which quite probably is precisely what Congress intended when it established the category. Given that the public would not stand for a ban on potatoes or coffee without overwhelming evidence of harm to humans, this categorization is a sensible way of allocating priorities towards those substances in food that can more easily be avoided if they are risky.

With the 1938 act, Congress also began subdividing the added-substances category by providing for tolerances for added deleterious substances that either are required to produce food or cannot be avoided even with good manufacturing practice (food contaminants). Congress created this subcategory because, as food technology became more sophisticated and packaged foods and the use of pesticides more prevalent, a safe, affordable, wholesome, and abundant food supply required the use of some chemicals that could be safely tolerated in small amounts. Unlike the authority for added substances generally, this category permits the FDA to balance the risks to the public health of a given substance against the extent to which it is required or unavoidable in the production of food and to set a tolerance for the substance. Tolerances are not set, however, for the additional subcategory of avoidable contaminants.

The FDA often translates the "unavoidability" element of the tolerance criteria into an assessment of the effect of various possible tolerances on the cost and availability of food. For example, in deciding what tolerances to adopt for polychlorinated biphenyls (PCBs) in freshwater fish, the FDA attempted to determine how much fish would be made unlawful at each potential tolerance level and to compare the dollar value of that fish against the estimated reduction in risk obtained by reducing consumers' exposure to PCBs. This type of exercise is often frustrated by a lack of important data and the prohibitive cost, in time as well as money, of obtaining those data.

Tolerance setting for food contaminants is also directly affected by an extrastatutory consideration. In order to enforce a tolerance, the FDA must have an analytical technique to conveniently and reliably detect and quantify the substance in foods. A tolerance will never be set lower than the capability of the analytical method. Through coincidence or otherwise, the balancing of risks against extent of avoidability often winds up at or very close to the limit of detection.

The tolerance approach to unavoidable contaminants illustrates the way in which the category approach of current law usually leads to desirable regulatory outcomes. Contaminants are subject to stricter regulation than inherent constituents of food because a reduction in exposure to the tolerance—and presumably a reduction in risk—can often be accomplished at an acceptable cost. Needless to say, however, this is not always easy. It is, for example, possible to eliminate all traces of the carcinogen aflatoxin from peanuts only by inspecting each peanut individually. Similarly, unless trace elements of the toxic compound PCB were to be permitted, most freshwater fish would have to be taken off the market.

In 1954 Congress again subdivided the added-substances category by creating the category of pesticide residues and establishing an elaborate scheme to determine what level of a pesticide residue in food could be safely tolerated. The Environmental Protection Agency (EPA), under the federal Insecticide, Fungicide, and Rodenticide Act (FIFRA), determines whether a pesticide may be registered for use, a process involving a comprehensive balancing of its risks and benefits. Once a pesticide has been registered for use on food (generally raw agricultural commodities), a tolerance for the residues must be established under the FDC Act (again by the EPA).

Pesticide residues are the first of the "unintentional food ingredients." Although pesticides directly applied to raw agricultural commodities are likely to appear in processed food, precise quantities are difficult to determine, which vastly complicates their regulation.

Food and color additives

Congress further divided the added-substances category in 1958 by creating a major category for food additives, along with two subcategories for substances that, while technically food additives, are excluded from the major category. In 1960 Congress created a category for color additives as well. These new categories represented a fundamental shift in the approach to added substances. With the exception of the pesticide residue authority, it was the first time Congress provided that an added substance should be excluded from food unless its safety were first demonstrated to the FDA's satisfaction by the proponent of use—either the additive maker or a food processor.

The food additive category is extraordinarily broad. It includes any substance that does or may reasonably be expected to become a part of food. For practical purposes, the FDA has divided the universe of food additives into direct additives, substances such as preservatives and emulsifiers intentionally added to food to achieve a technical or physical effect, and indirect additives, substances that may migrate to food from packaging or from use on processing machinery (unintentional food ingredients). All food additives must be shown to be safe and to accomplish their intended purpose. It is important to note that the FDA is not authorized to consider the benefits of an additive in deciding whether to permit its use.

Although color additives are essentially food additives used to impart color in foods, drugs, cosmetics, or medical devices, for historical reasons they have been treated as a separate category. Since 1960 color-additive regulation has been characterized by a seemingly interminable FDA effort to resolve the status of colors in use before premarket approval requirements were imposed. Congress chose to create a provisional list of colors in commercial use in 1960 that required additional testing before "final" decisions were made on their safety. Although Congress expected the transition from provisional to "permanent" listing to take two and a half years, it authorized the FDA to extend the time frame if necessary. The FDA has made the most of this authority, so that more than twenty years later numerous colors, including some important to the food, drug, or cosmetic industries, remain on the provisional list. Thus, a "provisional" category, intended to exist only temporarily, to this day continues to dominate the regulation of color additives.

GRAS substances and prior sanctions

Not all substances that are added to food or that migrate to food from packaging are regulated as food or color additives. The first subcategory created by Congress in 1958 contains substances generally recognized as safe by qualified experts (GRAS); the second contains prior-sanctioned substances. GRAS substances are exempt from the food additive definition, the premarket approval requirement, and the Delaney clause, ordinarily because of a substantial history of safe use on the basis of which experts acknowledge their safety. GRAS substances are not necessarily safer than food additives, but the perception of safety is more widespread. Salt, sugar, raw agricultural commodities, and other mainstays of the food supply have been considered GRAS since 1958. GRAS status is not permanent. If a substance ceases to have general recognition of safety, it will become subject to regulation as a food additive.

Also exempt from the food additive definition are substances in use in food before 1958 that were approved by either the FDA or by the U.S. Department of Agriculture (for substances used in meat and poultry products) under an informal and voluntary system in which some processors sought the opinion of the government on the use of food constituents. These opinions, often given by the agencies in letters and speeches, gave rise in 1958 to a "grandfather" exemption for substances with a "prior sanction." A single substance may have one use with a prior sanction and another use regulated as a food additive, which can result in inconsistent regulatory treatment.

Animal drugs

The final category of added substances contains residues of drugs administered to food-producing animals. Before 1962 these residues were regulated in a most confusing and illogical way: the drug use of the substance was subject to the drug portions of the FDC Act, and the residue portion to the food additive authority. This scheme involved two FDA bureaus and resulted in the application of two sets of regulatory criteria and procedures that simply did not mesh well. The current scheme, vigorously promoted by the animal health industry, regulates animal drugs under a single consolidated provision of law, although it has not eliminated the inefficiencies of the two-bureau problem; the FDA's bureaus of veterinary medicine and food retain pieces of the action.

Animal drugs are subject to premarket approval. A drug must be demonstrably safe and effective for the animal and its residues in edible tissues must be shown to be safe for human consumption. Like food and color additives, animal drug residues are subject to the Delaney clause, but with a twist that evolved when their peculiar nature became apparent. Unlike food and color additives, which are added directly to food or placed in contact with it, these drugs are administered to the animals, and the presence of their residues in edible tissue depends in large part on the sensitivity of analytical methods. Again, like pesticide residues, indirect food additives, and food contaminants, regulation is complicated by the uncertainty of how hard one should look to determine if they are there and what to make of the amount found.

CONTROL-BASED CATEGORIES

As the preceding discussion illustrates, the technology-based grouping of the statutory categories glosses over some fundamental differences in regulatory approach that a "control-based" grouping illuminates. Although there is no single "correct" control-based grouping, the following suggestion organizes the statutory categories according to the degree of regulation provided under the FDC Act:

Standard for adulteration not stringent; burden on the FDA to initiate regulatory action: food and its inherent constituents.

Moderately strict standard for adulteration; burden on the FDA; tolerances may be set: unavoidable food contaminants and prior-sanctioned substances.

General perception of safety required, but not FDA approval: GRAS substances.

Demonstration of safety required, but Delaney clause does not apply: provisionally listed color additives.

Strict safety standard and premarket approval required: pesticide residues.

Strict safety standard, including Delaney clause and premarket approval: food additives, color additives, and animal drug residues.

The control-based grouping exposes a greater number of the features of current law than technology-based grouping. For example, one might question why prior-sanctioned substances, GRAS substances, food additives, and color additives are not treated as a single category, since all substances in these categories are added to food (or, in the case of packaging materials, intentionally placed in contact with food) for a specific technical or physical effect. Indeed, if this article were written in, say, 1957, that is precisely the conclusion that would have been reached. In 1982, however, practical considerations lead to a different conclusion.

The GRAS, prior-sanctioned, and provisionally listed color-additive categories were established by Congress in order to make a sensible transition from the pre-1958 law, which contained no premarket approval requirements, to a new system that did. Without subcategories like GRAS and prior sanctions, substantial time and money (both public and private) would have been misspent on substances with a long history of safe use instead of being directed toward new substances of unproven safety. The task of consolidating these categories now, while rationally appealing, is probably not worth the administrative effort and cost—which would be considerable. It may be for this reason that adjusting the current categories has received little attention, beyond the National Academy of Sciences report, during the current debate over revision of the food safety laws.

The overriding and by far most refractory issue in food safety law and regulation is determining when a food constituent is safe. Congress has addressed this question in several ways, as the multiple categories demonstrate. In the case of food and color additives, which cannot be used unless approved by the FDA, the law does not define "safe." The law's legislative history, however, states that the term requires a "reasonable certainty of no harm" rather than proof of "absolute safety." The "reasonable certainty" test is stringent, but it clearly implies that some level of risk should be tolerated from a food or color additive, if for no other reason than the fact that science can never demonstrate definitively that *no* risk exists. Controversies often involve industry, consumer, and FDA disagreements over "how safe is safe enough."

Each portion of the law pertaining to food, color additives,

172 STUART M. PAPE

and animal drugs, respectively, contains one of the three Delaney clauses in the FDC Act. The Delaney clause, by far the most famous provision of the law, provides that no additive (or residue) shown to cause cancer in man or animal may be found to be safe, regardless of the actual risk, if any, from the substance. In the case of animal drug residues, a special twist permits the use of a carcinogenic animal drug if "no" residues are found in the edible tissue. In this context, "no" does not mean absolutely "zero" residue, but rather "no detectable residue using a sufficiently sensitive analytical method." Understandably, it has not been easy to define a "regulatory zero."

When it was first proposed, and for the twenty or so years thereafter, the clause was redundant with the requirement that additives be shown to be safe. The FDA would not have been reasonably certain of no harm from exposure to an additive if ordinarily, in tests involving laboratory animals, the additive were shown to induce cancer; therefore, even without the clause, a no-risk policy toward carcinogenic additives would have prevailed. In recent years, however, several developments have suggested that the FDA has altered its view that no amount of exposure to a carcinogen may be safely tolerated. Analytical methods now detect substances in parts per trillion (and possible parts per quadrillion), whereas at the time the Delaney clause was adopted the limit of detection was closer to parts per million. This means that we are now aware of substances in food at levels far smaller than could have been envisioned in 1958. This astounding increase in analytical capability places unbearable tension on a no-risk policy. Every carcinogenic molecule cannot be eliminated from food if we are to have a varied, affordable, and adequate food supply; and the costly and hopeless effort to do so would not necessarily achieve any significant reduction in risk.

There is some prospect of relief from the dilemma posed by overly sensitive analytical capabilities in the rapidly developing techniques of quantitative risk assessment. In the case of animal carcinogens, for example, the principal problem in translating results in test animals to humans is how to predict confidently what effects, if any, will occur at the much lower doses that approximate human exposure. Newly developed mathematical models to predict the magnitude of risks at the low end of the dose-response curve have increasingly been used by scientists, industry, and regulators to identify the upper bound in the risk from exposure to an animal carcinogen. The FDA has also used quantitative risk assessments in formulating regulatory policy on aflatoxin, PCBs, saccharin, and nitrites.

PROPOSED REVISIONS AND REFORMS

The process by which we identify substances as animal carcinogens (and thus potential human carcinogens), and the development and justification for quantitative risk assessment techniques, are important issues for food safety policy that are principally in the purview of scientists. What we do with the information, insight, and tools provided by the scientists is a question of social policy to be determined in the political and regulatory arenas. For example, when scientists identify a substance in the food supply as a weak carcinogen and the risk is calculated as no greater than, say, one cancer death per ten million persons over their lifetimes, we still do not know whether that level of risk is acceptable. How much risk is a reasonable price to pay for a varied, affordable, convenient, and wholesome food supply? There are risks in all aspects of contemporary life that can never be eliminated. Given that at some point further efforts at risk reduction achieve no significant effects, the question becomes when to stop trying.

Current proposals to revise the food safety laws, including

a comprehensive bill introduced by Orrin Hatch, chairman of
the Senate committee with legislative jurisdiction for the
FDC Act (S. 1442), invariably address the problem of deciding what "safe" means and its specialized application to additives shown to cause cancer in animals—the Delaney clause
problem. Some of these proposals would resolve the problems
in current law by creating an exception to the Delaney clause
for carcinogenic additives that present only insignificant
risks, utilizing quantitative risk assessment and redefining
"safe" to mean "reasonably certain" (the same probability of
an outcome now required) that the risks are indeed insignificant. Not surprisingly, these proposals are controversial.

Some critics focus on the techniques of risk assessment,
likening them to "black art" and rejecting their application
to food safety decisions, even though the FDA has employed
them for several years. Others assert that the risks of permitting *any* carcinogens to be added to food cannot be
justified—even though continuation of the Delaney no-risk
policy may, in future years, require the banning of important
additives whose risks are trivial. The success of proposals of
this sort will rest largely on how well risk assessment fares
during congressional hearings, and on the extent to which
the notion prevails that low-level, low-risk carcinogens are
not worth banning.

Faced with these controversial proposals that address the
risk side of food safety decisions, some legislative proposals
would authorize the FDA, in special cases, to consider the
benefits of an additive that presented risks deemed not acceptable. (Some proposals, including Senator Hatch's, would
combine a risk-and-benefit approach.) The FDC Act could be
revised, for example, to authorize the FDA to consider the
benefits to health—as in the use of nitrites to preserve foods
—of an additive with a risk greater than the safety requirement's minimal level. Because there would appear to be little
support for applying a benefit requirement to all additives
(the marketplace currently serves that function), this

statutory benefit authority would probably be limited to additives with a substantial history of use. The authority could further be limited to additives without practicable substitutes, thus preserving the approach of current law in all but the most exceptional case.

Aside from the recommendation of the National Academy of Sciences to restructure the food safety laws, current reform efforts all proceed on the assumption that the existing law is essentially sound and that the problems brought on by scientific and technological progress can be accommodated within its framework with relatively modest changes. The degree of support for much of existing law should not be surprising. After all, can a law whose basic provisions are seventy-five years old—and still going strong—be all bad? A fundamental rewriting of the food safety portions of the FDC Act might keep lawyers employed for the next decade or beyond, but the current attention to "tinkering" with existing law is likely to generate a far better law in a shorter period of time—a law that will enable the FDA to respond adequately to the food safety challenges in the next decade and beyond.

8

GEORGE C. EADS*

White House Oversight of Executive Branch Regulation

The scope of Executive Order 12291. The Office of Information and Regulatory Affairs. Oversight under Nixon, Ford, and Carter. Regulatory agencies and the White House. The need for improvement in regulatory analysis. Monitoring proposals as they develop. Public reaction to monitoring agencies. Flexibility in regulatory procedures.

*Senior Economist, The Rand Corporation. This chapter draws heavily from Eads 1981. The views expressed are the author's own.

The significant expansion of federal rule making over the last decade and a half, especially as practiced by executive agencies, has been matched by a growth in White House concern with bringing some coordination and coherence to the rule-making process. Since the federal government has engaged in something called "regulation," with direct or indirect grants of valuable rights often involved and politically well connected individuals sometimes standing to gain or lose from the outcome of regulatory proceedings, presidents and their close aides have taken an interest in such proceedings. However, *continuing* White House interest in the impact of federal regulatory activities on the economy as a whole, other than during wartime, is a new phenomenon dating from the early 1970s.

Presidents Nixon, Ford, Carter, and Reagan have each experimented with institutional and procedural reforms to bring executive branch rule making more firmly under White House control. These experiments—beginning with the Nixon administration's Quality of Life Review in 1971 and marked most recently by President Reagan's issuance of Executive Order 12291—have been highly controversial. They have been attacked as unwarranted and possibly illegal attempts by the White House to inject "political" considerations into the otherwise apolitical fact-finding activities of expert agencies. Others have defended them as legitimate and necessary steps to assure that federal regulatory activities are consistent across agencies, are giving due weight to important national concerns that otherwise might be overlooked, and are integrated appropriately into complementary federal activities. Both views have merit; there is a tension inherent in White House regulatory oversight activities that no administration has yet managed to deal with successfully.

If White House oversight of regulation is ever to become an accepted tool for assuring appropriate and efficient programs, steps must be taken to depoliticize the review process. To be sure, important regulatory decisions will always be made in a politically charged atmosphere. And, for all the talk of "analysis," certain decisions will turn out to be essentially political. Yet experience suggests that it is possible to make regulatory decisions on the basis of significantly more analysis, and to separate the preparation of analyses from political concerns. Experience also suggests that this will lead to better regulatory decisions.

This chapter concentrates on the Reagan administration's program, certainly the most comprehensive and probably the most controversial to date. The program concentrates power and authority in ways that previous presidents were reluctant to permit. It has the potential to allow the development of a coherent, consistent regulatory strategy, but it also has the potential for serious political abuse.

The Reagan program is still in its "shakedown" phase. It has suffered thus far from excessive attention to public relations at the expense of concrete achievements—a problem exacerbated by the program's highly visible role in the initial Reagan economic "game plan." This role has demanded that it demonstrate large—but largely unsubstantiable—regulatory "savings." The program has also suffered from the inexperience of several novice regulatory appointees. Agency analytical capabilities, already thinly stretched, have been further sapped by open warfare between the new Reagan appointees and professional staffs. Nevertheless, barring successful legal challenge or sufficient political indiscretions to undermine its credibility with Congress and the public, the essential features of the Reagan program are likely to survive, if only because they meet a long-felt need.

THE REAGAN PROGRAM

There can be no doubt that the Reagan administration has made the most thoroughgoing attempt yet to bring the regulatory activities of executive branch agencies firmly under White House control, by creating a new Cabinet-level regulatory appeals group headed by the vice-president and by issuing Executive Order 12291. In a real sense, the executive order marks the final stage of regulation's emergence as a governmental activity deserving the same level of attention as raising and spending money. It is impressive both in its comprehensiveness and in the extent to which it rearranges executive branch regulatory power relationships under previous administrations, both Republican and Democratic.

Substantive requirements

Certain sections of the order are only recapitulations or minor extensions of executive orders issued by Presidents Ford and Carter. For example, the order proposes that agencies subject proposed "major" rules to formal economic analysis and make drafts of these analyses (now to be called "Regulatory Impact Analyses") available for public comment at the time the regulation is formally proposed.

In many respects, however, the order moves far beyond the procedures employed by Carter and Ford. The Carter administration always took pains to stress that its analytical and procedural requirements should not be interpreted as "cost-benefit" tests. Costs and benefits were to be identified and, to the extent possible, quantified, so that cost-*effective* solutions could be chosen wherever possible. The burden of proof on an agency's proposed final rule lay with those in the White House who monitored the "post-comment" process. Senior White House aides who followed the development of major rules could take the cost-effective issue to the president, but this was rarely done. Furthermore, for both political and substantive reasons it was stressed that no attempt was being made to impose any *new* requirements on those responsible for issuing rules. Neither President Carter nor his principal advisers wished to take on the major struggle with the environmentalists and organized labor that would have been required to change substantive rule-making standards. By confining his program to changes that were ostensibly "procedural," the president avoided this fight.

Reagan, however, has moved where Carter had been unwilling to tread. Except where expressly prohibited by law,[1] the Reagan executive order *requires* that a cost-benefit test be applied and met. Regulatory action is not even to be proposed unless the agency can demonstrate that the potential benefits to society outweigh the potential costs. Among available alternative regulatory approaches, the one to be chosen is that which minimizes the net cost to society. Finally, agencies are to structure their regulatory priorities to maximize aggregate net social benefits, taking into account the condition of the particular industries affected by the regulations, the general condition of the economy, and potential regulatory actions contemplated for the future.

According to an interview with James C. Miller, published in *Regulation* (Weidenbaum and Miller 1981, p. 21), the agencies also will be required to consider the impact of regulations that other agencies might be contemplating.

Oversight procedures

The Reagan executive order consolidates the various White House oversight functions into the new Office of Information and Regulatory Affairs (OIRA) in the Office of Management and Budget (OMB). In effect, OIRA is to become the gate through which all important regulations must twice pass on their way to becoming law. This office will have extremely broad powers. For example, it will be able to overrule agency determinations concerning the "major" rule classification and can group a series of related rules together for purposes of meeting this classification. It is to receive all draft Regulatory Impact Analyses at least 60 days prior to an agency's publication of a Notice of Proposed Rule Making (NPRM) and, if unhappy with an agency's draft, it can delay publication of that notice until the agency has adequately responded to OIRA's concerns. No record of these contacts or of the agency's response will be kept. The only appeal an agency has is to the President's Task Force on Regulatory Relief or to the president himself.

It is important to note that all this activity is to take place, as in the Nixon Quality of Life Review, *before* a regulation has been formally proposed. As we shall see, there are both advantages and disadvantages to concentrating on this stage of the rule-making process.

The issuance of the Notice of Proposed Rule Making and publication of the draft Regulatory Impact Analysis begins the formal public comment period. Under the Carter procedures, it would have been during such a period that administration comments would have been prepared and filed.

Under the Reagan plan, it is unclear whether public filings by executive office agencies or by interagency groups are contemplated. In the original executive order, and in the Miller/Weidenbaum interview, a strong impression was created that such filings would not occur. However, a subsequent memorandum from OMB Director Stockman, issued 11 June 1981 to the heads of executive departments and agencies, refers to the development of "factual material . . . appropriate for the whole record of the agency rulemaking."[2] It is not known at this time how OMB or the task force staff intend to interpret the phrase "whole record." It still seems to be the case that, insofar as possible, OIRA will operate on an "off-the-record" basis, making it difficult for the public to know what its views—as distinct from the views of the agency proposing the regulation—might have been.

As was the case in previous administrations, once the formal public comment period closes, the regulatory agency will have the responsibility for summarizing the comments received and drafting the final rule. However, thirty days before the rule is to "go final," the agency must transmit its final Regulatory Impact Analysis to OIRA. If OIRA objects, the rule is held up until objections are resolved or until OIRA is overruled by the task force or by the president. In this case, the substance of any disagreement between OIRA and the agency, together with the agency's response to it, will be included in the rule-making file. It will thus be available to any reviewing court, though it will not, of course, be available to the public (or other interested parties) prior to the time the final rule is issued.

Another important difference relating to the Reagan "post-comment" procedures should be noted. During the Carter administration, care was taken to limit contacts between the White House and the agency to a small group of presidential advisers or their deputies. Within this group, it was informally arranged that a single person would be the principal point of contact between the White House and the agency. This was to minimize the possibility of *ex parte* contacts that would "taint" the rule making. The decision by the Reagan administration to broaden the circle of individuals potentially involved in post-comment discussions to include members of the President's Task Force on Regulatory Relief will make the policing of outside contacts significantly more difficult.

"Sunset"

The above process will apply to new rules. But there is a vast body of rules and regulations already in place that need to be reviewed. Although Carter's executive order required that agencies periodically review their existing rules and eliminate or revise those that were outmoded, this requirement was never formally put in place. Reagan's executive order gives OIRA the power to designate existing rules for their review and analysis. Revising such rules will require their formal reproposal. The new procedural and analytical standards will then apply to them as well.

Additional responsibilities

President Reagan has abolished the Regulatory Council and
transferred to OIRA the authority to oversee the publication
of the *Regulatory Calendar* and to identify and eliminate
duplicative, overlapping, and conflicting rules. OIRA has also
been given the duty of overseeing the Federal Regulatory
Flexibility Act (which directs specific attention to the regulatory problems of small business) and the Paperwork
Reduction Act. Finally, it has been specifically charged with
developing procedures for estimating the annual costs and
benefits of agency regulations, on both an aggregate and a
sector-of-industry basis, "for purposes of compiling a regulatory budget."

OIRA'S CAPACITY TO PERFORM
ITS MISSION

To be an effective institution, OIRA must achieve and retain
credibility in the eyes of the regulatory agencies, the Congress, the courts, and the general public. Merely asserting
power—and even demonstrating that it has power—will not
be enough. OIRA must show that it is capable of using power
in a responsible way.

Given the scope of its authority and the indication that it
intends to exercise that authority aggressively, OIRA will require large resources to carry out its principal mission. Unfortunately, this is not the case.

Staff resources

On paper, OIRA's resources appear to be considerable. According to the Miller/Weidenbaum interview in *Regulation*,
OIRA will have about 90 personnel slots. But this figure is

deceptive because few, if any, of these positions are new. OIRA is a consolidation of three existing units: the Regulatory and Information Policy office (RIP, already located within OMB), the Office of Government Programs and Regulations (from the now-abolished Council on Wage and Price Stability [CWPS]), and the Office of Statistical Policy (OSP, a unit now located in the Department of Commerce). Of these units, only the 20-person CWPS office is experienced in the techniques of cost-benefit analysis, regulatory impact analysis, and the analysis of cumulative regulatory impacts. The RIP analysts, while capable, are primarily trained to monitor paperwork burdens and to oversee agencies' technical compliance with the executive order. The job of the Statistical Policy Office is exactly what its name implies—to oversee the quality of federal statistics. While this experience may be of help in the development of standardized techniques for regulatory cost and benefit accounting, OSP analysts are not experienced in regulatory matters and are not likely to become so.

In the Miller/Weidenbaum interview, reference is made to the ability to use OMB budget examiners to monitor regulations. OMB has over 250 professionals working full time on financial budget review and oversight. While the talents of some of these individuals may be available to supplement those of the analysts in OIRA, the training (and professional inclination) of most OMB budget examiners is to focus on direct federal expenditures, not on the indirect costs resulting from regulatory requirements. In short, to oversee an area of responsibility that is considerably broader in scope than the federal financial budget, OIRA will have but a fraction of the resources OMB devotes to that task. Indeed, when account is taken of the loss in personnel due to the elimination of various units having some responsibility for regulatory oversight and other redeployments, it is clear that OIRA will have considerably less analytical horsepower than the agencies whose functions it has assumed.

Analytical capabilities

Considering that the Reagan program stresses the formal cost and benefit analysis of both individual and groups of regulations, the lack of technically trained personnel within OIRA to monitor agency analytical work adequately cannot help but undermine the organization's credibility. But the harm could be even greater. Lacking sufficient analytical resources, OIRA might miss important reform opportunities. These missed opportunities could be of two general sorts: first, significant issues that appear innocuous but will fall between the cracks because no one knows enough about their significance to challenge them, and second, important issues in major rule makings that no private party has the incentive to raise and that require considerable analytical effort to develop credibly.

An example of the first sort of issue arose during a 1980 Environmental Protection Agency (EPA) proceeding that was intended to define the term "source" for purposes of new source reviews in areas of the country not meeting national ambient air quality standards. In areas already meeting these standards, "source" had been defined to include an entire plant; for nonattainment areas, "source" was defined as an entire plant *and* as each of the major pieces of process equipment within the plant. The point at issue was whether to broaden the definition of source in nonattainment areas to make it consistent with the definition in attainment areas.

This issue came to the attention of White House staff very late in the rule-making process. Briefly stated, such broadening would have permitted replacement investment to occur free of EPA's new source review as long as the total *plant* emissions did not increase significantly. This would have considerably helped the steel industry, among others. But because the change also would have removed what EPA considered a valuable weapon for forcing steel firms onto compliance schedules, there was resistance from some within the agency to broadening the definition.

The White House analysts were able to develop estimates of the impact of the change on steel industry investment and they raised the matter at very high levels within the administration. After an extremely bitter controversy, the EPA administrator, who opposed the change, prevailed. (With the change of administration, however, the agency announced its intention to repropose the regulation to permit the issue to be reexamined.) In this instance, having a highly competent analytical staff strategically located within the White House with sufficient resources to prepare a well-documented analysis helped to assure that an important issue, which otherwise might have slipped by, was considered.

An example of the second kind occurred during the rule making for EPA's premanufacturing notification regulation for new chemicals and new chemical uses proposed under the authority of the Toxic Substances Control Act. The public filing primarily focused on the impact that these regulations might have on the rate of innovation in the chemicals industry—certainly an issue of national importance. Initially arguing against a Regulatory Analysis Review Group (RARG) review, EPA had contended that this was not an appropriate proceeding in which to raise the innovation issue and that insufficient information already existed to ascertain the regulations' likely impact on innovation. The chemicals industry, though concerned about the regulations, had not focused upon their likely impact on innovation, possibly because by substantially slowing down the rate of innovation of new chemicals and by making the development of new chemical uses more costly, the regulations could substantially enhance profits on the sale of *existing* products. Also, by differentially affecting costs in large and small firms, the regulations might raise entry barriers, again enhancing profits for existing firms.

Nevertheless, RARG voted to undertake a review. Working together, CWPS and the staff of the Council of Economic Advisers (CEA) were able to shed a great deal of light on the innovation issue and see that a critical issue got put on the agenda. It might be argued that in the Reagan administration, agencies such as EPA will automatically see that all such important issues are raised or that a thinly staffed and overworked OIRA will have enough time and resources to single out such innocuous-appearing and politically unappealing issues for serious attention. Or it might be argued that once the Reagan oversight process really gets rolling, EPA will not bother about trivialities such as premanufacturing notification. Congress may be in an antiregulatory mood right now, but if a chemical appears that eventually causes harm to someone, and such harm could have been prevented by tough premanufacturing notification and testing, it is dubious that this mood will prevail.

The importance of adequate resources

An effective and credible oversight process requires sufficient staff familiar with both the regulatory programs of individual agencies and the industries that these agencies regulate. It also implies the ability to develop priorities and to ask the crosscutting questions that would otherwise go unraised. Merely asking industries, trade associations, and other affected interests to submit "hit lists" of regulations they would like to see eliminated, as Vice-President Bush did last spring, may be good politics, but it is no substitute for independently developed views of which regulations make sense and which do not. Indeed, a flood of responses to such a request can inundate a thinly staffed office, increasing the chances that such an office will be seen as (and, in fact, may become) merely a conduit for special interests.

THE ROLE OF THE AGENCIES
IN REGULATORY OVERSIGHT

OMB will have help with regulatory oversight, just as it does with financial budget oversight. Indeed, the bulk of the responsibility for preparing analyses of the costs and benefits of individual regulations and entire regulatory programs must necessarily fall on the agencies themselves. No office in OMB or in any other central location can ever have enough knowledge of the detailed workings of a regulatory program to prepare an analysis from scratch; it generally must use agency-generated raw material, the quality of which is crucial. A major paradox of the Reagan program emerges when OIRA's extremely broad mandate, limited resources, and high political visibility shift a *greater* part of analytical responsibility to the agencies than was the case during the Carter administration. Unfortunately, the agencies' *incentive* to perform this role in a manner consistent with both the president's objectives and the requirements set down by the courts may be less. The sharp budget cuts have not spared the regulatory agencies' analytical efforts, and short shrift has been given to analyses suggesting that certain politically unpopular regulations might in fact meet the tests laid down in the Reagan executive order.

How are the agencies to be motivated? The quick answer is that President Reagan is appointing new agency heads who share his basic regulatory philosophy. But that answer is certainly *too* quick. Translating a general concern for reining in the regulatory system into an effective and consistent program of regulatory management is not a straightforward task. Simply paralyzing the regulatory process by refusing to push new regulations forward does not work, either. As noted earlier, one of the most urgent tasks facing the administration is to develop an effective and credible "sunset" process by which to review existing regulations. But that means that each existing regulation will have to be analyzed, evaluated, and redesigned. A guillotine will not work.

The need to improve agency analytical capabilities

Regulatory analysis is not a well-developed skill. Under the Carter administration, very few agencies were particularly good at it. Indeed, one of the most important (but perhaps least appreciated) objectives of both RARG and CWPS filing was to improve the capabilities of agencies to conduct meaningful regulatory analysis. An important by-product of the collegial RARG process was that the distinction between what constituted "good" and "bad" analysis was gradually being established and transmitted throughout the bureaucracy.

Agencies originally responded to the Ford and Carter executive orders by preparing analyses that were designed to "prove" their regulations actually generated few if any costs. Some concocted rudimentary cost-benefit analyses designed to support the option they had already intended to choose. Only gradually did these analyses come to be used for their intended purpose, i.e., to generate information to help decision-makers identify the likely impacts of a whole *range* of possible regulatory outcomes. It was usually not until after an agency had been through a number of RARG or CWPS reviews that its analyses began to be appreciated.

I am not aware of any dramatic improvement in agency capabilities that has occurred in the few months since I left the government. I expect that the ability to provide meaningful analyses of both existing and proposed rules is still a scarce talent, one that is unevenly spread. And, as noted, the budget cuts and hiring freeze have caused some of the best analysts to leave the government for employment in the private sector.

Moreover, the agencies not only have to analyze the impact of individual proposed or existing regulations, but also must develop priorities for their entire regulatory program. I am not aware of *any* agency that is prepared to do this adequately at the present time.

A further factor exacerbates the problem of obtaining good analyses. Considering the current state of the art in estimating both the benefits and costs of regulations, the new requirement that agencies demonstrate that their regulations meet a cost-benefit test is equivalent to an invitation to fraud. It would be much more sensible merely to require that agencies identify and quantify, to the extent possible, whatever costs and benefits they consider likely to flow from the proposed regulations. This, coupled with an elimination of statutory bars to the explicit consideration of cost-benefit analysis (such as the bars contained in the Delaney amendment and certain portions of the Clean Air Act), would be a powerful spur to sensible regulation. But not even the regulatory reformers in the Republican-controlled Senate seem willing to face this issue squarely. They would merely codify the procedural requirements of the executive order, thus tightening the procedural straitjacket that the courts have increasingly imposed upon "informal" rule making.

One of the major dangers of suddenly imposing a strict cost-benefit requirement on this gradual learning process is that regulations that make sense may be stymied for lack of adequate supporting analysis.

OIRA's actions and agency incentives

OIRA's success depends to a large extent on how the OMB chooses to interpret the requirements of the new executive order. *If* OMB is willing to be sufficiently tolerant with agencies as they continue to struggle to improve their estimating capabilities, and *if* it is willing to provide them with the resources to continue to upgrade their analytical skills, then improvement can continue. *If*, however, OMB intends to operate as a stern judge rather than an understanding teacher, then virtually all regulations that come to its attention will fail the test—and not necessarily because of their cost-effectiveness. It will be extremely tempting for a harassed and overextended OIRA to give agency-prepared analyses only a cursory review, permitting rule making to proceed if they produce politically desired results and bouncing them back if they do not.

Unfortunately, in the *Regulation* interview, Miller shows signs of embracing the latter approach. When pressed about whether OIRA would apply the full procedural requirements to a regulation that purported to *reduce* regulatory burdens by several hundred million dollars, he replied: "If OMB, again under task force direction, were convinced on the basis of evidence, *however sparse*, that such a reduction would occur, a waiver would be granted immediately" (emphasis added). On the other hand, regulations proposing cost increases, however small, are to be given the full "treatment." This may seem an appealing short-run strategy for changing certain regulations, but it runs serious risk of court intervention and undermines the incentive to do serious analysis. Indeed, it returns regulatory analysis to the period when its principal purpose was to justify predetermined outcomes.

THE DIFFICULTIES OF CONCENTRATING OVERSIGHT ATTENTION ON THE PRE-NOTICE STAGE OF RULE MAKING

This is a useful place to explore another concern about the new Reagan process: its concentration on the pre—Notice of Proposed Rule Making (NPRM) period. In both the Ford and Carter administrations, primary emphasis was placed on the public comment period—the time after a regulation has been proposed but before it has been adopted. Occasionally, and usually only at agency request, officials in the Carter or Ford White House did concern themselves with the shaping of a regulatory proposal. But the general policy was to leave that task to the agencies.

This had certain drawbacks. It has been noted by more than one observer of the regulatory process that agencies often tend to structure their proposed regulations in ways that severely limit their scope for final rule making. By carefully monitoring developing proposals, the public filings of RARG and CWPS assured that the range of rule-making discretion was not unduly narrowed. And, by targeting important agenda-setting regulatory actions, White House officials monitoring the process could further increase the range of open options.

While concentration on the preproposal stage permits, at least in theory, consideration of the broadest possible range of options, it is questionable how great an improvement this will represent in practice. One problem is that various agencies use the NPRM in different ways. Some use it to identify only those options that have a reasonably good chance of actually being adopted. In such cases, the agency may have devoted considerable time and effort to assembling data on the identified options and analyzing their possible consequences prior to issuing the formal notice. Other agencies, however, use the NPRM as an information-gathering tool. They publish notices as a means of generating basic data about the industries they intend to regulate and the possible consequences of their proposed rules. Once this information has been gathered and analyzed, the agency may then repropose the regulation—or it may move directly to issue a final rule.

When NPRMs are used primarily as devices to gather basic information, it often will be impossible to perform meaningful regulatory analysis prior to issuing them. Instead, all that agencies will have to work with are sweeping claims of what the regulation *might* do if the agency were actually to go as far as it conceivably could go under its statutory authority. The numbers generated by interested parties will represent "worst case" scenarios—useful for attracting headlines but relatively useless for understanding what costs or benefits the actual regulations might cause.[3]

The reduction in public participation

Ironically, moving executive office involvement to an earlier stage of the rule-making process might have helped quiet one set of fears expressed by certain "public interest" groups during the Carter administration concerning intervention by RARG and CWPS. These groups were concerned that they were unable to comment formally on input provided by CWPS and RARG since both organizations filed their opinions at the close of the public comment period.

Curiously, this concern is echoed by Weidenbaum in the *Regulation* interview where he dismisses RARG's influence by noting that its comments were filed "literally minutes before the comment period closed—which restricted somewhat their capacity for stimulating public dialog." In practice, this did not prove to be a serious problem. Months or even years can elapse between the close of the formal public comment period and the time a rule is made final. In one case I am aware of, an agency reopened a public comment period expressly to receive comments on RARG's analyses. In another case, a "public interest" group prepared detailed, formal comments on a RARG filing and asked that these comments be placed in the public record, even though the comment period had closed. The CWPS staff in this instance prepared a rebuttal and had both placed in the record. Under Carter, in short, opportunity for public comment on executive office interventions prior to the very last stages of rule making was liberal.

Contrast this with the opportunities available for the public to know what transpired between OIRA and the agencies under the Reagan process: no record will exist of the critical preproposal discussions; no public filing putting administration views on the record will be made. During the post-comment period, a record will be kept of agency and OIRA interactions, but this will be put into the file only at the time the rule is made final and nothing assures that this record will be in any way complete. It is no wonder that one commentator, writing in the *National Law Journal* (27 April 1981) has remarked: "An agency attorney should be aware that there may be highly significant conversations going on between agency heads and the White House at any point prior to or during the rule-making proceeding about which he knows nothing." His conclusion: "Now more than ever, it can be expected that the race will be to the swift, to the enterprising and to those with access to the levers of power, not only in the Congress and the regulatory agencies, but also in the presidential office."

WHITHER REGULATORY OVERSIGHT?

Those who believe that the only reasonable thing to do with the regulatory process is to "shut it down" will wonder why so much attention is paid here to trying to figure out how to make it work efficiently. As noted earlier, though it is tempting to believe that we can return to a time when general industry had relatively little to do with government other than to pay its taxes and to obey the antitrust laws, such dreams are unrealistic. The public may not like the way regulation has been handled, but it is likely to be unwilling to completely abandon such protection. Much needs to be done in order to reduce the burden of regulation. A great deal of attention needs to be paid to developing regulatory techniques that permit greater flexibility in meeting regulatory goals and that move the government out of the business of detailed day-to-day oversight of industry's production and investment decisions. Yet the nation also needs to develop procedures that confront the trade-offs between achieving goals such as the reduction of pollution while improving economic growth through greater investment. The Reagan initiatives have moved us one step closer to the realization of these goals. But to achieve such goals, these initiatives must be administered carefully and with great sensitivity, for they also contain the potential to move us back to an era in which the White House was seen as a block to legitimate attempts at social reform.

The Reagan initiatives are best seen as a logical but significant extension of the process of experimentation begun by President Nixon and carried on by his three successors. The form this experimentation has taken in each administration reflects each president's character, his views about the value of regulation, and his attitudes toward the regulatory bureaucracy. Each successive experiment borrowed from the previous ones and, rhetoric aside, would not have been possible without the earlier efforts. Reagan's version of regulatory oversight borrows much of its procedure from Nixon's Quality of Life Review, many of its analytical requirements from Ford's Inflation Impact Statement program, and many of its analytical capabilities from those established and nurtured by Carter. Moreover, it will rely heavily on what is perhaps his administration's most important innovation: the *Regulatory Calendar.*

But it also breaks from the past in a number of important respects. At least in its initial form, it discards the concept of public filings and detailed logging of White House/agency contacts during the "post-comment" period. It deliberately shifts the locus of regulatory decision making in the direction of the White House. It eliminates many of the consultative and coordinative mechanisms that were intended to demonstrate to the agencies that regulatory reform was as much in their interest as in the interest of the White House.

But an experiment it certainly is. It is bound to be tested in the courts and, over the life of the Reagan administration, is likely to undergo major changes. For this reason, it would be especially unfortunate to embody either its current structure or its current procedures into law. The Reagan process should prove itself by operating under the more flexible arrangement of the executive order. Congress should avoid writing into law the developing "common law" of hybrid rule making in the mistaken notion that slowing the regulatory process to a crawl will somehow produce deregulation. If Congress feels compelled to act, let it take on the task of designing major changes in the substantive standards that agencies apply in rule making.[4] This does *not* require writing into law a requirement that regulations meet a cost-benefit test, a requirement that could actually be counterproductive to regulatory reform. Congress should merely remove the existing statutory impediments to consideration of costs as well as to balancing objectives across programs. This, combined with an ability to employ reasonably flexible administrative procedures, is sufficient to assure reasonable regulatory reform.

The regulatory process indeed needs to be harnessed, but it does *not* need to be hobbled. Regulation is not inherently bad; it has merely been assigned tasks it is incapable of performing.

If regulation is to be harnessed, a strong, credible, and professionally run White House oversight process is a prerequisite. Only at the White House level can important crosscutting questions be asked and the proper degree of regulatory integration be achieved. However, the potential for abuse of this power also needs to be recognized, and steps must be taken to assure that it does not occur.

III

Private Sector Alternatives to Direct Regulation

9

LAWRENCE S. BACOW

Private Bargaining and Public Regulation*

The private market and state law. Health, safety, or production? Regulation by OSHA and by collective bargaining. Unions and job hazards. An intervention strategy to improve union action. The advantages and limitations of negotiation, occupational and nonoccupational.

In many cases, government regulates because it is unhappy with the outcome of private bargaining. Job safety and health is the prototypical example. If Congress had been satisfied with the level of health and safety being achieved

*This paper is adapted from Bacow 1980.

through private negotiation between labor and management, the Occupational Safety and Health Act never would have become law. Similarly, if builders and home buyers were combining to produce houses with adequate attic and wall insulation, low air-filtration thermal envelopes, triple-glazed windows, and fuel-efficient heating and cooling systems, states would not be rushing to enact residential energy codes. More often than not, when we find the outcome of private market transactions unacceptable, we pass laws that mandate more desirable outcomes: we fix the level of health and safety in each workplace by adopting mandatory standards, or we increase the energy efficiency of homes by prescribing specific changes in design and construction. Rarely do we attempt to correct deficiencies in market outcomes by altering the conditions of private bargaining. We don't try to stimulate the natural regulatory capacity of self-interested workers or consumers—instead, we substitute for it. As a result, we often overlook regulatory strategies that are potentially both more efficient and more effective than traditional command-and-control approaches.

POTENTIAL GAINS FROM ENHANCED PRIVATE BARGAINING—OCCUPATIONAL SAFETY AND HEALTH

Perhaps the greatest potential for achieving regulatory objectives through enhanced private bargaining lies in the area of job safety and health. Studies of the performance of the Occupational Safety and Health Administration (OSHA) suggest that it has been relatively ineffective because the command-and-control strategy embodied in the Occupational Safety and Health Act is ill suited to the task of regulating job hazards (see, for example, Mendeloff 1979 and Bacow 1980). It is virtually impossible for the government to promulgate uniform standards that work well in each of the nation's 5 million workplaces. Hazards differ from industry to industry and firm to firm. What may be a reasonable approach to noise abatement in a textile mill in South Carolina may be impractical in a foundry in Pittsburgh. Moreover, OSHA has relatively few resources at its disposal to ensure implementation. Inspections are infrequent and fines modest. As an outside regulatory authority, OSHA is powerless to influence the day-to-day behavior of workers and their supervisors. As a result, when compromises must be made, health and safety almost always take a back seat to other production objectives within the workplace.

In theory, many of OSHA's structural deficiencies could be remedied if we placed greater reliance upon collective bargaining to make the workplace safe. Much of what a labor union does is similar to what a regulatory agency such as OSHA does. Both institutions exist to alter the conduct of management for the benefit of labor. Both spell out in great detail the dimensions of acceptable management conduct, in one case through regulations and in the other through the terms of the collective bargaining agreement. And both the unions and OSHA attempt to ensure management compliance through inherently coercive processes.

There are also a number of significant differences between union activity and regulatory activity. First, a union exists almost exclusively to represent and to further the interests of its members. Contact between officers and members is frequent, especially at the local level. If the union ignores the needs of the rank and file, the leadership may be voted out of office. OSHA, on the other hand, represents a large and diffuse class of people who have little if any contact with the agency. It is insulated from its constituency—workers—by size and distance. Second, unlike OSHA, a union cannot unilaterally mandate changes in working conditions. Each change must first be negotiated with management. As a result, the rules governing the conditions of employment produced by this bargaining represent a reconciliation of com-

peting interests by the principals. In contrast, OSHA functions more like a judge, sifting and weighing evidence and
rendering decisions that often satisfy nobody. Third, unions
deal with a much broader range of issues than OSHA, including wages, hiring, layoffs, seniority, insurance, training,
education, promotion, incentives, and discipline, in addition
to some health and safety issues. Related problems can be
solved in a single forum. Fourth, the work rules developed
through labor-management negotiation do a better job of accommodating the diverse conditions encountered in different
workplaces than do uniform national standards. There are
approximately 150,000 separate collective bargaining agreements in force in the United States. A majority of organized
workers work under contracts negotiated with a single
employer or for a single plant. Fifth, labor-management
rule making is more flexible than government regulatory activity. Collective bargaining agreements are renegotiated
periodically, and the parties may modify rules during the
term of the contract by mutual agreement.

Sixth, and last, the coercive enforcement processes
employed by unions and OSHA differ substantially across a
number of dimensions. Collective bargaining agreements are
enforced by the workers they are designed to protect,
whereas regulations are enforced by relatively disinterested
inspectors. The union's presence in the workplace is con-
tinual and pervasive; OSHA's is severely limited. Unions can
vary and escalate their threats and sanctions; OSHA cannot.
As a participant in the operation of the workplace, a union
can influence events that affect the cost of implementing
changes in working conditions—something that OSHA is
powerless to do. Union demands are treated relatively
seriously by foremen and supervisors; OSHA regulations and
fines often are not.

Given these potential advantages, it would seem that we
have much to gain by encouraging labor and management to
take a more active role in controlling job hazards through

the collective bargaining process. While some unions have been very aggressive in pushing for improved health and safety conditions at the bargaining table, others have not.[1] Most seem content to place primary reliance upon OSHA, however ineffective it may be. Virtually every collective bargaining agreement contains some reference to health and safety, yet a serious commitment to the problem is the exception rather than the rule. Where labor and management have worked together to improve working conditions, they have been very successful. The United Automobile Workers (UAW) and the major automobile manufacturers, for example, have successfully implemented a system of union health and safety stewards to identify and resolve health and safety problems in conjunction with the plant safety officer. Similarly, the Steelworkers and the Oil, Chemical and Atomic Workers (OCAW) have negotiated agreements to control specific hazards in their industries. Before we can begin to specify, however, the steps that might be taken to encourage other unions to follow the models set by the UAW, the Steelworkers, and the OCAW, we must first have a better understanding of the factors that both motivate and inhibit collective bargaining over health and safety issues.

INFLUENCES ON THE LIKELIHOOD OF HEALTH AND SAFETY BARGAINING

Many factors influence what commands the attention of labor and management at any point in time. At the most basic level, technology, market structure, and the relative power of the parties shape the bargaining relationship. But within this context the substance of bargaining is determined largely by a union's bargaining priorities, and these in turn are determined by intraunion politics, by the institutional capacity of the union to bargain over specific issues, and by the cost to the union of achieving specific bargaining objectives.

Politics

Unions are political institutions. Bargaining agendas reflect not only the preferences of the membership, but the process by which these preferences get translated into action. It is tempting to explain the lack of attention to health and safety issues in many unions by a lack of interest or concern on the part of the rank and file, but the evidence is to the contrary. Studies of the preferences of workers consistently show that they are willing to incur substantial costs to improve their health and safety (see Bacow 1980, pp. 91–92; Herrick 1976).

A better explanation is that often there is little political return to the union leader who champions health and safety causes, notwithstanding the preferences of the rank and file. Consider, for example, a union leader interested in ridding a plant of numerous safety hazards. In practice, safety hazards pose risks only to those workers in the immediate vicinity of the hazard—faulty hoists threaten only hoist operators and their assistants, unguarded machines threaten only machine operators, narrow catwalks threaten only people who work at heights, etc. The political gains to a leader from negotiating the abatement of each of these hazards are small because so few workers will benefit from his actions. In most cases, our hypothetical union president would be better off expending scarce bargaining capital in ways that benefit the membership at large—e.g., on wages and fringes. Also, since workers are highly conscious of their relative positions within the workplace, agreements that disproportionately benefit specific groups within the union are politically unpopular. Further reinforcing this reluctance to tackle individual safety problems is the political weakness of the workers at risk. Those most likely to be injured in an occupational accident tend to be disproportionately young and inexperienced workers, not the power brokers in the intraunion bargaining process (Hagglund 1976, p. 111).

Similarly, there is often little political return to the leader who tries to improve working conditions that threaten the long-term health of the rank and file. In contrast to safety problems, health hazards like cotton dust and coke-oven emissions tend to affect everyone in a workplace. But because of the long latent periods for the diseases produced by these hazards, the benefits from negotiated reductions in worker exposure often will not be apparent for years to come, usually well after the union leader who negotiated them has retired. In theory, younger workers have the most to gain from such actions, but as noted before, they tend to be weak politically. And older workers sometimes prefer the union to direct its efforts to improving pensions and disability benefits instead of negotiating expensive reductions in health-threatening conditions that they will not be around to enjoy. In short, health and safety issues often take a back seat to wages, pensions, and fringe benefits because most unions lack a strong intraunion health and safety lobby.

Institutional capacity

When a union undertakes to improve health and safety conditions through collective bargaining, it labors under a number of handicaps that are not prevalent when it bargains over wages and other conditions of employment. For a union to successfully negotiate the abatement of a job hazard, it must have access to three different types of information. First, it must know that a potential hazard exists. For example, it must recognize that a chemical in common use is potentially harmful. Second, it must be able to monitor the magnitude of the hazard over time. Without access to monitoring data, a union cannot confirm or rebut a management claim that a particular substance (or condition) is safe

at the level commonly encountered. Also, a union cannot enforce a negotiated agreement to limit worker exposure unless
it can monitor that exposure. And third, a union must have
knowledge of cost-effective hazard abatement techniques.
Without access to this third type of data, a union cannot critically evaluate management proposals for reform.

In practice, each of these three types of information is
often in short supply, especially for occupational disease
hazards. Although many international unions have recently
hired industrial hygienists, information and expertise are
still scarce at the local level where workers actually confront
hazards. The vast majority of local unions lack the
knowledge needed to identify and monitor nonobvious
hazards. As a result, some unions don't push for abatement
of dangerous conditions because they are ignorant of them,
while others don't push because they lack the institutional
capacity to bargain over these issues with management. This
lack of technical sophistication plagues the contract-
administration process as well. Arbitrators generally lack
the experience necessary to judiciously resolve health and
safety disputes. In at least a few instances, labor and management have shied away from negotiating comprehensive
health and safety agreements because they did not trust arbitrators who were without health and safety training to
fairly interpret and enforce the agreements (see Bacow
1980, p. 99).

Cost

Another reason unions are often reluctant to pursue improved health and safety conditions through collective
bargaining is that it is costly. To win concessions on health
and safety issues directly from management, a union must
expend scarce bargaining capital, thereby forgoing other
bargaining objectives. In contrast, if the same improvements
are achieved through government regulation, the cost to the

union is considerably less. It is also cheaper for a union to enforce an OSHA standard than to police a negotiated health and safety agreement. Disputes over compliance with negotiated contracts usually are settled by mutual agreement of the parties during the grievance process or by appeal to third-party arbitration. A fair amount of bargaining occurs in the disposition of grievances. By winning concessions from management on health and safety grievances, labor may diminish its capacity to resolve non–health and safety grievances in its favor. Similarly, arbitration is expensive because the cost is shared equally by labor and management. In contrast, a union incurs few costs in enforcing an OSHA regulation. A complaint is filed and the rest is up to OSHA.

Bargaining over job hazards also is potentially expensive because it makes unions potentially liable for failure to enforce their negotiated agreements. A few unions have been sued by members who claimed that they suffered injury because the union failed to discharge its contractually assumed duty to inspect the workplace for hazards (see Bacow 1980, p. 97). While the unions have prevailed in nearly all of these cases, the threat of liability continues to discourage unions from assuming greater responsibilities in identifying and eliminating dangerous conditions. Unions are not legally obligated to negotiate health and safety agreements, so they can escape the threat of liability entirely by leaving the job of hazard regulation to OSHA.

In summary, we don't observe more efforts to improve the safety of the workplace through collective bargaining for a number of reasons. First, intraunion political processes are not particularly responsive to health and safety concerns. Second, unions often lack the institutional capacity to negotiate and implement comprehensive health and safety agreements. And third, from a union perspective, OSHA is a much cheaper alternative to hazard abatement than collective bargaining.

A STRATEGY FOR ENCOURAGING A LARGER ROLE FOR COLLECTIVE BARGAINING

Collective bargaining will never be a substitute for government regulation of job hazards. While none of the obstacles described above is insurmountable, labor and management realistically will never be able to achieve the level of technical sophistication necessary to address most health hazards on their own. Nonetheless, government can try to improve the meager performance of the federal regulatory effort by encouraging unions to play a larger role in enforcing health standards and in negotiating agreements to control safety hazards. The previous discussion suggests the broad outlines of an intervention strategy. Government must look for ways to make health and safety issues politically attractive to union leaders; it must try to improve the capacity of the collective bargaining process to address health and safety issues; and it must lower the cost of negotiation as an alternative to reliance on OSHA. Some specific suggestions for achieving these objectives follow.

Train union health and safety stewards

In most workplaces in the United States, OSHA is almost invisible. Inspections are few and far between. When an inspector does come to visit, his search for hazards is hampered by his lack of familiarity with the routine of the workplace. While violations may be cited and fines levied, infrequent inspections place little pressure on either labor or management to pay continuous attention to job safety and health. OSHA could take a large step towards remedying this deficiency if it trained a cadre of union health and safety stewards to inspect the workplace and work with management in abating job hazards. With a modest amount of training—on the order of 40 hours—a union steward could be taught how to recognize significant hazards commonly encountered in his work environment, some hazard-abatement techniques, the OSHA standards relevant to his workplace, and how to read a noise meter and take air quality samples for evaluation elsewhere. What the steward might lack in technical sophistication relative to a government inspector would be compensated for by his continuous presence in the workplace and familiarity with it. In addition to providing compliance pressure, training one person in each workplace to be a quasiprofessional health and safety inspector also provides a basis for a health and safety lobby within the union. Furthermore, a safety steward also gives the union the institutional capacity to negotiate agreements whose implementation demands a union monitoring capability.

The concept of a union health and safety steward is not a radical one. In Sweden, they are required by law (Boden and Wagman 1978, p. 43). Union health and safety stewards also have existed in the automobile industry since negotiation of the 1973 General Motors–UAW contract (see Bacow 1980, pp. 61–67). The GM–UAW experience has been highly successful. GM officials have praised the program because it has encouraged resolution of health and safety issues on their merits; one function of the steward is to explain diplomatically to his fellow workers when their complaints are not justified. The union also is pleased with the program because it has enhanced its capacity to bargain intelligently and effectively with management over genuine health and safety problems. OSHA would be wise to encourage other unions to copy this approach by investing heavily in a union health and safety steward training program.

Exempt from inspection workplaces with OSHA-approved stewards

Training alone does not ensure that union personnel will

either enforce OSHA regulations or independently pursue
the abatement of job hazards. To function effectively, a
union steward must have as much access to the workplace as
an OSHA inspector. He must be free to walk around the work
site, investigate complaints, and discuss health and safety
issues with foremen, supervisors, and workers. In practice, it
is difficult to legislate these rights because of the difficulties
inherent in enforcement. Moreover, such a move would no
doubt be politically unpopular, given the current mood of
Congress. A better approach would be for OSHA to negotiate
selectively, with employers and unions, agreements in which
exemption from OSHA inspection would be offered in return
for walkaround rights and funding for the health and safety
steward. The conditions for exemption should vary with the
size of the firm. Very large employers might be asked to fund
full-time health and safety stewards; smaller employers
might have to fund only part-time stewards. Since the union
would be a party to any exemption, weak unions that preferred the status quo could elect not to participate in the program. To avoid a situation where management might attempt to buy off the union leadership in return for exemption
from OSHA inspection, OSHA could require each firm to
demonstrate that its accident and illness rate improved
before renewing the exemption. OSHA could strengthen the
hand of participating unions by responding quickly and
decisively to complaints initiated by the union steward. Such
a strategy puts the steward in the position of being able to
say, "Deal with me or deal with OSHA."

The selective exemption program just described also is not
a radical idea. Cal-OSHA has negotiated an agreement with
Bechtel Corporation to suspend enforcement on a large construction site in return for a joint labor-management safety
program (Bardach and Kagan 1982, chap. 8). Such an agreement offers a little something to everyone. From the regulator's perspective, it frees up scarce enforcement resources so
that they may be redeployed in places where labor lacks the

capacity to protect itself. It also strengthens labor's hand in dealing with management over health and safety issues and encourages labor to concentrate its health and safety efforts on the problems of greatest concern to the rank and file. Exemption also offers management much more flexibility in complying with OSHA than does regular OSHA enforcement. Many managers would prefer to deal with their unions over health and safety issues because the union understands the practical problems of the workplace (Bacow 1980, p. 66). In contrast, OSHA is often viewed as naive, picayune, and unyielding (Bacow 1980, p. 108). And in practice, a union is likely to exercise much more discretion in assessing what constitutes management compliance than is OSHA.

Exempt unions from liability

Unions may be reluctant to participate in the exemption program just described if they fear that they will render themselves liable to lawsuits from their members as a result. The appropriate response for government is to statutorily exempt unions from liability except in cases of willful neglect. This action would not diminish the rights of workers who, under current law, must demonstrate a breach of the duty of fair representation to collect against their union. It would, however, remove the ambiguity from the current law, and in doing so would further lower the cost to unions of assuming a more active role in the regulation of occupational hazards.

Fund industry-specific morbidity and mortality studies

Government can encourage unions to give greater priority to health and safety through judicious use of information. Workers and their unions are acutely sensitive to differences that exist between industries or across firms in the terms and conditions of employment. If the wage scale for members of a local union, for example, is significantly below the industry average, pressure is automatically placed on the union leadership to do better at the bargaining table the next time around. The union leader who ignores such differences lays himself open to charges of complacency or ineffectiveness made by potential challengers for his office. The government can exploit this sensitivity for relative positions by collecting and disseminating data on the relative morbidity and mortality of large firms as well as of unions and industries. In practice, nothing grabs the attention of workers more than a government report stating that they have a significantly higher likelihood of contracting a dread disease than their cohorts in the population at large. Such studies also buttress the bargaining position of labor in health and safety negotiations with management. Even if additional government support for epidemiological research is not forthcoming, at a minimum government can require firms to prominently display to their employees the average lost-time injury rate of *both* the firm and the industry.

Promote swift and inexpensive resolution of health and safety disputes

The availability of a fast and effective means to resolve health and safety disputes is important to the development of collective bargaining over job hazards for three reasons. First, as noted before, collective bargaining agreements are implemented through the grievance-arbitration process. To the extent that the parties lack confidence in this process, implementation of hazard-limiting agreements will be inhibited. Second, arbitration acts to fill the inevitable gaps in a collective bargaining agreement. Since it is virtually impossible to anticipate all health and safety contingencies *ex ante*, arbitration permits resolution of future disputes without resort to economic conflict. And third—and perhaps most important—the availability of arbitration influences the significance of labor's rights to refuse hazardous work. From labor's perspective, swift arbitration protects against improper discipline a worker who rightfully refuses to perform a dangerous job, and from management's perspective, it guards against abuse of the walkoff right.

In 1980 the Supreme Court upheld an OSHA regulation that prohibited employers from disciplining workers who refused hazardous work, provided that the workers "reasonably believed" that the task threatened "death or serious injury and that there is insufficient time, due to the urgency of the situation, to eliminate the danger through resort to regular statutory enforcement channels."[2] The ruling was significant because, by expanding the right to refuse hazardous work, it strengthened the intraunion bargaining position of safety-conscious workers. Any time a worker refuses to perform a job, he places pressure on both labor and management to address the issues that underlie the work stoppage. In practice, however, the right to refuse hazardous work may be meaningless if the correctness of an employee's decision to cease work is not swiftly tested by arbitration. The language of the OSHA regulation invites management challenges: Was the employee's fear of death or serious injury reasonable? Was there, in fact, time to eliminate the danger through normal channels? If it takes a month to resolve these issues, during which time a worker may be shifted to a lower-paying job or even suspended, a worker may be reluctant to exercise his walkoff rights even if he is entitled to back pay and to reinstatement if he is ultimately vindicated.

Government can take a number of steps to promote rapid arbitration of health and safety disputes. First, it can offer special training to arbitrators in hazardous industries. At present, not only are most arbitrators technically ignorant, they also lack the practical knowledge of specific hazards that comes from working on a job for a number of years. Thus in many cases arbitrators are less well qualified to

resolve health and safety disputes than the parties themselves. OSHA can upgrade the quality of health and safety
arbitration through training programs that cover relevant
OSHA standards, conditions that pose extreme danger to
workers, the types of evidence commonly offered to establish
the existence of exceptional risks, and other technical subjects that would assist in the resolution of health and
safety—related disputes. Second, OSHA can underwrite the
cost of health and safety arbitration by these specially
trained arbitrators. If OSHA is to encourage unions to use
collective bargaining mechanisms to address health and
safety issues as an alternative to government regulation,
then arbitration must be priced competitively with OSHA
complaint procedures. Third, OSHA can make arrangements
to have these arbitrators available to labor and management
on short notice—ideally, within a day. And fourth, OSHA
can publicize the success of expedited arbitration procedures
in industries that have experimented with them.

ADVANTAGES AND LIMITS
OF BARGAINING

The changes described above will not by themselves eliminate job hazards. What they will do is increase the
equilibrium level of health and safety achieved through collective bargaining by making it easier for labor and management to bargain over these issues. All of the suggestions
operate at the margin by either strengthening the capacity
of the collective bargaining process to address health and
safety issues (the health and safety steward program, the
training of health and safety arbitrators), lowering the cost
to unions of obtaining health and safety concessions at the
bargaining table (free training for health and safety stewards, exemption from inspection for selected workplaces,

government funding of health and safety arbitration, union exemption from liability), or gently encouraging unions to give greater priority to health and safety issues (the steward program, epidemiological studies). The incremental nature of the reforms is characteristic of government attempts to stimulate private bargaining. Unfortunately, government cannot command people to bargain. All it can do is create an environment conducive to negotiation by removing small but significant obstacles and by enhancing the attractiveness of negotiated outcomes relative to the alternative. For example, government can make it easier for home buyers to negotiate with builders over the energy components of their homes by providing information in a form that permits comparison shopping. The Environmental Protection Agency (EPA) has adopted this approach in requiring publication of the mileage ratings of new cars. In some cases, government can also try to alter the outcome of private bargaining by strengthening the bargaining position of one of the parties. Some consumer statutes have this effect by mandating minimum warranties that can be waived with the knowing consent of the consumer.

The great virtue of bargaining is that it permits the parties to fashion outcomes that closely match their needs and circumstances. This flexibility is a highly valued but rarely encountered commodity in the regulatory arena. The political process that gives rise to command-and-control regulation invariably demands that it be administered in a tough, evenhanded fashion. While toughness and evenhandedness are admirable qualities in the abstract, in the highly diverse world in which we live they are synonymous with inflexibility and inefficiency. For example, requiring that every house be fully insulated and weather-stripped imposes needless costs on people who only want to build summer homes in temperate climates. Because truly decentralized regulatory alternatives like taxes and economic incentives are politically unpopular, we are often left with the task of trying to improve the efficiency of regulation within the context of command and control.

The collective bargaining strategy described above represents an attempt to enhance the capacity of the implementation process to reflect efficiency considerations. In effect, it constitutes decentralization through an enforcement process that is flexible by design. Rather than attempt to enforce regulations centrally, it capitalizes on the self-interest of the protected constituency—labor—to achieve compliance. It gives responsibility to unions for enforcing regulations while, at the same time, building their capacity to do so. In practice, unions are likely to enforce regulations that matter a lot to their members and to ignore regulations that matter not at all. And unlike OSHA, unions are also in a position to help management implement cost-effective hazard abatement programs.

A major drawback of this approach is its limited application—only 28 percent of American workers are employed in unionized workplaces. Aside from freeing some inspectors to look elsewhere, the suggestions described above would do little for nonunionized workers. This limited scope is also characteristic of strategies that seek regulatory compliance by altering the conditions of private bargaining. Such strategies are necessarily opportunistic. They often must capitalize on the existence of institutions like unions that help to organize the interests of the intended beneficiaries of regulation in a way that facilitates bargaining. Where such institutions do not exist, it is often impractical to create them. Before a health and safety steward program could be implemented in a nonunion shop, for example, representational elections would have to be held, some mechanism would have to be created to protect the steward from arbitrary dismissal, and labor and management would have to begin a joint problem-solving dialogue. In other words, many of the attributes of collective bargaining would have to be replicated. Notwithstanding its limited application, we should exploit the opportunities that are created by bargaining and look to other regulatory strategies to address aspects of problems that are not amenable to this approach.

NONOCCUPATIONAL BARGAINING

Perhaps the most promising nonoccupational application of bargaining as a supplement to regulation lies in the environmental field. All too frequently, environmental regulation gives rise to lawsuits. In many cases, these disputes drag out until the last available court has refused to hear the appeal of the last litigant claiming that the regulatory agency's action was either too harsh or too lenient. Unfortunately, even a final court order does not ensure resolution of the underlying controversy because the principles of judicial review discourage courts from addressing many of the substantive issues in such a case. Usually, courts seek to avoid issues that most concern the parties (generally questions of fact or policy), while issues that interest the courts (typically, narrow questions of law or procedure) by themselves are of little concern to the parties. Because of this mismatch, lawsuits rarely resolve the true underlying differences of the parties to an environmental dispute.

The expense of this process has encouraged a number of litigants to consider negotiation as an alternative. In contrast to litigation, face-to-face bargaining forces the parties to address the merits of a controversy. Like bargaining over job safety and health, environmental negotiation relies on the principals to fashion solutions to complicated environmental problems. These individuals generally possess a greater understanding of the technical and institutional dimensions of environmental controversies than do judges. They are usually in a better position to creatively explore alternatives and analyze the consequences of different proposals than a nontechnically trained jurist who may see only one or two similar cases in his career. Moreover, as with labor and management, these people have to live with any agreement they negotiate; consequently, they are likely to be sensitive to the realities of implementation.

Virtually all the attempts to date at environmental bargaining have been *ad hoc* procedures.[3] Only recently have states begun to experiment with institutionalizing bargaining as part of the environmental regulation process. The Massachusetts Hazardous Waste Facility Siting Act (Mass 1980) requires developers of hazardous waste facilities to bargain with host and abutting communities over environmental controls, mitigation measures, postclosure management procedures, and compensation to be paid to the communities in the event that the developer goes forward with plans to construct or operate a new facility. As of this writing, the act is in the early stages of implementation.

Early efforts have had to overcome a host of legal and institutional obstacles that arise because our regulatory procedures are designed to facilitate judicial review, not consensual dispute resolution. Often these procedures are divisive and encourage litigious behavior. For example, open-meeting laws and requirements that records and transcripts be maintained discourage the give and take that is the essence of successful bargaining. Similarly, limitations on *ex parte* communications sometimes prevent regulators from acting as brokers between competing interests. Given the potential contribution of bargaining to the resolution of environmental disputes, a serious reexamination of these procedures would appear to be in order.

10

MICHAEL O'HARE

Information Strategies as Regulatory Surrogates

The advantages of information strategies. Alternatives to regulation. Escape-from-freedom and market-failure regulation. Quality standardization. Enforced disclosure and liability. The economics of guarantees. Insurance premium regulators. News media as surrogates.

The sign "SPEED LIMIT 25" often precedes a stretch of road on which it is dangerous to drive fast. If the limit is enforced,

it does the job, more or less. But dangerous areas may be preceded by an entirely different kind of sign:

| LEFT LANE CLOSED AHEAD | | CONSTRUCTION 500 FEET |

These are much more useful than the first, for these reasons:
First, they work without further attention from the police.
Second, they allow the driver to prepare for the particular risk
at hand. Third, they do not activate the driver's aggressive
"Don't tell *me* what to do!" instinct; instead, they make his
perceived interests congruent with society's wishes.

This example illustrates the general principle of substituting information management for command-and-control
regulation. When this substitution works, it often works very
well—for the same three reasons exemplified above. Put
more generally, they are:

(1) Information strategies are frequently cheaper to
implement.

(2) Decision-makers who are well-informed and free to
choose different responses have the flexibility to deal with
varying situations differently, which is far more efficient
than if differently situated people with different preferences
are all obliged to do the same thing.

(3) Information strategies are noncoercive, at least as
regards the informee (someone may be required to provide
information to him), and life is better for everyone when
there is less ordering people around.

Not all information strategies are well advised. I have always wondered how to use:

> **DANGER:**
> **LOW-FLYING PLANES**

and the prospectus for my money-market fund just makes me feel guilty as I file it unread. As I discuss several examples of information policies that might be substituted for conventional regulation, my point of departure will be that information is *prima facie* better than coercion, and I will therefore emphasize pitfalls and problems in implementing such substitutions as exceptions to this general position.

COMPETITIVE STRATEGIES

Information strategies compete with tax/bribe incentives as alternatives to regulation. These two are usually appropriate for different kinds of regulatory purpose. In particular, regulation may usefully be separated into three general types. The first, which I will call market-failure regulation, seeks efficiency by forcing A to behave as he would if he were as interested in B's welfare as in his own. In this category we find air pollution regulations, which prevent drivers from dirtying air that is mostly breathed by others; the justification is that any single driver's benefit calculus will undervalue the welfare of all other breathers. Many of these regulations can be replaced by a tax on A pegged to the damage that would be done to B by A's unregulated behavior.

The second type, which I will call elitist regulation, attempts to force A to do what B thinks A should want to do. There are few pure examples of this kind of regulation in the

United States, but motorcycle helmet and seat belt laws are a mediocre fit: the seat belt is such a modest inconvenience, and the risk of driving without a seat belt is so great, that people who want to do it are believed by others to be mistaken (about their own preferences) or ignorant (of the relevant statistics).[1] These regulations are favored by Bs but often resented by As. They can be replaced by a tax pegged to the marginal benefit A derives from the regulated behavior, or—sometimes—by an information management policy.

A third type is imposed to save the individual time and effort. Food and drug regulation is of this type (though it may also reflect an elitist motive): each of us has something better to do than to test every bottle of aspirin for purity. Even though we all have different optimal balance points of purity against price for aspirin, our tastes are similar enough to make it worth hiring a third party to enforce a single acceptable level; the individual departures from optimality that result, plus the cost of paying the regulator, are less for (nearly all of) us than the value of the time it would take each of us to test our respective aspirins at every purchase.

In practice, this type of regulation is usually imposed on producers by consumers as voters, as in the case of various aspirins. But aspirin consumers, by being deprived of choice among aspirin purities, are just as much regulated, in fact, as the producers. The political judgment being made is an exchange of diversity (that would permit individual fit of actions to tastes) for free time or absence of anxiety, and the instrumental imposition of the regulation on producers should not obscure the essential difference between this "escape-from-freedom" regulation and market-failure regulation. We prevent the emission of poisons into the air because poison is bad for everyone; we prevent the sale of substandard aspirin and useful but incompletely tested drugs *despite* the fact that both are better for some people than what is permitted to be sold (Kelman 1981 discusses this model of regulation at length).

"Escape-from-freedom" regulation of this type can theoretically be replaced by a prohibitive tax on nonstandard items, but this solution is impractical. The management of information, however, can often be a genuinely useful substitute, and in many cases the information strategy will be decidedly more efficient than the regulatory approach. This chapter focuses on such strategies.

The most likely opportunities for information to replace regulation are those in which relative preferences for different properties of a good (such as price and safety) differ widely. Where a single regulated standard imposes the greatest aggregate compromise on all persons, it is more likely to be efficient for people to make up their own minds. If information can be provided that reduces to a manageable level the analysis involved in a consumption decision, information strategies will be the right policy. More precisely, the analysis must cost less than the average difference between individual optimality and the fixed level that regulation would provide. Another way to put this condition (as the contrapositive) is that if well-informed people would all choose to buy about the same item that the best-tuned regulation would restrict them to, an information strategy would not make much difference nor be worth much.

Other conditions favoring information strategies are that the consumption decision be rare (so analysis each time will not mount up to a large cost), and that the item in question be expensive and complicated so the range of reasonable choices will be wide.

A case in point is housing purchase, which meets the latter criteria and illustrates several possibilities for an information policy. At present, we regulate housing to strict minimum standards through building codes. Restricting our attention to single-family houses to avoid the externality issue, in what ways could information substitute for the code?

CATEGORIZATION

One of the problems a home buyer faces is that houses can vary in many different ways: durability of materials, livability of plan, image projected to neighbors, probability of fire, escape conditions if a fire occurs (size of exits, alarm system, etc.), cost of heating, and so on. Since houses are extremely complicated artifacts, purchasers find them difficult to evaluate according to their own particular interests.

The analysis a buyer needs could be much simplified if the house were evaluated on specific, partially aggregated dimensions and, within each dimension, into specified ranges of the quality variable. A government agency or a voluntary group, for example, might officially grade a house—much as tires are now rated—as follows:

Durability	A
Fire safety	C
Plan	B
Operating cost	B

People who cared a lot about safety would, at a given price, prefer an A,B,B,A house to an A,C,A,A house. Such a scheme raises plenty of questions, of course: How should the same consumer think about an A,B,A,A house compared to an A,A,C,A house? What is he to make of an A,A,A,A house that costs $10,000 more than an A,B,A,A house? But such questions also beset a buyer without a categorization scheme, and at least the various factors bearing on safety have been collected and combined for the purchaser by a technical expert.

STANDARDIZATION

Information is carried by one language or another, and an information policy can standardize this language to be more useful than what an uncontrolled market would provide. Just as the Food and Drug Administration establishes standards of identity so that the range of things designated on a label by the word *mayonnaise*, for example, is extremely narrow, one could standardize the language of housing by defining words describing architectural styles. Even such apparently simple concepts as *room*, now used to describe almost any sort of space, could be restricted to denote "a space not part of the path to another space, isolable by walls and doors, greater than X ft.," and so on (O'Hare et al. 1979). At least some such standardization is essential to commerce; where would we be without legal standard definitions of the inch and the liter?

Note that such standardization by law tends to entrain regulation; not only must you use the official liter when you promise the consumer a liter of intoxicant, but you now may offer only certain bottle sizes. (Another way to look at this latest step is as standardization of the implicit terms *small bottle, medium bottle*, etc.)

Where standardization is not enforced by law, it is often established voluntarily by producers or customers, as in the case of screw threads. Yet however willing they are, private actors may not be able to establish a useful standard without government action. As an automobile manufacturer reportedly testified before Congress, "We would be delighted to make our bumpers at the standard height if someone would only tell us what that height is!"

Language is not the only thing that can usefully be standardized; each of the summary measures suggested in the preceding section requires an operational definition that

gives the testing procedure used to determine the grade.[2] For
at least some qualities of housing, this is practical: low-cost
tests for energy efficiency could be used instead of obligatory
energy conservation standards, and would probably result in
more efficient buildings (and happier home owners) overall
(O'Hare et al. 1979).

ENFORCED DISCLOSURE

So far, I have discussed only voluntary standardization,
possibly with a minimal government role in identifying a
"focal point"—such as the standard bumper height—
without forcing anyone to use it. Government may have a
larger role in providing information as well. When a government is casting about for alternatives to direct regulation,
the obvious information strategy is to enforce disclosure of
what the regulatee (usually a producer) is doing. The concept
of enforced disclosure is seductive to the theoretical economist with a full tool kit of simplifying assumptions; but as
Bardach and Kagan (1982) explain, it is not so easy to deliver
a workable and reasonable enforced disclosure strategy as it
might appear. Nevertheless (as in the case of energy standards for buildings), when the consumer's decision justifies
large allocations of analysis time and effort and a rich array
of choice confronts him, it is probably the preferred option
unless specific obstacles prevent its implementation.

One consistent problem with enforced information is the
tendency of regulators to require too much information. I
have discussed this problem at length in the context of Environmental Impact Statements and the information management process for public decisions (O'Hare 1981c).[3] Here I
offer a more qualitative analysis. A most important information problem is to make realistic estimates of the practical
limits on a consumer's information intake. It seems cheap to

force a drug seller to add, at the margin, just a little more information to the package insert; surely the *production* cost of this information is not significant. But the consumer who would read ten words in large type ("Don't take this drug if you have had a drink") will ignore a piece of paper with ten paragraphs of small print; the cost of *consuming* the information counts here.

An experiment related by Bardach and Kagan (1982) should be more widely known: a bank recently inserted in its electronic funds transfer disclosure statement a sentence offering $10 to anyone writing the words "Regulation E" on a postcard and sending it to the bank. Out of 115,000 recipients, not one responded. An experiment like this is damning evidence that an enforced disclosure policy constructed without a realistic appreciation of the recipient's rational allocation of his time is not necessarily preferable to regulation and may be worse than nothing.

Even a well-meaning and perspicacious regulator is likely to become tangled in a web of perverse incentives; since he is enforcing disclosure that the regulatee would not otherwise want to make, his rules have to meet legal and practical standards of enforceability that drive all kinds of regulation in the direction of tedious specificity, loss of proportion, and irrationality. What we really want to do is force a seller to be as imaginative and clever in telling the consumer what the consumer wants to know as he is when he presents his own pitch in advertising. Indeed, the essence of the enforced disclosure problem is captured in the contrast between bank advertising to attract new credit card customers on the one hand, and the boilerplate the bank mails out under duress to disclose its operating rules on the other. The poor performance called forth when the regulatee is forced to act counter to his desires is a constant of regulation generally and should motivate us to dream up Zen strategies that "use the enemy's strength against him" wherever possible.

GUARANTEES

One such strategy is a performance warranty, which is required to some extent from all sellers by liability law and is willingly offered by some sellers by contract. Enforced liability, or required warranties, eliminates the incentive for a seller to deceive a customer about quality; both parties' interests are closely aligned. But why would a seller offer a warranty voluntarily?

In a deservedly famous paper, economist George Akerlof (1970) describes the problem of the seller who knows more about his product than the buyer. How can a used car dealer persuade his customers that a "cream puff" (a good car) is really a cream puff? One solution is for the seller to guarantee performance. The buyer reasons (1) if this item fails to perform as promised, restitution will be made; (2) if the product generally does not perform as promised, the seller will lose money by making good on guarantees. The law of contracts, and some statutes requiring specific warranties, establish a framework for commerce that direct regulation could not possibly provide.

The economics of guarantees, voluntary or required, have been investigated theoretically by Harvard economist Michael Spence (1977, p. 561), with the important result that a guarantee can, under appropriate conditions, provide efficiency-increasing—even optimal—information to a consumer about a product's reliability. He also discovers the surprising, hence valuable, result that if consumers are risk averse, a seller's warranty alone is not efficient but requires, in addition, a liability to the state for nonperformance.

Guarantees seem to have potential outside the normal channels of commerce as well. For example, the Commonwealth of Massachusetts recently enacted legislation establishing a process of negotiated compensation whereby local opposition to the development of hazardous waste processing and disposal facilities might be overcome (Massachusetts General Laws, chap. 21D). The compensation can take many forms (a new fire truck, direct cash payments, extra-strict monitoring procedures, etc.). Property-value guarantees by the operator have been recommended by the state agency supervising the process as a particularly valuable part of such compensation agreements. Such guarantees substitute directly for government regulation of the hazardous waste processor's activities, at least in part.

The reasoning behind such guarantees is as follows: apprehension of accident or hidden health damage from a hazardous waste facility is likely to reduce property values for neighboring houses. Since a neighbor's house is usually his principal asset, realization of such fears would leave him unable even to leave the vicinity, since he would lack the capital to buy another house elsewhere. Thus, protection of property values responds to a significant part of the neighbor's concerns: if things get bad around the new plant, he can, at worst, pack up and move on.

From the developer's point of view, such a guarantee is likewise valuable. In the first place, unlike the fire engine, it can be provided without significant up-front expenditures. In the second place, the developer's expected cost of the guarantees is low even in the long term, since he plans to run such a fine operation that fears of property-value reductions will prove groundless. This means that even if he has to buy a few houses early on, he will at worst have to hold them until they recover their former value as his operation establishes a good record and becomes accepted as just another industrial neighbor. Of course, the neighbors will want to be sure that the developer has bonded resources to make good on such guarantees.[4]

INSURANCE AND COMBINED STRATEGIES

Guarantees of performance or compensation for nonperformance are sometimes provided by third parties, as through insurance policies. The premiums for properly underwritten insurance contracts frequently carry information about the relative risks imposed by different actions: fire insurance for homes already distinguishes crudely between such grossly different risks as approved (e.g., asphalt-shingle) and unapproved (e.g., cedar-shake) roofs, or residence in towns with better or worse fire departments. But other risks that might be reflected are not. For example, cigarette smoking causes about a quarter of residential fires.[5] About a third of the population smokes,[6] so smokers have almost 50 percent more fires than other people. Smoking is an addiction extremely difficult to conceal; it is verifiable enough to allow lower life insurance rates to be charged at present to nonsmokers. Fire insurance premiums should also reflect the large relative risk smokers impose on their dwellings.

The benefits of insurance premium fine tuning as a substitute for health and safety regulation are potentially large. Investigation of its costs and practicality, and of government policies that would encourage it, is a high-payoff research investment.

One especially attractive feature of insurance premiums for regulatory purposes is their flexibility. Let me illustrate how they might be used to avoid an ethically troublesome regulatory problem by returning to the example of automobile seat belts (the example applies as well to motorcycle helmets). We are apparently not going to mandate the use of seat belts; we may yet mandate the purchase of extremely expensive passive restraint devices. Legitimate objection has been raised to either type of regulation on grounds that it is the driver's business to protect himself if he wants to. The counter to this objection is that an unbelted driver risks imposing external costs on others, as when he is crippled and drains public medical care funds, or dies and forces his family onto the welfare rolls.

We might simply refuse public funds (or forbid accident-liability awards) to drivers who were seriously injured because they failed to wear belts, but it is hard to imagine a jury turning away a paraplegic or a widow on grounds that the driver had fair warning and, for public policy reasons, we have to make an example of him. The time to make adjustments is before a catastrophic event occurs. Consider instead a law requiring seat belt use unless the driver has purchased an insurance rider, at its proper price, protecting the public against the external costs that unbelted driving imposes.[7] No one would be required to wear a seat belt; what would be forbidden would be to make society pay for one's not wearing it.

Such a law probably would not require external evidence of the seat belt's use (such as an indicator light outside the car): seat belt requirements seem to be enforceable in Europe, and a shoulder belt makes it enormously easier to observe compliance from outside the car. But it certainly requires evidence of the extra insurance, probably in the form of a windshield sticker. It is interesting to speculate whether the principal motivation to wear seat belts under this scheme would arise from (1) the information about the costs of beltlessness provided by the insurance premium, (2) the disincentive of paying the premium itself, or (3) the obligation to inform the world via the sticker that one is not only rash, but foolish enough to pay for the right to a particularly unrewarding form of rashness (driving without a seat belt is much less fun than hang gliding).

THE ROLE OF THE PRESS

The industry whose stock-in-trade is information has not appeared in the forgoing discussion. What do news media have
to do with information strategies as regulatory surrogates?
On the whole, government should stay out of defining or dic-
tating that role, so I will not suggest government policies to
force the media to inform better. But news purveyors are
widely agreed to have special responsibilities to the public.

The seat belt issue raises one such responsibility that has,
I think, been misunderstood technically by the media
(O'Hare 1981a). On the whole, newspapers and broadcasters
do a respectable amount of preaching about the use of seat
belts and publishing statistics on their effectiveness. What
they tend not to do is note whether the victims of a particular
accident were wearing seat belts or not.

Editors apparently think people decide whether to use seat
belts on the basis of statistics accumulated by government
agencies or nonprofit groups. Indeed, these statistics are
dutifully published when the press release of a new study or
some legislative testimony appears.

But it would be more realistic to think of us as accumulating a little table in the back of our minds for each life-saving
strategy. The table for "consult doctors when sick" looks
like this:

	Got better	Did not get better
Went to a doctor	Many	Few
Did something else	Very few	Some

(I choose medical care to contrast with seat belts because, though it is costly, inconvenient, and less effective for its purpose than seat belts for theirs, many more people go to doctors than wear seat belts.) We add to this table as we learn of specific cases. The updating is sporadic and approximate, and such a table may be completely wiped out if formal statistical evidence turns up to contradict it. But these are the data that will motivate the decision whether or not to seek medical care when ill.

We all know from personal experience (ourselves and friends, family, etc.) of cases to include in the medical care table. But death by automobile accident is a rare event, so nearly all the experiments that might be entered in such a table can be known only from news reports, and the current conventions for reporting omit the essential fact.

The appropriate policy here is, in the first instance, one that news media should adopt: always report whether accident victims were wearing seat belts or not. But a government policy suggests itself as well: police departments should include seat belt use by victims in the official accident reports from which reporters assemble stories. This noncoercive policy would make it easier for the press to do what it generally wants to do as well as what we want it to do.

CONCLUSIONS

Many kinds of behavioral regulation can usefully be replaced by clever use of information. The best opportunities are regulations designed to avoid the cost of individuals' analyzing consumption decisions.

Information management is not necessarily best done by government; in most cases, the appropriate information policy is most efficiently implemented by private parties (warranties, insurance premium fine tuning, news-reporting practice, etc.). Often a modest intervention by government can accomplish the desired purpose where heavy-handed government action would be dysfunctional. In particular, the common tendency to replace behavioral regulation with enforced disclosure regulation has pitfalls not greatly different from those that generally beset behavioral regulation.

Any information management strategy requires careful consideration of the costs of information *consumption*; existing enforced disclosure strategies would be more effective if they took into account information receivers' rational allocations of their time. All too often, increasing the amount of information helps nobody. I am indebted to an opossum for the best statement of this last insight:

Howland Owl: What's wrong with advice?

Pogo Possum: If you ask for it, nothin'. If you don't, ever'thing.[8]

11

EUGENE BARDACH

ROBERT A. KAGAN

Liability Law
and Social Regulation*

The incentive effect of liability judgments. Regulation as a supplement to the law. Toxic substances, the chemical industry, and Japan. Specialized agencies. Reforms and prevention. Multimillion-dollar verdicts and the costs of litigation. No-fault "enterprise liability." Defensive medicine. Tort liability. Judges as administrators, as regulators. The surrogate defendant.

*This chapter is adapted, with slight editorial changes, from Eugene Bardach and Robert A. Kagan, *Going by the Book: The Problem of Regulatory Unreasonableness*, a Twentieth Century Fund Report (Philadelphia, PA: Temple University Press, 1982).

Socially irresponsible behavior can be deterred by the prospect of private lawsuits as well as by the threat of regulatory inspections and fines. The liability law system, however, is better shielded from the political and bureaucratic pressures that often make direct regulation unreasonably rigid, and it encourages enterprises to tailor protective measures to the specific combination of risks and abatement costs in each particular operation. To some observers, therefore, liability law, as it is or as it might be reformed, is the superior regulatory mechanism. In this chapter, we explore its potential and its limits as well as the concept of combining regulation with liability law.

THE LIABILITY SYSTEM

Court-ordered damage awards for injuries and illnesses caused by dangerous products or pollutants often extend into the hundreds of thousands of dollars and occasionally into the millions. Even smaller liability judgments usually outweigh the fines typically imposed for most regulatory violations. The mere threat of such lawsuits, therefore, would seem to provide strong incentives for enterprises to control any aspect of their activities that might lead to damage claims, even if the protective measures needed to avoid liability are not mandated by direct regulations. The prospect of large recoveries encourages aggressive legal action against violators of liability law. While overworked government enforcement attorneys may be inclined to back off from certain difficult cases, the injured plaintiff's lawyer has a contingent fee arrangement that encourages diligent prosecution of claims. Through pretrial discovery processes, he can compel defendants and their managers to disclose the contents of their files, the technical and economic basis for their decisions, and even their thought processes.

Where the threat of such damage suits is present, enterprises establish their own safety staffs and quality control units to conduct intensive internal inspections, or they submit to inspections by the loss control representatives dispatched by liability insurance companies. These private inspectors are present more often than government inspectors and are more knowledgeable about specific risks posed by each facility. Also, largely because they are free of the legal constraints and accountability pressures under which their government counterparts operate, private inspectors can tailor protective standards more closely to the hazards presented by the particular enterprise and thus minimize unreasonableness.

Similarly, liability standards applied by the courts usually are more generally worded and open ended (and hence, more sensitive to the particular context) than the detailed specification standards enforced by regulatory agencies. Courts impose liability only for behavior that actually has caused harm, not for behavior that might cause it. The adjudicatory process and private negotiations that accompany it tend to elicit evidence and focus attention on the risks and equities in each specific case. Judges and juries are less susceptible than regulatory officials to charges of capture or selling out if they decide in favor of a business enterprise, and they are under less pressure to apply the law legalistically so as to shield themselves from blame in the event of some future catastrophe. Similarly, compared to regulatory enforcement officials, plaintiffs in private lawsuits have more freedom to negotiate compromise remedies that depart from the letter of the law without being accused of subverting the public interest.

On the other hand, the liability law system has certain weaknesses that impair its potency as a deterrent to irresponsible behavior. Liability rules place the burden of proof on the injured plaintiff, and even when the plaintiff's claim is just, proof is often difficult to obtain. Litigation is always very costly and very slow; hence many plaintiffs, especially those with smaller claims, may be discouraged from bringing suit or induced to settle quickly for less than their due. Many valid claims never reach court because the victims are poor, uneducated, timid, ignorant of their rights, or fearful of contact with lawyers and courts. Others, who know litigation for the unpleasant experience it is, may decide that the protracted struggle, expense, and animosity associated with lawsuits are not worth the trouble. From the standpoint of enterprises whose activities might cause harm, the deterrent threat of lawsuits is partially blunted by liability insurance, especially when insurance premiums are not quickly adjusted to penalize less responsible firms to any significant extent. Recalcitrant enterprises can exploit the numerous opportunities for delay afforded by pretrial discovery rules and the complexities of court procedure. For all these reasons, the liability system probably does not in reality force enterprises to "internalize" all the social costs that result from their negligent or otherwise irresponsible actions.

Programs of direct regulation, in fact, typically have been enacted because the liability system by itself seemed to afford inadequate protection. But direct regulatory programs also may be somewhat ineffective in practice and are likely to lead to considerable unreasonableness. Hence further questions arise: Can the liability law system be changed or adapted to overcome its weaknesses as a regulatory mechanism? Can it be made to work better than direct regulation, to substitute for it in some areas, or to complement it more fully in others?

Consider, for example, the reforms in liability law represented by the state workers' compensation statutes enacted fifty to seventy years ago—absolute employer liability for all work-related injuries, a fixed statutory schedule of damages, adjudication by specialized administrative tribunals, limited counsel fees, and mandatory insurance for employers. These reforms greatly facilitated claims by injured workers. They impelled employers to make substantial improvements in worker safety, improvements that direct regulatory programs such as the Occupational Safety and Health Administration (OSHA) have found hard to supplement. Moreover, further liability law reforms have been proposed, such as increased workers' compensation benefit levels, sharper merit rating of employers by insurance companies, new standards of liability for occupational illnesses and diseases, and tax penalties for employers with above-average liability experience. Such changes might actually lead to more effective worker protection than OSHA achieves. By pushing liability costs up, they might provide employers with an incentive to do more than OSHA rules require (if doing more would cut liability costs). And they might have that effect without causing nearly as much site-level unreasonableness because they do not depend on strict enforcement of overinclusive specification standards. Law journals currently abound with proposals to increase the deterrent effect of liability law with respect to other perils as well, such as dangerous products, consumer deception, and employment discrimination. But can the regulatory potential of liability law be achieved without greatly increasing its propensity for unreasonableness? Or, in comparative terms, can liability law, if made more fearsome and effective, still operate more reasonably than comparable systems of direct regulation?

AN EXAMPLE: THE PROBLEM OF
TOXIC SUBSTANCES

Many of the more than 30,000 chemicals in common use are known to be toxic, a great many more are under varying degrees of suspicion, and still more have effects that are simply unknown. And even chemicals once thought safe have turned out, with disturbing frequency, to be dangerous. Through carelessness, ignorance, or occasional indifference, many of these hazardous substances invade the environment (e.g., transformers containing PCBs deteriorate or seepage occurs from poorly designed industrial waste sites), then find their way—through groundwater, the food chain, or direct contact—into man with sometimes horrifying results, such as the severe neurological disorders found among employees of a plant producing Kepone in Hopewell, Virginia, and among their families and area residents (see Stone 1977; Soble 1977, pp. 694–96).

Sometimes such effects are discovered in time to enable victims to sue for relief. Their exposure to the chemical and its responsibility for their illness are reasonably clear, and there is evidence that a particular manufacturer was negligent in not preventing or reducing the hazard. In such cases, which may be occurring with greater frequency, private lawsuits—often class actions involving millions of dollars in liability—would seem to provide a strong incentive for adequate care by chemical companies in the future.[1] But the requisite conditions for such lawsuits do not always apply. The discovery of a hazard may be delayed for years, pinpointing responsibility for its dissemination may be difficult, or it may be impossible to prove in a legally acceptable manner that a particular chemical substance (as opposed to heredity, smoking, diet, or other environmental causes) is responsible for certain symptoms. Because toxic substance suits can lead to massive liability awards, manufacturers, along with their insurers and lawyers, can be expected to challenge every scientific and legal weakness in the plaintiff's case, adding months or years of delay and expense to an already slow and costly litigation process.* The liability system alone, therefore, may fail to compensate many funda-

---

*The same problems of proving causation can also frustrate claims under workers' compensation systems concerning workplace exposures to chemicals whose effects are not well established.

mentally valid claims of injury from harmful substances; hence it may fail to provide an adequate financial incentive for manufacturers, users, and disposers of chemicals to invest in expensive scientific studies concerning possible toxicity or in the controls needed to ensure careful storage, usage, and disposal of known toxic chemicals. Not surprisingly, therefore, in the 1970s direct regulatory controls were demanded.

In 1976 Congress passed the Toxic Substances Control Act (TOSCA) to curb the introduction of toxic chemicals and other substances into the human environment (see, generally, Portney 1978b). The regulatory approach taken by TOSCA was adapted from the realm of pharmaceuticals, putting the burden of proof on industry to show that a substance is safe before it is put on the market. But the lesson of pharmaceutical regulation—that full testing for all new drugs could inordinately delay the introduction of new and useful products (see, for example, Seidman 1977)—was perhaps even more powerful when applied to the entire chemical industry with its rapid rate of innovation. Thus TOSCA added a new twist: full testing by the manufacturer is not automatically required for each and every new chemical. The manufacturer submits limited information. The Environmental Protection Agency (EPA), the enforcing agency, after reviewing this information must demand full testing of substances it believes might pose substantial risks and must do so within a reasonable period of time. Moreover, the EPA can demand safety testing of chemicals already on the market, but TOSCA limited such demands to fifty substances per year. All this seems quite reasonable, but effectiveness depends on the EPA's scientific and bureaucratic capacity to judge the substances most in need of testing. Predictably, the EPA has been bogged down in data and scientific controversy, slow to make decisions, and locked in conflict with both the gigantic chemical industry and strident consumer groups. Manufacturers, moreover, have been cautious about

supplying information for fear that the EPA will not be able
to keep valuable trade secrets from their competitors (see
Martin 1978, p. 40; Kirschen 1977, pp. 1220–24). Direct
regulation, clearly, has its problems too.

Stephen Soble (1977, pp. 729–53) has proposed a scheme
that would substitute indirect regulation via a modified
liability process for direct regulation via TOSCA. First,
Soble's proposed statute, which reflects some provisions of a
Japanese law enacted in 1973, would divert compensation
claims for injuries caused by toxic substance pollution from
courts of general jurisdiction to a specialized administrative
tribunal. Second, it would alter the burden of proof. In the
traditional tort or workers' compensation action, the plaintiff must show to a considerable degree of certainty the
causal connection between the defendant's conduct (or product) and the claimant's symptoms or injuries, a burden that
often cannot be met even by presenting epidemiological
studies (assuming they exist) showing a correlation between
certain pollutants and a heightened incidence of disease
among exposed populations. Soble's proposal, however, would
require the claimant to provide only plausible evidence of
causality—for example, epidemiological studies indicating
statistical correlations. Then, to avoid liability, the *defendant*
would have to prove that injuries plausibly linked to exposure to its chemicals in fact stemmed from other causes.
Third, the administrative tribunal and its staff explicitly
would be assigned responsibility for helping claimants to
meet their initial burden of showing a plausible causal link;
the staff would gather and analyze epidemiological data on
the health effects of various classes of chemicals, would look
for patterns among the claims submitted by discrete claimants, and would publicize those patterns. Fourth, should
the tribunal ultimately find the defendant's product the actual cause of a claimant's injury, it would make a certification to that effect, binding in subsequent cases; all "second
wave" claimants would be entitled to compensation simply

on a showing of similar symptoms and similar exposure to the substance. Fifth, if the causal link is certified, the manufacturer would be strictly liable; having undertaken standard tests and precautions in light of existing scientific knowledge or standard industry practice would not be a defense. Moreover, damages would not be limited to a fixed amount, as under workers' compensation statutes, and therefore might be quite substantial.[2]

Although a number of legal and practical problems would have to be ironed out, Soble's scheme seems to have certain advantages over current practices. Unlike the conventional liability system, a specialized regulatory agency shoulders some of claimants' proof problem and transfers other parts of it to defendant corporations, which are better able to generate the relevant information (on the health effects of exposure to chemicals) or to afford the discovery costs of developing alternative explanations of plaintiffs' injuries. More important, the obligation to disprove possible adverse effects would provide an incentive for chemical companies to track the uses of their more suspect products in society and to gather epidemiological information concerning populations exposed to those substances. And unlike direct regulation under TOSCA—where government officials must ultimately decide which chemicals to investigate, how much certainty is enough, and hence how much time and money must be expended on investigations—the proposed liability scheme places the burden of correct research and judgment on the private firms: unlike EPA officials, they would ultimately pay for their mistakes either in damage claims arising from too little caution or in forgone profits resulting from too much (Jason 1981, p. 29).[3] There would be no arbitrary limit on the number of substances that would be subject to intensive investigation; perhaps many more than fifty would be studied. Furthermore, there would not be so many pressures to standardize the approach to investigating any given substance—the usual result of research mandated by government regulations.

What of the smaller company that might be out of business by the time liability claims come in? To ensure financial responsibility for claims, and hence incentive to take adequate current precautions, the government might require mandatory insurance structured to "survive" the insured, if necessary, or posting of thirty-year liability bonds for firms that market certain classes of chemicals. There is a precedent for liability bonds in the regulations requiring stripmining firms to post bonds covering the cost of restoring strip-mined lands. Insurance firms also would apply pressure. EPA recently issued regulations under the 1976 Resource Conservation and Recovery Act requiring all companies engaged in the manufacture, disposal, and storage of hazardous chemicals to purchase "environmental impairment" insurance policies; insurance firms, it was reported, began requiring applicants for coverage to conduct and submit detailed engineering surveys of chemical storage facilities.

Because the Soble approach substitutes an administrative and rather specialized tribunal for the regular court system, the result is likely to be a reduction in litigation costs, a greater number of effective claims, more compensation granted to deserving victims, and the accumulation of a body of useful epidemiological data that would contribute to social learning. In these respects, it is superior to the traditional liability system while managing to retain that system's distinctive advantages. It is mobilized by the forces of private self-interest, and is backed by a penalty structure based on damage actually caused rather than on a politically negotiated system of fines. The threat of very substantial damages would encourage enterprises to take precautionary measures not limited to those called for by preexisting regulatory rules. Conversely, firms would not be forced—as they often are under direct regulation—to take precautionary measures based on risks that are very remote in the specific instance.

THE LIMITS OF LIABILITY
AS A SUBSTITUTE FOR
DIRECT REGULATION

It is very difficult to make general comparisons between liability and direct regulation. Any real-life system of social control, which always involves a complex interplay between the controllers and the various parties who might wish to evade control, is quite sensitive to small details in the rules of the game, variations in market structure and incentives, imperfections in technical capabilities, and other basic conditions. The liability system, in which enforcement is in the hands of thousands of private parties and rule application is decentralized to hundreds of semiautonomous judges and juries, is especially sensitive to such conditions. Broad generalizations, therefore, about which sort of system would work better under what conditions, would have to be so abstract that they could well be misleading in particular cases.

There are other problems as well. For one thing, liability is never absent; all producers are subject to ordinary suits for negligence. We can never choose between direct regulation and liability, but between direct regulation and some reformed version of the current liability system. Yet which particular sort of reform should be held up for comparison? Reforms can emphasize quite different social values—for example, maximally preventing harm regardless of cost, minimizing the financial costs to producers, facilitating the payment of compensation to injured victims, assuring that all cases are decided justly, minimizing the transaction costs in the system (e.g., lawyers' fees and court costs), and minimizing the sum of transaction costs plus the costs of preventing harms plus the costs of harms that eventually occur anyhow. This last criterion is preferred by many of those commenting on the social policy uses of liability law (see, for

example, Calabresi 1970; Posner 1972, chap. 1, n. 41). Yet it
is certainly not the only defensible criterion, and a number of
plausible alternative liability reforms could be constructed
for the sake of comparison with a direct regulation policy.

Moreover, liability law by its nature is constantly reforming itself. "The" law is the array of practices and legal rules
in numerous state and federal jurisdictions, in hundreds of
separate court districts, and in the minds of thousands of individual judges (not to mention the many more participants
like lawyers, jurors, plaintiffs, and defendants who move in
and out of the system). It is always evolving, therefore, in a
rather decentralized way, with new legal theories popping up
here and legal defenses there, looser rules of evidence in one
jurisdiction and longer plaintiff-discouraging delays due to
crowded dockets in another. To reform such an amorphous
social system can be quite difficult. The most available
leverage for a state legislature, say, is usually to change the
rules defining who is liable to whom for what, although certain procedural changes, like those that facilitate the bringing of class actions, are also possible. Other changes that
may be at least as important, such as those in the business
practices of the liability insurance industry or in the
way particular courts manage their calendars or attorneys charge their clients, are harder to bring about by
central direction.

In addition, the scope of social problems for which liability
law reforms—even arguably—would represent an improvement on direct regulation is, in fact, rather limited. Although
a liability approach to regulation should never be ruled out *a
priori*, a good many of the problems with the liability system
that led government to undertake direct regulation in the
first place are not likely to be solved by any presently con-
ceived reforms. Thus liability law probably is irretrievably
inadequate where damages are very remote in time, collective in nature, or impossible to quantify, as in the case of the
destruction of dolphins by tuna fishermen, the scarring of

beautiful countryside by strip-mining operations, and the gradual depletion of the earth's ozone layer by the release of chlorofluorocarbons from countless sources.

Even when damages are economically tangible, the liability system's transaction costs seem insurmountably high in many spheres. Consider air quality regulation, for instance. Usually a large number of potential plaintiffs (victims of pollution) would have to be joined in a class-action suit against a pollution source, since the amount of damages suffered by any single individual is in general relatively small and successful litigation is expensive. Class-action suits, however, have become more difficult and costly to launch in recent years.[4] The difficulty of aggregating plaintiffs, moreover, is overshadowed by the difficulty of aggregating defendants. If, as many scientists believe, the harm done by certain air pollutants increases disproportionately with their degree of concentration and in combination with other pollutants, then one cannot assess damages against any single polluter in a crowded air basin without simultaneously proceeding against all other polluters who contribute significantly to the background conditions that make the first polluter's emissions damaging. Yet the difficulties of finding and joining the appropriate defendants in a legally defensible fashion and, in the event of a victory for the plaintiffs, of allocating damage responsibilities among many defendants, pose the same dilemmas for a judge that are now faced by regulators—and the judge would be technically less well equipped to confront them. Direct regulation, emission taxes, or other government-operated schemes thus seem preferable to liability law as the primary strategy for dealing with most air and water pollution problems, although the utility (and the essential justice) of suits for compensation in some cases should not be dismissed.[5]

In other fields, it seems quixotic to expect private citizens consistently to muster the persistence and courage to sue delinquent enterprises. For example, most nursing home residents are far too poor, infirm, and vulnerable to reprisals to instigate a lawsuit against the owners of a facility that mistreats them. Even if the families of a few residents or public-interest advocates do bring such suits, the problems of proof are forbidding. Courts might be willing to acknowledge a cause of action for breach of contract, much as they have read an "implied warranty of habitability" into the rental transaction, enabling tenants to sue or legitimately withhold rent from landlords for very poor maintenance. But what would a similar implied warranty to the nursing home resident contain, how would its breach be established, and what would be the measure of damages for incremental additions to the discomfort already suffered by unemployed and infirm old people? Poor housing maintenance leaves tangible evidence, such as broken plaster and door latches and plumbing facilities. Success in nursing home litigation, too, would turn on proving nonperformance only with regard to the most easily documented, objectively measurable harms. Although the absence of loving care might be the main source of dissatisfaction, a judge is no more likely to be able to hold a nursing home operator liable for this situation than is a regulator. Moreover, whatever its weaknesses, direct regulation is far easier for patients and their families to activate, and carries less risk of acrimony and reprisal.

Problems of proof are very difficult to overcome in other fields as well. Victims of certain kinds of food poisoning often cannot determine which ingredient caused their illness or which enterprise in the chain of distribution was at fault. Hence government enforcement of *ex ante* regulations concerning additives, sanitation, and storage would seem to be a far more consistent deterrent to irresponsible food processing than the prospect of lawsuits alone—although lawsuits predicated upon proven regulatory violations might add to the deterrent effect of regulation. For the same reasons— difficulty of tracing injuries to their causes with certainty, or lag time between negligent behavior and injury—the threat

of private lawsuits cannot fully replace government enforcement of direct regulations for many kinds of water pollution
or fire code provisions concerning the adequacy of electrical
wiring in buildings.

Finally, even if one could somehow eradicate the problems
of cost, delay, plaintiff ignorance, and difficulties of proof,
the liability law system, viewed as a deterrent to irresponsible behavior, suffers from a vital theoretical weakness.
Like the pure deterrence theory of direct regulation, it rests
upon the assumption that business enterprises are perfectly
calculating profit maximizers for whom an adequate threat
of liability will induce adequate preventive measures. But
many accidents occur, not because enterprises deliberately
cut corners on safety, but because of error. New or marginal
companies, short on management expertise and short of
capital, may fall far short of accepted industrial practice.
Many accidents occur despite a sophisticated enterprise's attempt to install an appropriate quality, safety, or pollution
control system; preventive routines occasionally break down
from overconfidence, from unexpected shifts in personnel, or
from sudden crises that divert attention. Though one could
hardly imagine a greater deterrent to airplane crashes than
the resulting multimillion-dollar liability claims, crashes
sometimes do occur. The same is true for other infrequent
but catastrophic harms, such as coal mine explosions, hotel
fires, and derailment of trains carrying dangerous chemicals. In such industries, it is neither politically nor morally
acceptable to rely entirely on liability law for the requisite
margin of safety; a fail-safe layer of direct regulation and inspection is often necessary to prevent slippage in established
liability-avoiding routines.

LIABILITY REFORMS AND
UNREASONABLENESS

In recent years, many reforms to strengthen the liability

system have been instituted. Legislatures have authorized and facilitated class-action suits in several specific fields, including securities law, antidiscrimination law, and certain consumer protection matters. Lawmakers have subsidized plaintiffs' attorneys' fees, sometimes by direct provision of legal aid, sometimes by requiring defendants—including the government—to pay litigation expenses of successful plaintiffs.[6] To provide an incentive to sue even when individual damages are very small, the federal Truth-in-Lending Act guaranteed individuals who successfully sued violators a minimum recovery of $100 from the losing party, as well as attorneys' fees. At the same time, to reduce the court congestion and delay that discourage lawsuits, several jurisdictions have required diversion of certain cases to mediators or arbitrators,[7] or have devised mechanisms for penalizing defendants who unjustifiably refuse early settlement offers.

Changes in substantive law, too, have been designed to reduce plaintiffs' burdens of proof and thus increase deterrence. Product liability law, for example, has moved in many small increments—and more rapidly in some states than in others—away from a negligence standard and towards a strict liability standard.[8] In many states, if the injured plaintiff can show that his injury stemmed from a defect in the product, he need not prove the manufacturer or seller to have been negligent; the defendant can be held responsible even if it had taken normal or reasonable quality control precautions. "Defect" has been expanded to include "design defect." Manufacturers have been held liable for failing to incorporate in the product known or readily imaginable safety devices or to include warnings that would help prevent foreseeable accidents, even if those accidents arose from misuse of the product or the plaintiff's own negligence. In the decade following the late 1960s the number of product liability suits in the courts increased tenfold and jury awards (based on a sample of cases appealed to higher courts) rose to an average of $221,000 between 1971 and 1976 (U.S. Department of Commerce 1970, pp. II-56, III-3).[9] Although less frequent in statistical terms, a considerable number of highly publicized multimillion-dollar verdicts and punitive damage awards (the most famous of which was a $125 million verdict against Ford Motor Company in a case involving an exploding Pinto gas tank) sent shock waves through the business community. One result, the Interagency Task Force on Product Liability concluded, was that producers made noticeably greater efforts to install better quality control systems and to redesign products in order to prevent liability (U.S. Department of Commerce 1970, pp. IV-2, IV-5–8, VI-47).

Even with such changes, of course, the costs and difficulties of litigation undoubtedly leave a great many legitimate plaintiffs out in the cold; therefore, some legal reformers, such as Jeffrey O'Connell, have called for absolute, no-fault, "enterprise liability" (but with certain limits on the amount of recoveries) as applied to producers of high-risk products (thus eliminating plaintiffs' burden of proving the existence of a defect), and even as applied to physicians who perform certain medical procedures (such as spinal fusions) that present special risks of harm.*[10] Such reforms to lighten plaintiffs' burdens and stimulate risk-reduction measures, however, can easily go too far. In effect, they can impose unreasonable demands on potential defendants, compelling them to invest in costly defensive strategies both before and after the fact of a lawsuit. Like direct regulation, indirect regulation by means of the liability system can easily become unreasonable.

*O'Connell's model "enterprise liability" statute would read, "Any enterprise is subject to enterprise liability for bodily injury to any human being resulting from the operation of typical risks arising from the operation of the enterprise." In return for such "no fault, automatic" liability, producers in O'Connell's scheme (as in workers' compensation) would face, he asserts, lower and more predictable payouts; compensation would be limited to medical expenses and lost earnings, thus excluding emotion-based jury awards for "pain and suffering," and would be reduced by compensation received by the victim from other private or social insurance sources.

Consider, for instance, the area of medical malpractice. There has recently been a phenomenal increase in malpractice litigation—for example, in New York State by 1974 a malpractice suit was pending against one in every ten doctors, in contrast to one in twenty-three in 1969. Strong evidence indicates that this increase has changed the traditional (that is, previously accepted) practice of medicine. Doctors have begun to order more laboratory tests, more X-rays, more consultations, and more or longer stays in hospitals. An ingenious statistical study by Bruce Greenwald and Marnie Mueller (1978, p. 83) estimated that in 1975 the practice of such "defensive medicine" consumed sufficient resources to account for $2.3 billion in the national medical care bill.

This increase in "defensive medicine," as it is often called, undoubtedly produces some benefits. Fear of leaving any stone unturned because of an expensive lawsuit, with all the attendant personal anguish and financial cost, surely leads in some cases to important, even life-saving, diagnoses. Hospitals have worked harder to institute more rigorous quality control procedures, a field in which improvements certainly can be made, as indicated by the success of consultants in hospital risk management (see "Doctor Fail-Safe," *Newsweek*, 26 July 1979, p. 79). Yet many critics have strongly suggested that the costs far exceed benefits and that the added tests, hospital stays, and expensive procedures mainly prevent lawsuits—or, more accurately, successful lawsuits—rather than actual medical malpractice. One reason, although the point is certainly debatable, is that most physicians attempt to serve the best interests of their patients no matter what the liability requirements; added malpractice exposure may well prod them to undertake additional tests or procedures but is unlikely to increase their sense of duty or diagnostic or surgical competence. Another is that improvements in medical care have come, not from deliberate liability avoidance, but from better and continuing medical education and from the movement toward hospital-centered care, which forces private physicians into regular contact with peers and induces exposure to more sophisticated practices. Finally, since most of the costs of additional hospitalization and tests have in recent years been passed on to third-party reimbursers (Medicare, Medicaid, private health insurance companies), there was not much incentive for doctors or hospitals to economize on medical tests and consultations, even before defensive medicine became more widespread.

Like the unreasonableness associated with direct regulation, unanticipated consequences of the liability law's attempt to do good may go well beyond excess precautions or expenditures. One possible perverse effect is inducing people to run away altogether from social responsibility because they fear exposure to excessive liability or aggravations; because of the inherent unpredictability of law applied by scores of judges and juries, the liability system can be quite threatening to providers of products and services. For example, in addition to the unnecessary procedures sometimes induced by the threat of malpractice suits—a practice that has been called "positive defensive medicine"—commentators have perceived an increase (although how pervasive is unclear) of "negative defensive medicine" whereby doctors shun certain risky but possibly therapeutic procedures or, worse yet, turn away high-risk patients because they present too great a liability exposure. Negative defensive medicine could also mean hesitating to adopt new medical procedures or to implement more efficient organizational techniques, such as relying on physicians' assistants or delegating certain functions.*

Withdrawing or limiting activities to reduce the possibility of lawsuits is not restricted to the malpractice field, although

*There are arguments, too, that the growing threat of litigation has helped to erode whatever trust between patient and doctor has survived until now, and hence whatever component of therapeutic care that depends on trust.

systematic data on such effects are not readily available. Landlord/tenant law reforms have curtailed a landlord's ability to evict tenants promptly for nonpayment of rent, and have authorized a tenant to withhold rent pending an adjudication of his claim that the landlord has breached a judicially implied warranty of habitability. According to Roger Starr (1979), these legal changes have been significant contributing factors in the disastrous withdrawal of rental housing from the market and the failure to build new units. In a few cases, courts have held insurance companies liable to persons injured in insured buildings or factories as a result of defects that were not detected or remedied by insurance company loss control personnel. The insurers, in short, were held to be liable for negligent inspection. But if these precedents were to become a general rule, as Victor P. Goldberg (1977) has observed, the result might well be that some insurance companies would withdraw inspection services entirely.

Untrammeled expansion of liability also can increase the price of certain risky services or products beyond the means of consumers, some of whom, if given the alternative, might prefer a lower-cost—albeit riskier—alternative. It has been estimated that the rapid rise of medical malpractice—liability insurance premiums are fully passed on to purchasers of medical care services (see Greenwald and Mueller 1978). Product prices would increase significantly if we adopted absolute "enterprise liability" rules such as those advocated by O'Connell. For example, if sunlamp manufacturers were liable for the thousands of injuries each year that stem from use (or misuse) of their products, they would certainly be induced to install expensive automatic shutoff mechanisms and other devices on every lamp sold rather than merely to offer such mechanisms (estimated to add $14 to the price of each lamp) as an option for more risk-averse consumers willing to pay more (see "Safeguards for Sunlamps Ordered," *San Francisco Chronicle*, 9 November 1979, p. 22).

Finally, the tort-liability system can unreasonably shift to defendants (producers) the responsibility for suppressing risks that can more easily and inexpensively be avoided by the relevant class of plaintiffs (e.g., consumers and workers). In the products liability field, Richard Epstein (1977, p. 19) observes:

> The expansion of products liability was [deemed] necessary to give producers the proper incentives for developing safe products. Yet . . . in many situations, incentives belong elsewhere in the chain of distribution. A manufacturer of machine tools cannot compel purchasers to keep them in proper maintenance and repair; he cannot prevent the removal of safety guards and warnings; he cannot compel individual workers to observe all the required safety precautions. Yet manufacturers . . . have been held fully liable for damages in precisely these situations. Employers are often in a better position than the original manufacturer to prevent worksite accidents by controlling the work environment or by giving individual employees warnings and instructions about a product's hazards and proper use.

Unreasonable effects stemming from court decisions perhaps are more easily reversed than regulatory excesses, as indicated by recent legislative efforts to limit medical malpractice litigation and make product liability rules more moderate and uniform (see Jenkins and Scheinfurth 1979, pp. 829, 838–39).[11] The point here is simply that liability law reforms designed to overcome very real costs and obstacles to legitimate claims can quickly spill over into the same kind of overinclusiveness, unreasonableness, contentiousness, and perverse consequences that characterize legalistic direct regulation.

GETTING THE BEST OF BOTH WORLDS

Can liability law be made into an effective deterrent against irresponsible behavior *without* producing overdeterrence and unreasonably costly precautions? One set of possibilities, suggested by the workers' compensation system and Soble's toxic substances control proposal, would entail a combination of regulatory and litigation strategies, drawing upon the particular strengths of each.

In contrast to regulators, civil court judges traditionally have taken no responsibility for "following up" their decisions. If, following a damage award, the defendant delays payment or even continues his misconduct, the judge may never even hear about it. Could judges act more like regulators and find a way to keep up the pressure even after they have rendered their decisions? Judges have done so, increasingly, in the public law sphere. In suits against school districts, prison systems, and mental hospitals for violations of constitutional rights, courts have been called upon to compel reforms rather than payment of damages. They have responded with a flexible array of equitable remedies, often worked out in negotiation with the defendants, and have enforced and adjusted these remedies through a variety of monitoring arrangements whereby steps toward compliance are reported back to the judge (see Chayes 1976 and cases cited therein; also Berger 1978, and Diver 1979). Christopher Stone (1975, chap. 17) points to a case in which a judge, noting that a petroleum plant was before him the second time for illegal spillage into a waterway, suspended sentence and put the plant "on probation," requiring the company to set up a preventive program and report back to him. The judge also threatened to appoint a special probation officer to monitor progress (*U.S.* v. *Atlantic Richfield*, 465 F.2d 58 [7th Cit. 1972]).

One could imagine statutory authorization for such prospective and ongoing remedies in private law damage actions as well. Suppose, for example, judges responded to the most egregious medical malpractice cases not only by awarding restitution but also by demanding and reviewing the defendants' "malpractice history" and, when it seemed warranted, initiating delicensing proceedings—which physician-controlled state licensing agencies have traditionally been slow to do—by ordering defendants to take special continuing education courses or requiring hospitals to establish and report on certain preventive procedures. Judges, properly authorized, similarly could compel defendants in product liability suits not merely to pay damages but to undertake and report on improved quality control or product redesign efforts.

To be sure, there are many difficulties involved in encouraging judges to think and act more like administrators. When they have taken on this role in the context of reforming schools and institutions for the mentally ill, the results have often been disappointing (see Glazer 1978, p. 64). Yet we are not free to choose among ideal alternatives. Given the problems of the liability system as it stands, it is not clear that society is better off if judges continue to act like traditional judges.

Consider, further, the limitations of judges in their role as definers of liability standards. Appellate court judges are generalists, usually untrained in the technicalities of either safety engineering or economics. They decide on regulatory matters infrequently, and when they do, they usually see an unrepresentative sample of cases in which dramatic injuries have occurred. Judges lack ongoing familiarity with the regulated industry, differences among the firms in it, its economic problems, and whether it has been "improving" over time. Courts cannot systematically monitor the consequences of particular changes in liability law and readjust the standard in light of experience. Some of these weaknesses can be overcome by good lawyers, but many cases are argued by counsel who fail to provide judges with adequate information.

The decentralization of the judicial system also means that each state's standards will be applied by scores of trial judges and juries, each likely to weigh competing values with a somewhat different calculus, often in light of the emotional impact of the injuries sustained by the particular plaintiff. After a jury recently held an automobile manufacturer liable for a driver's severe injuries because of "defects" in the car's design, a federal judge noted that, through the accumulation of such suits, "individual juries in the various states are permitted, in effect, to establish national safety standards." But the result, he lamented, is "incoherence in the safety requirements set by disparate juries." In the particular case before him, the judge said, the automobile manufacturer was found liable for not producing a sufficiently rigid frame to protect the passenger from injury; yet, because more flexible "energy absorbing" frames are advocated by some auto safety specialists, the producer of cars with more rigid frames might be found liable by a jury in another case.

Specialized regulatory agencies, on the other hand, enjoy at least a comparative advantage in information gathering and the preparation of standards that reflect an overview of the relevant industry as a whole. The Consumer Product Safety Commission (CPSC), for example, uses a computer-based system for monitoring hospital emergency rooms throughout the country to determine what products are major sources of personal injuries. In considering appropriate safety design standards, CPSC staff members can assemble data from many manufacturers (not just the defendant) on costs and design alternatives and market trends. The National Highway Traffic Safety Administration (NHTSA) gathers data about the accident and injury frequency associated with various automotive models and their components. When an NHTSA official looks at the individual case of an injury from an exploding fuel tank or erratic carburetor, he knows whether it is a freak event or part of a larger pattern. He also might know something about the performance of comparable components industrywide, about trade-offs among different designs for protecting fuel tanks, and about the adequacy of industrywide practices in this regard.

Agency officials can consult competent and representative (although, of course, not disinterested) parties from both large and small firms, independent engineering bodies, and consumer groups, and can solicit their views on the most desirable trade-off between safety and other design features.

One approach to making the liability system more predictable and balanced, therefore, might be to facilitate the flow of information from regulatory agencies to lawyers, judges, and juries. Suppose, for example, that *all* attorneys (not just the especially competent ones) had regular and easy access to NHTSA data and analyses concerning the frequency of accidents associated with various components of all car models, and that judges (and juries) therefore were regularly exposed to such data in deciding whether one component had been designed in an unreasonably dangerous way. Specific standards established by regulatory agencies could also be used to impose limits on the juries' impulses. A defendant's compliance with applicable regulatory safety standards might be treated as a presumptively conclusive defense (which it is not under most existing law. See, for example, *Hubbard-Hall Chemical Co.* v. *Silverman*, 340 F.2d 402 [1st Cir. 1965]; Pasztor 1980), rebuttable only by evidence that such regulatory standards are substantially out-of-date and clearly behind the best cost-effective current practices in the industry. Conversely, while juries now often take violation of safety-related standards as conclusive or near-conclusive evidence of negligence,[12] the courts might accord stronger consideration to defenses based on the unreasonableness of regulatory standards as applied to a particular context.

In addition, if the standards and information assembled by regulatory agencies could be incorporated more reliably into the liability process, regulatory agencies might be relieved of the pressure to apply ever-tougher preventive requirements on their own. If auto manufacturers faced a more predictable and informed liability system, they would have an incentive to voluntarily recall vehicles that had higher-than-average fatal accident or component failure rates rather than face enhanced liability exposure. Yet they would be more likely than NHTSA to refrain from recalling vehicles whose repair costs, in the aggregate, would be high but from which relatively few serious accidents and lawsuits were anticipated. NHTSA, on the other hand, might be able to stop recalling so many vehicles for which the costs of recall and repair probably outweigh potential dangers (see Altshuler et al. 1979, pp. 228–29).

Under the Soble proposal for dealing with toxic substances, an administrative agency would assist claimants in overcoming problems of linking their injuries to specific chemicals and responsible sources. In other fields, the mandatory record-keeping and labeling requirements that regulatory agencies have imposed, or might impose, could serve a similar function, and thereby substitute liability claims for direct regulation. For example, recovery by consumers injured by contaminated packaged food, and hence the deterrent effect of the liability system, is facilitated by regulations requiring food processing firms to maintain detailed production records and to label cans from each batch. Similar labeling and processing regulations for blood plasma products and intravenous solutions make it far more likely today that patients harmed by defective batches of such products could track down the culprit, establish liability, and collect large judgments. We are not certain how adequate such enhanced liability systems are to deter carelessness, but they suggest an important line of inquiry. To the extent that mandatory labeling and record keeping make it difficult for producers to avoid the massive liability judgments that can stem from sending contaminated products out into the world, it may be possible to relax some of the inflexible direct regulations that prescribe specific facilities, machines, sanitation, or sterilization procedures. Indeed, one could imagine a desirable regulatory life cycle in which regulators mandate detailed safety-oriented technologies or procedures at an early stage in the development of new productive processes, only to deregulate or relax enforcement later as the liability system is made more capable of maintaining quality control pressure.

In dealing with the problem of exposure to disease-causing agents in the workplace, too, regulatory record-keeping rules could help make the liability system more effective and reasonable than direct regulation. Workers and their families often have difficulty tracing an illness or disability to exposure in a particular job, for the effects may not be visible for a long period and the worker may have been employed elsewhere in the interim; it becomes unclear whether or not intervening exposures (or congenital health problems) caused the illness. The effectiveness of the compensation system for such problems (as well as the collective bargaining system) could be improved if employers were obligated to keep and make available to employees records showing the levels of designated chemical exposures associated with specific jobs and specific workers.[13] This would facilitate epidemiological analyses by regulatory agencies and help claimants' lawyers establish the probability of adverse exposure in particular cases. The costs of such record keeping might be considerable. But it still might present advantages over direct regulation by OSHA which, encumbered by judicialized rule making, is terribly slow in developing standards for suspected hazards and is rigid and over-inclusive in prescribing control technologies when it does act. A government-assisted information system to facilitate valid claims, moreover, would increase incentives for employers and insurance companies to develop early-warning systems and appropriate control technologies.

Where substantial obstacles to private lawsuits against producers remain, government agencies might serve as surrogate defendants, paying compensation directly to injured individuals and funding such payments by suing responsible private sources themselves or by levying taxes on those sources. In Japan, individuals who live in areas designated by regulatory authorities as special high-pollution zones can claim compensation from a government body for validated illnesses that are statistically associated (according to government-sponsored research) with the specific pollutant.[14] The government body collects its funds by taxing major pollution sources, including automobile owners, according to their estimated contribution to the level of each pollutant in the designated zone. Similarly, in the state of Maine, a 1970 law established a revolving fund via license fees on all facilities and enterprises involved in the transfer of oil between seagoing vessels and between vessels and shore. Persons claiming property or other injury from oil spills may apply to the fund for compensation, thus sidestepping costly and slow judicial proceedings—assuming they know who might be named as defendant in the first place. If the government body can then establish responsibility for the spill, the polluter must reimburse the fund for all claims the fund paid out for the spill in question (see Post 1974, pp. 524, 538–41; Stewart and Krier 1978, pp. 612–15). David Leo Weimer (1980) argues that a specialized compensation board consisting of medical practitioners and researchers might effectively be substituted for *both* prior licensing of drugs by the FDA and the normal tort-litigation system. Drug manufacturers would have to deposit funds with the board in an account established for each drug product. This account would be used to indemnify claimants who sustain drug-related injuries for which the manufacturer had failed to issue a warning. Manufacturer payments into the account would continue for twelve years (perhaps even longer would be desirable, in our view) unless the manufacturer were able to demonstrate, in postmarketing studies whose technical quality satisfied the board, that the drug was safe and effective for the conditions for which it was being promoted. In order to increase its own confidence in the results of this postmarketing surveillance, the board would have the authority to pay physicians to send in fully documented adverse reaction reports.

REGULATION AND LIABILITY

Liability law is a form of regulation, and regulation is a form of liability law. The one can be made to substitute for the other under certain conditions, and they can sometimes be made to complement and reinforce one another.

It is sometimes claimed that liability law would be less prone to regulatory excess than is direct command-and-control regulation: the common-law rules of liability are more open ended and flexible; penalties are not invoked unless actual harm has been done; and judges and juries are less susceptible than regulatory officials to charges of softness or corruption if they do not apply the law strictly and legalistically. At the same time, liability law, being mobilized by private plaintiffs pursuing their own self-interest, could mount stronger pressures for harm prevention than would likely come from regulators motivated only by an abstract dedication to "the public interest."

In this chapter we have concluded that liability law could indeed be superior to direct regulation in some applications—but only if the institutions that were to administer it would be better designed for the purpose. In particular, it would be necessary to improve the courts' ability to decide complex technical and scientific disputes about what sorts of conditions cause what sorts of harms, and to ascertain how the facts of particular cases fit these generalizations. This might mean making judges act more like regulators, or at least expediting the flow of information and knowledge between regulatory agencies and courts. And in some areas it might mean establishing specialized tribunals and boards to

carry out the research and data collection efforts necessary to administering the liability system intelligently
and efficiently.

12

JOSEPH FERREIRA, JR.

Promoting Safety
through Insurance

**Liability insurance and risk. Regulating liquefied
natural gas. Risk assessment and insurance. A National
Disaster Relief Fund? Safety standards for automobiles.
The insurance approach to vehicle safety.
Make-and-model rating. Governmental intervention
and the insurance option.**

This chapter examines the circumstances under which insurance
might replace direct command-and-control regulation
in reducing risks. For this purpose, we shall focus on
two specific examples involving public safety: the storage
and transportation of dangerous chemicals (e.g., liquid
natural gas [LNG] facilities), and the crashworthiness of
automobiles.

HOW INSURANCE INFLUENCES THE
LEVEL OF RISKS

At first glance, insurance appears to be a poor substitute for safety standards. Since insurance guarantees compensation to accident victims and/or indemnifies those held liable for the accidents, it encourages risk taking by reducing the consequences of rash behavior. However, aside from the fact that encouraging risk taking is not always undesirable, the effect of insurance on such behavior depends on how the insurance is priced and how accident costs would be distributed without it.

Liability rules have traditionally been the cornerstone of strategies for controlling risky behavior: those who undertake risky activities are often held financially responsible for their actions, even without evidence of intent to cause harm. This approach satisfies a sense of justice by compensating the innocent and encouraging risk-takers to weigh the full costs of their actions.

In practice, however, such liability rules do not always work so well. Identifying the "cause" of an accident is often complex and judgmental. Insolvent parties may be unable to pay damages for which they are liable. Difficulties in assessing risks or incorporating them into decision making may lead to problems. Potential victims may be exploitable (when economic conditions leave them with no alternative to accepting undesirable risks) or powerless (when the risks, while large, are so dispersed that collective action is needed to mount a case for compensation). Finally, financial risks caused by the liability rules themselves may inhibit undertaking economically viable activities. Solutions involve specific protective regulations—such as safety standards and traffic laws—and a variety of indirect approaches that provide financial incentives, change risk-sharing arrangements, or supply risk-related information and analytic capacity.

Liability insurance addresses two of the limitations: it provides resources for compensating innocent victims even if the guilty party cannot pay, and it can prevent the financial uncertainties of legal liability from discouraging economic activity that, on average, is well worth the risk. But insurance also removes some of the caution that liability laws are intended to induce. Whether, on balance, insurance is beneficial depends critically on the accuracy with which risk can be assessed.

Suppose, for example, that an insurer provides automobile liability insurance to a group of motorists whose aggregate claims can be accurately predicted. Lacking information to distinguish high- from low-risk motorists, the insurer would charge an annual premium reflecting average costs (plus a loading for expenses, profit, etc.). Such insurance—priced without regard to individual driving care—redistributes the costs of accidents to all motorists regardless of fault. Hence, the financial incentive to drive carefully is lost and, with it, part of the fairness concept that motivated interest in liability rules.[1]

If, on the other hand, the insurer were able to monitor each motorist closely, insurance would need not detract from the justice and efficiency goals of liability rules. Motorists would pay premiums that corresponded precisely to their risk-taking behavior. A decision to drive on a particular trip would then reflect the direct costs and benefits of the trip plus the expected costs per trip resulting from accident risks. The insurance would protect against the uncertain timing and costs of accidents. Such protection has a beneficial risk-spreading effect without undesirable incentives for unnecessary or reckless driving.

Accurate risk assessment is crucial. Insurance premiums that reflect accurate risk assessment[2] help the incentive effects of liability laws by providing a swift and certain response to risk-taking behavior regardless of the timing and cost of accidents. In fact, if risk assessment could be trusted, liability rules and insurance would by themselves provide a rational basis for regulating safety, addressing all the normative problems. What remain would be questions of acceptable risks (involving risk perceptions and alternatives to risk/benefit analyses in evaluating the worth of risky undertakings), and institutional problems involving possible exploitation or lack of influence. While these issues are both difficult and important, their discussion would focus on a different set of concerns from the principles of justice and efficiency that have occupied us thus far.

Unfortunately, accurate risk assessment is difficult—if the causes of accidents were not complex, we would not refer to them as accidents. The same issues of causality that complicate assignment of liability make it difficult to monitor and classify risks. What is more, the impact of safety standards (in addition to or in place of liability rules and insurance) likewise depends upon the quality of risk assessment. Hence the choice of a regulatory strategy also must be determined by seemingly secondary information issues, such as whether the regulator or insurer is in a better position to assess and monitor risk. As we shall see in the examples, this perspective on the role of risk assessment in promoting safety can lead in directions different from the usual debates about public safety.

Example I: Regulating LNG safety

Liquefied natural gas (LNG) is one of several liquefied energy gases, including butane, propylene, and naptha. Energy gases are liquefied in order to facilitate transportation and storage. Chilled to −260 degrees (F), natural gas becomes a liquid with about 1/600 of its gaseous volume at atmospheric pressure. Natural gas is liquefied both for import via tanker and for "peak-shaving" use during periods of high demand. Typically, LNG is off-loaded from large tankers into storage tanks at import terminals and is later shipped by truck to smaller storage facilities where it is gasified and added to pipelines as needed.

Safety hazards of LNG have generated considerable public interest. While the risks are probably no greater than those associated with many other chemical industries, the consequences of LNG accidents are potentially catastrophic. LNG is a highly flammable fuel that, when spilled, spreads and evaporates quickly. If ignited immediately, a pool fire results. Otherwise the flammable vapors spread laterally as a cloud that may disperse harmlessly or, if ignited, cause a serious fire. For accidents involving storage facilities, a dike around the storage tank will contain some or all of the liquid; containment is not possible for LNG spills on water or from trucks. Land spills pose additional hazards, since LNG may enter storm drains, sewers, subway tunnels, and so forth.

Various federal, state, and local government agencies and laws regulate the manufacture, storage, and use of LNG. In addition, liability laws are generally interpreted to imply that handlers would be held strictly responsible for any accidents. Justification for such regulatory action usually involves arguments that safety is a "public good," individuals are not well informed, LNG operators act rashly in accepting or perpetrating risks, or neighbors and workers are too easily exploited since their economic situation leaves no alternative to undesirable risks.

A 1978 General Accounting Office (GAO) study of LNG risks questioned the adequacy of existing safeguards. One of the concerns was that LNG handlers had little incentive to try to limit the size of serious accidents. The corporate structure of businesses handling LNG shielded the assets of parent companies from liability claims. Serious accidents were likely to bankrupt the firms directly involved and exhaust their liability insurance coverage. Either the size of large accidents would have to be controlled by additional safety standards (e.g., restricting trucks to nonurban streets or nonrush hours, or increasing distances from LNG tanks to bordering property) or insurance coverage for LNG operators would have to be increased.

In order to focus on the relative merits of safety standards and insurance as a means of controlling LNG risks, let us accept the GAO conclusions as stated and examine LNG trucking options. Efforts to control LNG trucking risks directly via safety standards face the spectrum of difficulties that in other chapters have been identified with command-and-control strategies: informational problems with assessing risks, monitoring compliance, and forecasting the impact of safety standards on LNG activity; administrative problems with reconciling the need for simple regulations and the reality of multiple jurisdictions, varied individual circumstances, and ever-changing regulatory agendas; and political problems with achieving consensus on specific rules without wide acceptance of the social objectives that motivate them.

Consider, for example, a ban on LNG trucking through urban areas. The severity and even frequency of trucking accidents is plausibly related to population density, vehicular congestion, and other such factors. Hence, one would expect considerably higher risks in urban than in rural areas. If switching from urban to rural truck routes brought the risks within the financial resources of the LNG operators, the GAO objections might arguably be addressed.

In a hypothetical circumstance, such a regulation is quite plausible. But as a general rule, it becomes much more problematic: How is "urban" defined? How often can urban changes, safety improvements, and the like be the bases for reconsideration? Who resolves disputes, enforces the rules, measures the risks? Even if these issues are resolved, are the consequences of the rule easily forecast? Does the enhanced safety warrant the added economic cost? Moreover, the economics of energy supplies may be such that liquid propane gas will be substituted for LNG as long as the use of propane trucks is not equally restricted. Would the net risks be reduced in this case? Should propane (and other materials hazardous to transport) be included in the rule? Varied local circumstances suggest local control, but federal authorities are more likely to have technical expertise. What mix of jurisdictions is politically and administratively feasible?

Even if this litany of difficulties is surmountable, it suggests pause for careful consideration before adopting even a rule as apparently straightforward as a limited ban on truck routes. However simple, such an approach offers little opportunity for matching regulatory incentives to the varying circumstances that inevitably arise. With this problem in mind, let us consider the use of insurance as an alternative means of internalizing the social costs of LNG risks.

Liability insurance coverage could provide LNG handlers with the financial resources to cover whatever compensation for accident losses is considered appropriate by the courts. To the extent that such coverage is priced to reflect the risk-taking behavior of individual LNG handlers, it provides a convenient means of linking risks and economic costs.[3] In the ideal insurance arrangement, both LNG handlers and the insurers have a financial interest in LNG safety. The potential for insured losses provides an incentive for the insurer to closely monitor actual risks; and the fact that insurance premiums track risk-taking behavior encourages the LNG handlers to be safety minded. While there may still be an incentive to hide risk-related information from the insurer, a mutually beneficial contractual arrangement between insurer and insured should make monitoring easier than it is for the government regulator. Moreover, insurance seems to offer a better means of fine-tuning LNG operators' risk-taking behavior to reflect local circumstances, changing technologies, or evolving public standards of compensation.

The insurance alternative does, of course, have its own set of practical difficulties. The insurer has just as much need for risk assessment information as did the government reg-

ulator. In fact, the consequences of poor risk assessment are
quite similar in each case. The regulator might overestimate
risks and unduly constrain LNG activity or he might fail to
control certain risks, thereby providing no incentive for the
LNG handlers to obtain adequate protection. Similarly, the
insurer might hedge against risks by pricing insurance considerably in excess of actuarially estimated costs, or he might
neglect to include a specific risk-taking activity in the premium computation. The former action would restrain LNG
activity since the high limits of liability insurance would be
compulsory, and the latter action would produce a disincentive for safety similar to the omitted regulatory standard.

Another practical complication with the insurance approach involves determining the circumstances under which
the insurer must pay claims. Most state laws are likely to be
interpreted so that handlers of hazardous chemicals are held
strictly liable for any accident damages. However, LNG activities, like other complex technologies, involve many
different corporate entities performing various functions.
When accidents are large, the multiplicity of incidents, consequences, and causes surrounding them raise questions
about the extent of responsibility for any single party. In an
LNG trucking accident, for example, potentially liable parties might include the driver, the driver's employer, the
owner of the vehicle, the lessor of the vehicle, the manufacturer of the vehicle or its components, the owner of the LNG
in the vehicle, the operator of the terminal at which the
truck was loaded, etc. Even when strict liability rules apply,
long costly court battles are virtually inevitable before the
responsibility of individual parties is determined.

Delays in settling claims coupled with problems of risk dis-
tort the ideal insured/insurer relationship. The effect is that,
under present arrangements, insurers have less incentive to
be concerned with safety and accurate risk assessment than
one might expect. First, the long delays in paying claims shift
insurers' attention from underwriting to financial plan-

ning—especially in these times of high interest rates. Moreover, the long payout period enables premiums to be adjusted upward between the occurrence of a large accident and its financial settlement, which reduces the importance of accurate risk assessment at the outset and diminishes an insurer's incentive to promote safety. As long as the insured—or the industry of which they are a part—are likely to survive a major incident, these financial considerations are consequential. As a result, the pricing of trucking insurance is likely to depend more upon the trucking firm's size and reputation and simple measures of exposure (miles driven or gallons shipped) than upon route-specific risk estimates. Since there is also likely to be a correlation of a firm's size and years of experience with prudent risk taking and technical expertise, it is no surprise that a large trucking firm operating along urban routes may obtain high-limit liability insurance at a more favorable rate (as a percentage of transportation costs) than a much smaller trucker operating along less urban (and presumably safer) routes.

Additional institutional factors reinforce this effect. The higher limit "layers" of liability insurance are generally placed with domestic and international insurers via brokerage houses. No one insurer wants to be exposed to catastrophic losses from a single incident. The broker, who acts as a skilled intermediary in arranging the insurance package, has considerable influence over its availability and cost. These brokers are also likely to emphasize the size and reputation of prospective insureds—especially since brokers generally offer an assortment of commercial insurance coverages and may view larger firms as attractive accounts for much broader reasons than route-specific risks of liability claims.

If accurate risk assessment were economically available, one might expect the estimates to overshadow these institutional considerations. However, for the case of potentially large LNG accidents, risk assessment technology is neither sufficiently accurate nor inexpensive.

Nevertheless, one should not conclude that compulsory liability insurance for LNG operators is less desirable for promoting safety than direct regulation. Where debate focuses on the advisability of an entire technology (as with nuclear power) or where monitoring risks is exceptionally complex and technical, the government may have no choice but to become directly involved. But to fine-tune risk-taking behavior in a variety of circumstances, the standard-setting approach is imprecise, and it may be easier and more effective to change liability insurance rules and incentives.

A brief discussion will serve to identify some of the possibilities and issues. Unfortunately, the problem of promoting safety in areas of hazardous technology is not commonly viewed in these terms, so the analyses and debate needed to investigate the possible approaches in detail have, for the most part, not yet occurred.

Many institutional difficulties associated with the insurance alternative stem from the long delays in settling claims. There is evidence that these delays also work to the disadvantage of the most deserving victims, so steps to hasten the settlement process would be especially attractive. Since delays arise largely because of debate over the liability of various LNG handlers, compensation funds are often suggested as a means of reducing them. The establishment of a National Disaster Relief Fund for losses due to a variety of hazardous materials has, in fact, been debated before Congress. However, such a fund would be burdened with the same risk assessment problems that face insurers, without the mutual financial interests of the insurance situation. Such a publicly controlled fund not only invites political criticism as evidence of government's accepting rather than controlling undesirable risks, but in the event an accident should arise, it makes extremely difficult the denial of coverage to anyone remotely eligible.

An alternative requiring considerably less government administration would be to reform the liability rules so that a single, identifiable LNG handler would be held responsible for each possible type of LNG accident. By "channeling" liability in this manner, the claims of accident victims could presumably be resolved quickly. Most foreign countries use such liability channeling approaches in connection with nuclear risks.[4] So-called "wrap-up" insurance policies provided to prime contractors in the U.S. construction industry utilize similar ideas.

Liability channeling approaches do not resolve liability debates, nor do they represent a no-fault approach. Rather, they attempt to pay injured parties quickly and leave LNG handlers (owner, driver, lessor, buyer, seller, etc.) to resolve the allocation or liability among themselves. Such a strategy involves some new risks: will the primarily liable party settle the original claims appropriately? Will the fast initial payout make insurers more reluctant to write the insurance? Will those held primarily liable have control over the risk-taking actions of secondary operators? The answers to most of these questions look promising, especially if large LNG handlers linked to an incident have the liability channeled to them. (For example, the storage facility where truckers pick up LNG could be designated the primary party for accidents along the truck route.) Contractual arrangements among LNG handlers might also reduce the multitude of insurance policies that must now be written in order to cover each potentially liable party.

Other government strategies could address the difficulties in assessing risks. Rather than regulate individual risk-taking decisions directly (e.g., by prohibiting LNG trucks on urban routes), one could set the required liability insurance coverage according to LNG handlers' specific choices (for example, city routes might require $50 million coverage per truck per trip, whereas rural routes might require only $25 million). Such a strategy does not eliminate the need for regulatory risk assessments, but it does enable more flexibility than go/no-go decisions. It also leaves the economic consequences of business decisions in an arena where (with liability channeling) the involved parties are most likely to face financial incentives for useful exchanges of risk-related information.

Demonstrating the viability of these insurance-oriented strategies would require more extensive discussion.[5] However, the example illustrates both the circumstances under which insurance may substitute for direct regulation of risks and the sort of government action that must be contemplated and researched in order to make the insurance option viable. The automobile safety example in the next section will illustrate similar principles in a second context.

Example II: Automobile crashworthiness

The federal government has for more than a dozen years actively regulated safety standards affecting the design of automobiles. Examples include uniform bumper heights, damage limitations resulting from 5 mph test crashes, and mandatory seat belts, air bags, or other restraint mechanisms. Developing such standards is one of the principal duties of the National Highway Traffic Safety Administration (NHTSA), and their debate and enactment has generated considerable interest in Congress, in the automobile industry, and among the public. The standards are generally justified with arguments that safety is a public good or that some form of mutual coercion is needed for design features, such as standard bumper heights, whose safety benefits depend upon wide acceptance.

In order to focus on the relative merits of safety standards and insurance, we shall examine some of the issues and alternatives concerning bumper heights, air bags, and 5 mph test crashes. The rationale for standards in each case is straightforward. Bumpers are designed to absorb impacts with minimal damage but, when two cars collide, much of the benefit is lost if the bumpers do not contact one another. Air

bags can substantially reduce personal injury in most accidents—especially if passengers do not wear seat belts. The
damage restrictions on 5 mph test crashes provide assurance
that low-speed "fender-benders" are neither costly to repair
nor likely to cause personal injury.

The drawbacks of such standards are likewise readily
identified, and are typical of command-and-control strategies. The standards establish thresholds that inevitably involve some degree of arbitrariness—determining the "right"
bumper height, "adequate" air bag performance, or "tolerable" crash damage. In each case, administrative complica-
tions arise involving eligibility, certification, flexibility, and
enforcement. Do the special uses of jeeps and pickup trucks
warrant exemption from the standard bumper heights?
Must all cars meet the same air bag performance standards
(speed of inflation, impact absorbed, etc.)? What sanctions
should be applied when they do not?

Even if the costs of meeting the standards are known, the
overall effects of safety improvements and price adjustments
are difficult to evaluate, since the willingness of consumers
to invest in safety features is poorly understood and the
merits of limiting voluntary risk taking are endlessly debated. Moreover, the standards necessarily focus on limited
aspects of vehicular safety. As a result, changing vehicle
designs in order to meet standards inexpensively may result
in adverse safety effects elsewhere (such as sacrificing integrity or cost in 10 mph or angular collisions in order to
meet the standard for 5 mph head-on collisions). Hence it is
difficult, both conceptually and politically, to link the standards to cost considerations or public safety goals. To the extent that accident causality is complex and not well understood, the standards are all the more difficult to design—and
easier to circumvent.

Some of these safety requirements could be replaced by an
insurance price structure that reflects the crashworthiness
of vehicles. Traditionally, automobile insurance pricing has

been based on the age and original cost of the vehicle. However, in recent years several insurers have developed so-called make-and-model classification schemes that base the insurance premium on the specific vehicle model rather than on its sticker price. Such schemes permit differentiation among car models that sell for the same price but have different accident frequencies or repair costs. Charging higher insurance prices for vehicles that are less safe or more costly to repair should provide financial incentives to purchase safer cars and competitive pressure to improve vehicle safety.

Make-and-model rating does, nevertheless, have some practical difficulties. The accident experience of a particular type of car depends upon more than the physical design of the vehicle; when, where, and how it is driven also matters. Unless insurance pricing distinguishes vehicle safety factors from driver and usage factors, the premium differences across vehicle makes and models can provide distorted or even perverse incentives. Suppose, for example, that the safest vehicles were driven more often, in more congested areas, or by the least safe drivers. Then they could compile a poorer accident loss record than dangerous vehicles that are used more sparingly or with more caution. Trying to sort through the pros and cons of the resulting incentives leads to complicated causality issues and moral debates. Do the drivers favor the safe cars because they know they are safer? Is the incentive to buy the less safe vehicle desirable because those who buy the vehicle then drive less often, or is it undesirable because each mile of driving is then more risky? What if the same type of vehicle is used differently (or for different reasons) by various drivers?

However one resolves these questions, most analysts agree that accurately distinguishing driver, environmental, and vehicle effects would be ideal. Since most automobile insurance classification schemes already include driver, usage, and vehicle factors, the potential for such distinctions exists.

The statistical problems are, nevertheless, troublesome. Since individual vehicles and drivers are rarely involved in accidents—averages of one every four to twenty years are typical—and since accident costs vary widely, considerable data are needed to link driver and vehicle characteristics to average costs. For example, reliable detection of a 10 percent difference in average annual accident costs between two types of vehicles driven under similar conditions would require, under the best of conditions, observing several thousand such vehicles for a year. Identifying the individual contribution of various driver, usage, and vehicle factors, and distinguishing the ways in which the factors interact, increase the data requirements astronomically. In addition, the insurance prices represent forecasts of future costs. How past experience with a particular type of car relates to future experience may depend upon a host of economic factors (such as inflation) and causal relationships (e.g., is this year's new Chevrolet Impala as safe as least year's was? Will those who drive Chevrolets next year be similar to this year's Chevrolet drivers?).

There are other difficulties with the insurance approach to vehicle safety. More than half the cost of a typical automobile insurance policy protects against liability claims for damage to someone else's person or property. This cost depends more upon the car an insured hits than the car he or she drives. Suppose, for example, that a durable, cheap-to-fix vehicle equipped with air bags collides with a fragile luxury car in which the occupants are unrestrained. If the driver of the first vehicle is held liable, his insurer would likely have to pay considerably higher damages than would the insurer of the luxury car (should that driver be held liable). Hence, much of the benefit of driving the safer vehicle accrues to drivers of other vehicles.[6]

Another difficulty with the insurance approach concerns motorists' risk perceptions. Understanding the safety differences among vehicles requires a certain amount of

faith. Since accidents are rare events, even a relatively unsafe or easily damaged car is likely to go several years without any accident, and much longer before having an accident
linked to risky or expensive-to-repair aspects of the car's
design. Hence, the personal experiences of one's friends and
neighbors are of little value in assessing the relative risks of
vehicle design. In this respect, capitalizing the safety
differences into premium differentials for insurance coverage
makes the choice more direct and immediate. However, insurance premiums vary according to a number of factors, and
most motorists do not take the time to obtain a quote before
purchasing a vehicle. Amidst the myriad other factors influencing the choice of a particular car, safety and repair cost
aspects are easily dismissed or heavily discounted.

As difficult as these problems are, steps can be taken to
overcome them. Traditional actuarial techniques for pricing
insurance have tended to ignore the interaction of the major
classification factors—driver category, rating territory,
vehicle type, and past accident experience. The techniques
evolved before computer analyses of very large data bases
with multiple factors were practicable. The resulting cost
estimates for the disaggregated classifications have often
been wide of the mark and the ability to recognize and fine-
tune different classification schemes has been limited. The
result has been a reluctance to experiment with new
schemes—such as make-and-model rating—that require
sophisticated statistical models to sort out vehicle driver and
usage effects.

However, modern multivariate statistical techniques for
analyzing multiple-factor, small-effect data are just coming
into widespread use. For example, recent analyses at Massachusetts and New Jersey rate hearings have used disaggregated data and newly developed statistical techniques to
redefine territories, price vehicle-classification factors, and
combine driver-class and rating-territory factors. Such
studies examine the simultaneous effects of many rating fac-

tors and, as a result, require specially compiled cross-company data in order to have enough information.

Compiling such data is a formidable task. However, the use of make-and-model rating schemes would not require such efforts every year in every state. A few large-scale, carefully designed studies done, say, every four to six years would be sufficient to provide the stimulus for innovation, the analytic basis for judgmental rate making, and the feedback on past performance that individual companies need.

State and federal government agencies can assist in this regard. Most state insurance departments require automobile insurers to report their experiences broken down by classification categories according to a standard statistical plan. Similarly, state motor vehicle departments collect automobile insurance information, and federal funding rules encourage states to maintain such records in accessible and standardized formats. These data, however, are of limited use for the type of statistical analyses just discussed. Motor vehicle data generally record accidents by drivers, whereas insurance data count claim payments of policies that insure vehicles. Moreover, both types of data lack the controls or multiyear consistency needed for researching classification schemes. Data needed to translate information about accidents into risk measures (for example, accidents per million vehicle miles for each type of car or driver) are typically lacking. Likewise, standard statistical reporting of insurance data does not permit identification of multiple claims against the same policy or multiple-year records for individual policyholders, and tends to favor complete data at a common level of aggregation across companies rather than less comprehensive but disaggregated data suited for specific research purposes.[7]

The second problem with make-and-model rating was that liability insurance shifted some of the financial disadvantages of hazardous or costly-to-repair vehicles from their owners to the drivers who hit them. The advent of no-fault laws and comparative negligence statutes has shifted some of the claim-cost factors back to the insured. Also, direct (rather than liability) vehicle protection coverage accounts for roughly one half of the typical insurance premium. Since about one third of the premium represents overhead, taxes, and insurer profits, the expenses inflate any financial incentive to purchase safe vehicles to an amount that more closely approximates the aggregate safety differential (i.e., the total expected savings in accident costs for the vehicle owner and those who may hit him). In urbanized areas (where the standards for low-speed crashes are likely to have the largest impact), collision, theft, and no-fault protection coverages amount to several hundred dollars per year for a typical new vehicle. Crash studies and other make-and-model analyses report differences of 20 percent or more in accident repair costs for similarly priced vehicle models. More detailed studies are needed. Nevertheless, saving even 15 percent would mean an annual saving of $50 to $80 per year on moderately priced new vehicles in cities like Boston, New York, or San Francisco. For older cars the savings are less — but often represent a higher percentage of the car's value.

One cannot expect such differentials to have dramatic impacts on the selection and use of vehicles. But, if widely used and understood, they can help. For several years, some insurers have offered discounts of 5 to 15 percent on theft coverage for approved antitheft devices, inducing a number of customers to install them. Influencing the choice of a vehicle rather than what to add to it later is, admittedly, more difficult. However, antitheft discounts are much smaller in dollar terms, since theft coverage itself typically costs less than $100 per year; if the differences among makes of cars could be expressed to car buyers in simple percentage terms, one could expect at least as much of an effect from make-and-model rating as from antitheft discounts.

Like the LNG example, the automobile crashworthiness case is not clear-cut—and the insurance alternative needs some help to get off the ground. The detailed analysis has revealed strengths and weaknesses of each approach. Moreover, it has indicated how the situations in which regulatory standards are least desirable are situations where the insurance alternative is likely to be workable. The regulatory approach is most promising when standards are simple and straightforward and safety benefits are well understood, direct, and perhaps even synergetic. Standardizing bumper heights is an example.

Standards may also make sense if there is a consensus that specific automobile safety features are being inappropriately ignored. For example, economically and technologically feasible safety improvements might be overlooked by an automobile industry preoccupied with cost or other design features that are more attractive to a public known for discounting accident risks. Given the evidence about seat belt usage, such an argument is conceivable in the case of air bags. Of course, such reasoning requires a willingness to legislate greater limits to voluntary risk taking than motorists would themselves choose. The debate over the wisdom of such social policy, and over who should make the judgments, goes far beyond the scope of this chapter.

The insurance approach offers hope of a more realistic, economical measure of alternative vehicle designs where there is no logical threshold for the safety standard or the link between design and safety (or repair costs) is problematic. Low-speed crash tests fall in this category. Simple design changes are unlikely to produce significant safety benefits without an important increase in costs or a sacrifice of safety in other areas. It is more likely that a spectrum of design changes with varying costs is possible to improve safety—each change with different safety implications in differing contexts (such as angular or high-speed crashes). In such a case, the insurance approach offers the *only* practical prospect of fine-tuning design incentives to reflect appropriate safety and repair cost options. At some point, promoting meaningful incentives for safe designs in the marketplace becomes the more practical alternative.

The debates involved in setting safety standards have undoubtedly increased public risk awareness by dramatizing crash effects—a benefit not considered in the above analysis. However, maintaining adequate public concern should be possible by publishing test crash results (as is now done by the Insurance Institute for Highway Safety) and disseminating information about insurance cost differentials in understandable terms. Over an extended period, the 5 mph crash standard will either become unnecessary, because competitive pressures result in widespread demand for such performance, or increasingly difficult to rationalize, as safety, cost, or marketability problems burden the standards with administrative complexities.

The task now is to institutionalize the safety considerations fostered by the federal government in ways that require minimal government supervision. As the analysis shows, make-and-model rating is promising in this regard. However, developing such classifications is not easy, and the government can play a helpful role by facilitating data collection and analysis and informing the driving public of the insurance price differences that result. Doing this requires coordination among government agencies, and a shift in focus from direct control of vehicle design to active promotion of competitive behavior and accurate risk assessment in the automobile and insurance industries.

THE NEED FOR GOVERNMENT INVOLVEMENT

The examples indicate that insurance is a viable alternative, given good risk assessment, financially responsible parties, and enough information. While these conditions are never ideal, in a number of situations they offer a better chance of success than directly regulating risks. A minimal amount of governmental intervention often can do much to make the insurance option work.

To assess the potential for insurance to solve a safety problem and the actions needed to make it work, one should consider the following checklist:

- Is the claim settlement process likely to be straightforward or would it be complicated, expensive, time consuming, and inflammatory?

- Will insurance redistribute accident costs to those who can act directly to reduce the risks?

- Who is in the best position to assess risks (what data are needed, and what types of risk assessment are practical and desirable for the insurer and for government)?

- How well does objective risk assessment compare with underwriting judgment, size of firm, payout delays, and other factors in determining the insurance premium?

- Is there a compelling argument for setting safety standards that consumers would not voluntarily accept?

- Is an accident likely to be so catastrophic in the eyes of the public or so large in relation to the size of the insurers, broker, or insured that a single incident could ruin them?

At the core of this checklist is a host of risk assessment issues:

- How precisely can one identify accident causes before— and after—an incident?

- How do individuals assess and respond to risks affecting themselves?

- How do the inaccuracies of risk assessment translate into ineffectual, perverse, or unfair safety standards and insurance pricing incentives?

Since risk assessment is typically quite limited, this last issue is especially important, though often neglected. Accurate risk assessment is helpful for both regulatory standards and insurance alternatives, but the insurance approaches are likely to be much more sensitive to the quality of risk assessment. Even if accurate risk assessment is possible, the complexity of accident causation limits the value of administratively feasible regulations. On the other hand, insurance priced on the basis of poor risk assessment creates new problems of moral hazards and perverse incentives.

Recent improvements in risk assessment methodologies are beginning to make automobile crashworthiness a viable insurance rating factor. At the same time, a still limited—but improving—understanding of LNG risks hinders the ability of liability laws to apportion blame in a timely fashion. In both cases, improved risk assessment can be translated into improved safety but, for institutional or data analysis reasons, progress is likely to be slow without federal or state government help. Government actions should pay more attention to making insurance (and liability) mechanisms work and to collecting, analyzing, and disseminating risk assessment data. With effort, such action can stimulate viable private sector substitutes for direct regulation of safety, and it offers a reasonable prospect for a diminished government role in the future.

13

GEORGE C. EADS

Increased Corporate Product Safety Efforts: A Substitute for Regulation?

Support for product safety programs. Organization and function of unit models. Three prototypes. Trade-offs in the design process. Incentives, documentation, and defense against liability claims. Liability litigation. Federal regulatory agencies.

During the 1970s a new box appeared on the organization charts of many of the nation's corporations. The job title in this box was not always the same. And the box itself was not located at the same place on every organization chart. But each appearance signaled the recognition by one more firm of the need to assign formal responsibility for overseeing the safety of its products.

Table 1, compiled from information collected by the Conference Board in a 1979 survey of 300 large manufacturers, shows the proportion of firms reporting that they had established full- or part-time product safety activities at various levels over the course of the decade. It supports the view of Kenneth Randall, Conference Board president, that "until the early 1970s, relatively few firms maintained a separate, formal product safety function. More often, safety responsibilities were assigned internally on an informal basis and were judged to be the implicit concern of those scattered units who designed, produced, and sold its products" (McGuire 1979, p. ix).

What caused this change? There is no lack of claimants for the credit. Federal regulators, anxious to deflect charges that their activities have been ineffective, point to the increase in corporate product safety efforts as evidence of their success in inducing business to modify its behavior. Defenders of current tort law, opposing attempts to narrow the grounds under which parties injured by products can sue, cite the increased efforts of corporations as proof of the law's deterrent effect. Corporate officials, while mindful of these claims, suggest that the change has really been more evolutionary than revolutionary. They note that firms were taking actions to improve the safety of their products long before the creation of the Consumer Product Safety Commission (CPSC) or the rise of the doctrine of "strict liability."

The fact that everybody claims credit for stimulating the creation of corporate product safety units suggests that this event is considered good. And indeed it is. In its *Final Report,* the federal Interagency Task Force on Product Liability (U.S. Department of Commerce 1977, p. xlii) cited the in-

Table 1

**Proportion of Firms Reporting Either Full-Time or
Part-Time Product Safety Function at Level Indicated**

Period	Nondivisionalized companies (%)	Divisionalized companies		
		Corporate level (%)	Group level (%)	Major division level (%)
Early 1970s	26	25	22	33
Late 1970s	79	73	58	74

Source: Adapted from McGuire 1979, pp. 5, 12.

creased incidence of formal corporate product safety efforts
as a positive step in remedying unsafe manufacturing practices—one of the three identified causes of the product liability "problem" of the mid-1970s.[1] A House subcommittee, concluding a major study of product liability issues, also
remarked favorably on the trend (U.S. House of Representatives 1978, p. 75). Public policy scholars, seeing corporate actions as a possible substitute for regulation, have added their
voices to the chorus of approval.

The message of this chapter is that things are not so
simple. The product safety function has become well established in the overwhelming majority of larger manufacturing
firms. But its impact on product safety is not clear, and
neither is the extent to which it can serve as a regulatory
substitute.

A "NAIVE" MODEL OF THE ROLE OF CORPORATE PRODUCT SAFETY EFFORTS

Those claiming credit for the creation of product safety units,
as well as those applauding the fact of their creation, have
been using an implicit model as shown in figure 1. Depending
upon who is telling the story, product safety regulation, pressures from product liability claims and suits, or a desire on
the part of business to make products safer have led to the
creation of product safety units. This in turn has produced
changes in design and manufacturing practices, and these
changes have led to safer products.

To the best of our knowledge, no one has attempted to test
this "naive" model. That is understandable, since it turns out
to be extremely difficult to test. The only directly verifiable
element in it is the increase in the number of product safety
units; other hypothesized linkages are much less clear.

This chapter reports on research presently under way to

Figure 1
"Naive" Model of Product Safety Improvement

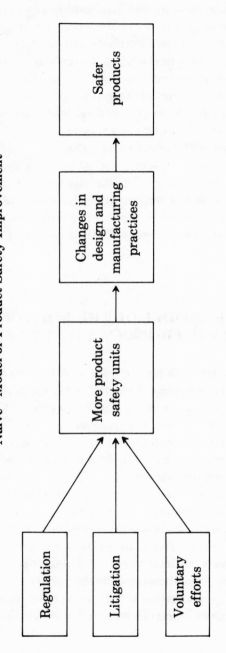

provide an indirect test of this model. To carry out such a test, it is necessary to make the model somewhat more complex so that it reflects the great diversity in the organization and operation of actual product safety units. To a certain extent, this diversity reflects different product and customer markets facing different firms. But more is involved. Corporate product safety units in fact perform multiple functions, not all of which clearly lead to the sorts of design and manufacturing changes necessary for safer products. Indeed, some functions may conflict sharply with the goal of improved product safety. Can the existence of more product safety units be associated with safer products? To answer this question, we will have to explore more deeply the organization and operation of product safety units.

A MORE COMPLEX MODEL OF THE IMPACT OF FORMAL PRODUCT SAFETY ACTIVITIES

The way a firm organizes itself reflects its perception of the strategic issues it must deal with, and organization, both formal and informal, clearly has an important influence on outcomes. These two insights suggest that the "naive" model needs to be made more complex, as illustrated in figure 2.

The same three environmental forces are operating: product safety regulatory activities, the pressures of litigation, and voluntary efforts by firms to incorporate new safety-related design and manufacturing techniques into their operations. But this time these forces are hypothesized to operate on an intermediate variable—the firm's perception of the "product safety problem." This problem can be seen primarily as a technical issue, a legal issue, or a design issue (or, in fact, a combination with various weights attached to each). The firm's perception of the so-called "product safety

Figure 2
More Complete Model of Product Safety Improvement

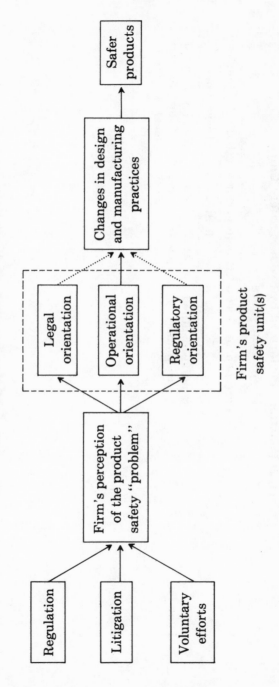

Table 2
Principal Functions Performed by Product Safety Units: All Companies

Function	Percent of product safety units performing indicated function:				
	In nondivisionalized companies (%)	In divisionalized companies			
		At corporate level (%)	At group level (%)	At major division level (%)	At minor division level (%)
Evaluating the safetyworthiness of new products	87	46	24	55	41
Investigating product safety failures	87	46	65	30	62
Liaison with safety regulatory agencies	80	62	39	20	77
Evaluating and/or preparing product use instructions	76	43	57	26	57
Auditing and testing the safety-worthiness of existing products	70	35	53	25	48

Setting safety performance standards for finished products	70	41	50	25	54
Evaluating patterns and trends of safety failures	67	38	43	22	51
Educating company employees in product safety matters	67	52	49	28	65
Processing product liability claims	65	72	33	19	85
Setting quality control standards for manufactured products	65	23	30	59	48
Setting safety standards for raw materials	63	50	53	25	42
Regulatory record keeping	58	33	40	19	44
Reporting safety defects to regulatory agencies	52	46	25	15	55
Planning safety education programs for products users or other outsiders	50	47	43	22	57
Managing product recall campaigns	4	3	2	1	3

Source: Reproduced from McGuire 1979, p. 53.

Note: Based on reported practices of 242 divisionalized and 46 nondivisionalized firms, for both full-time and part-time product safety units.

problem" affects how it structures and operates its product safety units. As table 2 reveals, these units can and do serve multiple functions:

• They are catalysts for increasing the firm's concern with safety issues.

• They act as the principal organizing focus for the firm's product liability defense efforts.

• They are focal points of liaison between the firm and various regulatory bodies with responsibility for product safety.

Product safety units can therefore have an "operational" orientation, a "legal" orientation, or a "regulatory" orientation.

The conceptual problem can be seen by working from the right-hand side of figure 2 toward the center. Safer products—the presumed goal—result only from changes in design and manufacturing practices. A product safety program with an operational orientation seeks to work directly on these practices and so ought clearly to have a positive impact on product safety, provided the program itself is run effectively. But the impact of a product safety program with a legal or regulatory orientation is less clear, since these programs operate only *indirectly* on design and manufacturing practices. And there are reasons to believe that their impact can sometimes be neutral or even negative, even if they are effective in their primary functions of enhancing legal defenses or developing an effective (from the viewpoint of the firm) regulatory response.

The "typical" product safety program probably does not exactly fit any one of these three prototypes but contains elements of all three. Yet the pressures of the middle 1970s, when the majority of product safety programs were being set up, tended to reinforce the regulatory and legal orientation. After all, this was not (to the best of our knowledge) a time when design or manufacturing standards slipped and products became distinctly less safe than before. Instead, it was a period when injured parties were increasingly willing to exercise their legal rights aggressively, when courts looked with more and more favor on such parties, and when governmental regulatory activity was increasing rapidly.

It is necessary, therefore, to assume that many if not most product safety programs have a significant (but not necessarily exclusively) legal or regulatory orientation and to consider the implications for product safety.

How do the three orientations affect product safety activities? To answer this question, it will be necessary to look at each of the orientations in greater depth.

ALTERING THE FIRM'S OPERATING PRACTICES TO GIVE GREATER EMPHASIS TO PRODUCT SAFETY

It has never been easy to create a product that is safe in its intended use and does not fail catastrophically even if it is misused. But this job has become enormously more difficult as products have become more complicated, the materials with which they are made, more exotic, and our understanding of how human factors can interact with a product to create hazardous situations, more complete.

It is increasingly coming to be recognized that the design decision-making process must be formalized. As John Kolb and Steven S. Ross (1980, p. 77) put it:

Sole dependence upon the decentralized design engineering function is not a valid method of assuring product safety, even within the smallest of corporate groups. There are too many regulations, too many potential hazards, and there is too much at stake to depend on the competence of a single person.

The situation becomes even more critical in large companies that are often multimarket, multidivisional, and sometimes multinational. . . . If different divisions in a company all have separate safety programs and all work in different ways, some will perform to excess, some inefficiently, and some not at all.

So, while the design engineer is the prime mover of safety concerns, the basic assumption should be that he or she cannot ensure product safety alone.

Thus the problem of assuring adequate attention to product safety involves more than just the design engineer: a variety of units within the firm have a role. Standards for materials and components to be used in a product's manufacture must be established and enforced. Appropriate quality control levels in manufacturing must be set and maintained. Advertising must be monitored to ensure that it does not inadvertently suggest a product to be capable of performing feats beyond its capabilities. The performance of products in the field must be watched, and the results collected and analyzed to permit appropriate changes.

These decisions involve numerous trade-offs between such factors as cost, durability, and appearance. And not all parties to the decision approach the problem from the same point of view. Marketing may resist a design that sacrifices appearance for safety or displays too graphic a warning about possible hazards. Production may object to stiffer quality control standards that lead to higher reject rates, or may find more durable materials excessively time-consuming or difficult to work with. The expense of maintaining an elaborate system to track and diagnose product problems in the field and feed this information back to design, production, and marketing may be viewed by sales as an unnecessary drain on earnings.

An organized product safety effort can provide the means of exposing and resolving these conflicts. It does this by uncovering the actual and presumed trade-offs, forcing their examination, and requiring explicit resolutions.

This result is far from automatic, however, for it requires the firm to solve one of the most novel organizational issues, creating an effective structure for formal liaison; as Henry Mintzberg (1979) notes, the rise of crosscutting issues within firms has increased the amount of mutual adjustment required for coordination. This mutual adjustment used to take place informally, but in recent years firms have established a number of devices to encourage liaison between individuals—devices that can be incorporated into the formal structure. Mintzberg (1979, p. 161) has called this innovation "the most significant contemporary development in organizational design, indeed the only serious one since the establishment of planning and control systems a decade or two earlier."

The sort of liaison arrangement a firm develops is a function of the degree of mutual adjustment required. When conflicts are few, establishing a liaison position—an individual responsible merely for facilitating interunit contacts—may suffice. Where more structure is needed, creating a temporary task force or a standing committee may be the appropriate organizational response. However, where even more coordination is required than these structures can provide, the organization may find it appropriate to designate an integrating manager—a liaison position with formal authority. Mintzberg stresses that to be successful, the integrating manager must rely a great deal upon his powers of persuasion and negotiation. His formal powers must always, of necessity, be quite limited.

There is a wide range of opinion as to the proper organization and placement of firms' product safety activities. Some strongly support formal product safety committees, arguing that only in this way can the necessary range of responsibilities and skills be brought together (Chandran and Linneman 1978, p. 36). Others, believing that committee control inevitably results in divided responsibilities and divided responsibility leads in turn to no responsibility, favor more centralized organization.

There is a similar range of disagreement about where to

locate primary responsibility for the firm's product safety activities. Some companies, noting the degree to which the functions performed are legal in nature or involve insurance-related issues, favor lodging primary coordination responsibility in their legal or insurance sectors. A larger number, noting the technical nature of the activities and stressing the central role of the design engineer, favor placement on the technical side. Indeed, some observers go so far as to warn that, unless the individual with primary responsibility for product safety coordination comes from the technical side of the firm, the activity is doomed.

Given Mintzberg's insights, it is now clear that this debate over organizational form and placement reflects a divergence of views as to the level of conflict resolution required in dealing with product safety issues and the proper role for the integrating manager. It is not surprising that those favoring the operational orientation for product safety efforts want authority to accrue to someone from the technical side of the company, while those with legal orientation favor someone with different skills and argue for a different placement of the function.

Changing the incentives

The mention of the need for conflict resolution raises another important function of product safety activities: restructuring intrafirm incentives to reduce the conflict between product safety and other corporate goals. Such restructuring is key if significant improvements in product safety are indeed to be realized. It is common in U.S. industry to view safety improvements and other quality-related features as a potential drain on earnings. But this may be mistaken. In a recent provocative article in the *Harvard Business Review*, Steven Wheelwright (1981, pp. 67–74) argues that within an extremely broad range—encompassing the present operations of most American firms—improved product quality is consistent with (and is, indeed, a *sine qua non* of) higher profits. It is the inappropriately designed management incentive systems, which fail to perceive improved product quality as having a strategic function, that prevent this from being realized. In Japan, however, where "operational" functions are viewed as having an important strategic element, higher profits and higher product quality are deemed quite compatible. In Wheelwright's opinion, this difference in management perception of the profit-to-quality trade-off may account for a significant proportion of the superior Japanese manufacturing productivity.[2] The struggle by firms to enhance product safety may therefore, viewed appropriately, have a far greater impact than improvements in the safety of firms' products, as important as the latter might be.

One point that commentators universally agree upon is the need for thorough documentation of safety-related decisions, beginning preferably at the concept stage where design changes are the easiest and cheapest to make. Such documentation assures that certain issues that otherwise might be overlooked indeed get raised. It also enables the firm to trace at some future time how earlier safety-related decisions were made, to determine whether new information should lead to these decisions' being changed.

Most firms have formal policies, developed and enforced by their product safety units, on documentation of safety-related decisions. But firms also characterize the enforcement of these policies as a "never-ending battle."[3]

This should not be surprising, for documentation is clearly a two-edged sword. As will be discussed in more detail in the following section, thorough documentation of safety design decisions can aid decision making and can help a firm rebut charges that its design decisions have been inappropriate, but it can also be the weapon for a clever plaintiff's attorney in destroying a company's defense in a product liability trial.[4] Companies deciding to increase the amount of safety-related documentation they require thus run a legal risk. It is not surprising, therefore, that some firms have attempted to increase their formal safety-related design efforts while severely limiting the amount of documentation generated.[5] Other firms, while recognizing these risks, seem to have decided that there are compensating operational—and even legal—benefits of formalization and documentation. Which view is right depends largely on individual circumstances.

ENHANCING THE FIRM'S ABILITY TO DEFEND ITSELF AGAINST PRODUCT LIABILITY CLAIMS AND SUITS

There is no doubt that an extremely important motivation for formalizing product safety efforts has been the firm's fear of product liability claims and suits. And not only during the 1970s. Firms in certain industries had "product liability problems" long before "strict liability" and "consumerism" became matters for industry in general to worry about. During this earlier time, a typical response to the product liability problem was to formalize a firm's (or industry's) product safety efforts—specifically, toward improving its legal defense posture. Consider the program established in 1958 by Clark Equipment Company, a major manufacturer of industrial trucks. The individual reciting the history of the program refers to an industry concern with safety that goes back to the period immediately following World War II and Clark's efforts, along with other manufacturers, to establish a safety standard for powered industrial trucks. But he cites the following as the proximate cause for the establishment of Clark's formal "product liability prevention" program.[6]

During the middle 1950s, we were shocked to observe that our insurance company was making some very substantial out-of-court settlements on accidents involving products which we did not consider defective. Furthermore, we were continuing to make the identical products and put them on the marketplace. . . .

[Our insurance carrier] explained to us that they [*sic*] felt there was great difficulty in defending this type of case in court, but they agreed to try out a change in policy if we would cooperate by supplying sufficient engineering assistance so that they could prepare a strong defense for each case. . . . We try to preach this wherever we go because we feel that when any manufacturer needlessly loses a case, it hurts us all by creating a bad precedent or even bad common law.

Similarly, the organized product safety activities of the Grinding Wheel Institute (which date back to the early 1950s) seem to have been motivated in large part by a desire to improve the defense posture of its members.

After World War II, the Grinding Wheel Institute became concerned about the increasing frequency of costly product liability losses. . . . The group developed a two-phase program to hold down insurance costs. The initial phase was aimed at reducing the number of grinding wheel accidents through strict loss control standards. The second focused on the development of an aggressive legal defense.

Before offering insurance to a grinding wheel manufacturer, the insurer handling most of the grinding wheel business surveys the design, testing, fabrication, and labeling procedures followed. . . .

In conjunction with [this] development . . . the Institute identified a number of attorneys capable of representing it and its members in the defense of bodily injury suits. These attorneys spent 2 to 3 days on the shop floor to gain a firsthand understanding of the grinding wheel manufacturing process. The insurer cooperated with this effort and agreed to use the attorneys identified by the Institute. Further, it appointed a senior claims adjuster to supervise the handling of all grinding wheel claims. (McKinsey and Company 1977, pp. 3–27)

There are several ways in which an organized product safety effort can improve a firm's defense posture. First, it provides a structure around which to organize the firm's product-related legal efforts. Table 1 confirms the frequency with which product safety units are concerned with such activities as processing and settling product liability claims and controlling product liability litigation. This organizational and tracking role seems especially important at the corporate and minor division levels, which should not be surprising. Individuals at the minor division level almost certainly know the most about the particular products against which claims have been filed—how they were designed, tested, and manufactured; how they should and should not be used; the characteristics of users, etc. Such knowledge is essential to a credible defense. However, it is likely that, except in rare instances, relatively few claims will be filed against any one company's individual product. Product liability prevention units at the corporate level, therefore, can tap the experience of the entire corporation and also call on the services of staff offices—the legal department, corporate research and development, etc.

A second way for an organized safety effort to bolster a firm's defense posture is to ensure that the firm's own standards and procedures are being followed. Nothing demolishes a firm's legal defense faster than the revelation that a slipup has occurred. Thus product safety units, especially at higher organizational levels, are often assigned "auditing" functions.

To be sure, an effective audit procedure can serve other objectives as well. Firms that lay great stress on modifying their operating procedures to improve product safety also employ audits. But all audits are not alike, and some seem to be far more "defense-oriented" than others. Firm D in Alvin Weinstein's study employed an elaborate audit checklist to assure that certain steps had been followed in a product's design, production, and marketing. But the information generated by Firm B's audit seemed designed to reveal instances of violation of procedure rather than to check on whether safety-related decisions were indeed "reasonable"—the focus of an operations-oriented audit.[7]

A third activity of formal product safety units that can improve a firm's defense posture is the thorough investigation of product safety failures. Many observers stress the importance of an active investigation effort to defend against fraudulent and inflated claims, and stories are common of allegations that, upon investigation, proved unfounded (see, for example, Nelson 1980, pp. 614–16).

This activity too can be compatible with an operations-oriented product safety program, but it need not be. Many firms, even with effective operations-oriented programs, seem to value accident investigation only for its defense-enhancing value. Both Firm A and Firm B in Weinstein's study delegated accident investigation to insurance adjusters. (Firm B, which was self-insured, actually contracted with outside claims adjusters for this investigation.) By doing so, these firms lost potentially valuable information for spotting design problems in both existing and new products.

Other companies, however, assign responsibility for monitoring the actual performance of their products (including the investigation of product-related accidents) to their field service offices, which have instructions to feed such information back to design, manufacturing, and marketing as well as to the individuals specifically responsible for coordinating product safety activities. This creates a greater risk of "smoking guns" in the firm's files, but it also generates safety-related information that cannot otherwise be obtained.

Clearly, the operational and legal objectives of a firm's product safety activities are likely to be substantially—though not totally—in conflict. Given current legal incentives, this conflict is unavoidable. The operational objective requires increased formalization and documentation of design-related decisions. For the legal objectives this is dangerous, however, as it requires limiting documentation only to what is absolutely necessary to avoid suspicions of a cover-up. How might the two objectives be reconciled?

An interesting suggestion in this regard has recently been made by Weinstein and his colleagues.[8] Product liability litigation currently emphasizes the reasonableness of the particular design decision related to the defect that led to the plaintiff's injury. This leads to battles of "experts": the plaintiff attempts to show that a different decision was possible that, had it been taken, would have prevented the injury, while the defendant attempts to show that the decision was reasonable, given the state of the art at the time. These researchers strongly argue, however, that product safety will not be substantially improved unless firms are given both an incentive to bring safety considerations more explicitly into their decision making—which requires more formalization and documentation of design procedures—and a degree of protection against "second-guessing" what at the time appeared to be "reasonable" decisions. They therefore propose that firms be able to raise a "process defense." In exchange for opening their safety-related decision-making processes (and presumably their ways of assuring they were in fact followed) to scrutiny, firms would be entitled to have their procedures—in contrast to individual design decisions—assessed. If these procedures, judged presumably against a professionally established set of standards, were deemed "reasonable," the decisions resulting from their use would also be presumed "reasonable." This prescription could be rebutted only if a plaintiff could show, by weight of "clear and convincing" evidence, that the design was defective.

In a sharply-worded critique, James Henderson (1982)—himself no admirer of the current system of product liability litigation—argues that the Weinstein suggestion is impractical.[9] In particular, the risks to the firm—both in the particular instance being litigated and in other potential cases—are so great that no responsible defense attorney would ever advise his client to use a "process defense."

The exchange between Henderson and Weinstein and his colleagues, though inconclusive, highlights the inherent conflicts between design decision-making improvement and defense enhancement. The former works on the theory of improving the average and, if effective, works primarily at the margin: newly designed products benefit the most by its application. The latter focuses on aberrant cases—presumably on the low end of the product quality distribution—and stresses the dangers of products already in the field, so its impact on design practices is, at best, indirect. Bringing these two objectives into closer congruence, though difficult, is vital to significant improvements in product safety.

Federal regulatory agencies, whether concerned directly or indirectly, are key actors in product safety. To what extent do their activities reinforce—or compete with—the two objectives on which we have been concentrating to this point? Might these agencies serve as catalysts to resolve the conflicts we have been discussing? We now turn to these questions.

THE REGULATORY LIAISON FUNCTION

Over the last decade or so, federal regulatory interest in product safety–related matters has grown enormously. Several new agencies with an important interest in product safety have been established, including the Consumer Product Safety Commission (CPSC, established in 1972), which is the best known, the National Highway Traffic Safety Administration (NHTSA, 1970), the Occupational Safety and Health Administration (OSHA, 1973), and the Environmental Protection Agency (EPA, 1970). And a number of existing agencies with product safety responsibilities have been strengthened, including the Federal Trade Commission (FTC), the Food and Drug Administration (FDA), and the Department of Agriculture (USDA). As shown in table 2 above, dealing with these agencies—learning about their proposed activities, developing company responses, seeing that regulatory requirements are implemented, and, inevitably, regulatory record keeping—is an important function of many product safety units.

To a degree, this liaison serves a purpose akin to that of

the legal function—it is defensive, although in another arena. But more than "damage limitation" may be involved, especially for the company that structures its product safety program appropriately.

Although most people associate federal regulatory agencies primarily with their rule-making activities, their activities in fact are far broader. Many agencies collect important information on the characteristics of product-related accidents. While the data provided by the CPSC's National Electronic Injury Surveillance System (NEISS) are probably too aggregated to be of much use to product planners, the in-depth accident reports collected by the agency may prove valuable in helping a manufacturer spot how his product might be improved or test whether a proposed design change might significantly reduce accidents.[10] Given potential competitive and litigation problems, the collection and exchange of detailed data on product performance by manufacturers themselves would probably be impractical.

Several federal regulatory agencies such as CPSC and NHTSA also have the power to force manufacturers to recall products that they deem defective. The exercise of this authority can sometimes seem—and indeed, may be—highly arbitrary. However, the requirement that firms be able to locate and notify their customers of potentially serious product defects—and refund their money or repair or replace the products—can reinforce manufacturers' incentives to monitor the performance of their products in the field. Indeed, the product safety activities of Weinstein's Firm C, a retailer, were keyed closely to these recall requirements.*

This requirement can cut two ways. The law requires firms to inform the government of a potential defect as soon as it is discovered. But determining whether a particular incident

*However, the firm made no attempt to utilize this information to enable the manufacturers of the products it purchased for resale — with whom it shared legal responsibility for product performance—to improve product design.

can be linked to a pattern of similar incidents, thereby creating the presumption of a defect, sometimes requires considerable investigation. Fearful of an arbitrary response, the firm is reluctant to inform the agency before it has completed its investigation. Thus some firms have in the past deliberately distanced their accident investigation from the employee responsible for regulatory liaison. In an effort to counteract this trend, agencies have been broadening the definition of "responsible individual" for purposes of defect reporting.

The Consumer Product Safety Act also requires the maintenance of records to ensure that firms are complying with its provisions and grants the CPSC access to these records. This requirement may encourage formalization and documentation of design-related decisions, or it may be seen as enhancing the danger to the firm's defense posture posed by increased quantities of potentially incriminating paper. Much depends on how the commission chooses to exercise its powers in this regard, and on how a firm's product safety managers choose to interpret the requirement.

Federally established standards play a mixed role in product safety activities. Although they provide goals for the firm, meeting them has, at least in the past, provided little or no protection in a product liability suit—while failing to meet them, even if they make little sense, may be treated as *prima facie* evidence of liability.[11]

How, then, should we evaluate regulatory agencies' contribution to the goal of improved product safety? In his new book, *The Strategy of Social Regulation*, Lester Lave (1981*b*, p. 3) proposes a useful test. Observing that the number of safety-related decisions society makes (many of which relate to the design and use of products) is far too large for any hope of direct regulation, he suggests that,

[the first task of the social regulatory agencies] must be to curtail the worst abuses, not wasting time on unimportant issues, and their second task must be to influence *but make no pretense of con-*

trolling the decisions of manufacturers and consumers. The latter depends on presenting these nongovernmental decisionmakers with facts, analyses, and a framework for making decisions and changing the perception of the importance of health and safety. [Emphasis added]

There is little evidence to support the proposition that the agencies have been successful in "curtailing the worst abuses," and much to suggest the opposite. However, the agencies may have played a useful role—and perhaps a more constructive role than the courts—in raising the level of the debate on product safety; that is, in "presenting ... nongovernmental decisionmakers with facts, analyses, and a framework for making decisions and changing the perception of the importance of health and safety."

As regulatory agencies seek responses to the current barrage of criticism, both they and Congress—which, after all, bears much of the blame for reinforcing unrealistic expectations of what they might accomplish—would do well to ponder how they might enhance this "safety consciousness—raising" aspect of their activities. Perhaps, rather than emphasize business failures, these agencies might look for ways of reinforcing firms' incentives to accept what may seem like increased legal risks to improve the quality of their decision-making processes.

A SUBSTITUTE FOR REGULATION?

Increased corporate product safety efforts deserve to be cheered—but they deserve one or one and a half, not three cheers. They may, on balance, have improved product safety, but it is hard to know by how much, relative to what would have occurred in their absence. Certainly incentives created by litigation have had mixed results. For all their seeming attractiveness as an alternative to regulation, they appear to have proved an extremely blunt instrument, at least in the current legal environment. Perhaps they could be made more congruent with the requirements of improved safety, but as the Weinstein/Henderson exchange shows, this will not be easy.

How does regulation fare in all this? If we believe, with Lave, that regulation can be no substitute for decentralized decision making but, at best, can only reinforce it, then regulation and corporate product safety efforts must be seen as complements rather than competitors. As operated to date, this complementarity has been far from maximized. But regulation may, in the end, turn out to have a genuinely positive role in promoting product safety—a proposition that will surprise those who view it as inherently useless.

14

EUGENE BARDACH

Self-Regulation and Regulatory Paperwork

Regulatory and compliance paperwork, statistical surveys, evaluation and research. Paper as an enforcement mechanism. Site visits. Plans and reports, variances and exemptions, rationality, relevance, due process and participation. The deterrent value of documentation. Data collection and display. Controlling the costs of paperwork. Regulatory competence.

Protective regulation always entails some form of inspection procedure; otherwise there would be no way of knowing whether rules and standards are actually producing the conduct demanded of citizens. A good many programs dispatch their own inspectors to travel around from site to site and directly monitor compliance, e.g., to make sure that machine guards are on punch presses or that milk storage vats are kept at appropriately low temperature readings. However, most regulatory enforcement is really based on self-inspection accompanied by some type of reporting or certification to the regulatory agency that the citizen has complied with the law. Nursing home inspectors do not stand around twenty-four hours a day observing the administration of medications to patients or the serving of "adequately nutritious" meals. Instead, they rely on doctors and nurses to keep charts about patient treatment and on administrators to keep a record of the items and quantities of food bought and served. Inspectors for the Bureau of Motor Carrier Safety unit of the U.S. Department of Transportation (DOT) do not actually ride with truckers to enforce the rules against their driving too many hours without a rest. Instead, they require that truckers keep logs of their "hours of service" and that these be retained by the driver or his company so that DOT inspectors *could* audit them and thereby check for compliance. Inspectorial visits thus give way to "paperwork."

And the more that on-site visits are replaced by a regime of "self-regulation," or regulation by means of an improved system of liability law, the more paperwork is likely to increase and multiply. If and as we move towards the more indirect methods of regulation indicated in previous chapters, therefore, we will also find ourselves burdened with a different kind of regulation.

It is not clear that the public likes regulatory paperwork more than it likes regulation by direct on-site inspection. Practically no one has a kind word to say for paperwork, and many an official report—from the Commission on Federal Paperwork (1977) to a current series of General Accounting Office (GAO) studies to the congressional preamble to the Paperwork Reduction Act of 1980—has borne testimony against it. On the surface, the numbers certainly do appear large. The federal Office of Management and Budget (OMB) estimated in its recent Information Collection Budget for fiscal 1981 that the public was spending nearly 1.3 billion hours annually on federal paperwork, or nearly 600,000 work-years, which "equals or surpasses work years for the entire steel industry or the entire newspaper and periodical industry" (U.S. OMB 1981, pp. 1−2). And these are figures for the federal government alone. State and local governments impose their own paperwork requirements, and these could very well add yet another 50 percent or more to the burden.[1]

PAPERWORK FOR REGULATION

The focus of this chapter, however, is only on *regulatory* paperwork, which is but a fraction—albeit a large one—of all paperwork. "Regulatory and compliance" paperwork is estimated by OMB at about 72 percent of the federal total including taxes, and 40 percent of all non-tax-related paperwork. A good example of the sort of paperwork of special concern here is the driver's daily log, referred to above, which is one of the two most burdensome federal regulatory requirements (the other is the motor vehicle accident investigation and reporting requirement). The log requirement is estimated by OMB to consume 31.5 million hours per year (U.S. OMB 1981, p. 10). The Commission on Federal Paperwork estimated that it uses up 1.2 billion sheets of paper annually (U.S. GAO 1981, p. 13). Yet the log accounts for only about 15 percent of all non-tax-related federal "regulatory and compliance" paperwork which, according to OMB, comes to about 250 million hours per year. Other examples of regulatory paperwork are the weekly payroll reports filed with the Department of Housing and Urban Development (HUD) by contractors and subcontractors who must show compliance with the Davis-Bacon ("prevailing wage") Act,

and documentation showing compliance with the requirements of the Real Estate Settlement Procedures Act that
obliges sellers and lenders to impose a burden of some 11.3
million hours on the public, mainly on businesses (U.S. OMB
1981, p. 30).

Some categories of paperwork that are not ostensibly
regulatory and do not get counted as such by OMB or many
other observers clearly deserve to be included under this
rubric. Applications for benefits, grants, and reimburse-
ments frequently have a regulatory component, in that many
details included in the forms are intended to deter or detect
instances of waste, abuse, and fraud. Perhaps most important, application forms and associated reports requesting
grant or contract *renewals* try to monitor and prevent the
shifting of funds away from targeted objectives to more
general uses. Local school districts, for example, that apply to
the California State Department of Education for federal
Title I funds for "educationally disadvantaged" students
must go into some detail about their numbers, their location
by school site, the sort of program offered, the number of dollars spent per participating student, and so on. Partly in
order to supplement these reports, the department also relies
on several varieties of mandated school advisory councils to
review programs and reports. The logical extension of this
procedure, of course, is for the department to monitor the
composition of these councils as well, lest the councils
become stacked with district employees at the expense of
genuine parental "consumer" interests. Hence each member
of a school-site council must be categorized in the school's
annual report according to whether he or she is employed by
the school district, the parent of a student in the School Improvement program, the parent of a Title I pupil, the parent
of a student in the preschool program, the principal, a
classroom teacher or other school staff member, a community representative, a student, or "other" (see California
State Department of Education form 4–001 [rev. 2–81]).

While by some definitions the school district's paperwork on these points is part of an "application" or "program management and planning" process and would not, therefore, be chalked up to the "regulatory" portion of the OMB paperwork budget, most people in fact perceive the purpose as regulatory — which indeed it is.

The OMB categories "statistical surveys" and "evaluation and research" comprise together some 11 percent of non— Internal Revenue Service (IRS) paperwork, and in many cases these also may contain "regulatory and compliance" elements. "Evaluation" is often connected with the attempt to enforce "accountability" on service delivery programs in order to try to ensure that the agencies or their contractors are complying with the mandate that some statute or executive order has laid down. A state-mandated evaluation of a privately operated but publicly funded drug treatment program, for example, is likely to be seen by the program operators as an effort to hold them to some sort of performance standard. And many a statistical survey conducted by a regulatory agency is just one phase in the development of a new regulation or targeting strategy for enforcement efforts.

But the main problem with regulatory paperwork, however it is defined, is not always its costs in time and money; for some people it is the psychological burden of frustration, alienation, and demoralization. This is especially true of professionals, who resent the loss of autonomy that comes with all regulation, and who chafe at diverting their productive energies into "proving" through paperwork, to an audience of anonymous and probably unsympathetic "outsiders," what they *already know* (or believe) to be their competency. Consider the testimony of one elementary school teacher (Peretti 1980):

In a typical day an elementary teacher deals with sign-in sheets, lunch counts, hall passes, absence slips, rollbooks, attendance cards, class count forms, parent communications, textbook and materials requests, lesson plans, student evaluations, documentation, [and] paperwork relating directly to teaching students. Additionally, different levels of the bureaucracy frequently request distribution and collection of questionnaires, ethnic surveys, free lunch applications, permission slips, walking trip permits, emergency cards, class schedules, federal forms for Impact Aid, home language surveys, audio-visual surveys, needs assessments, nine-week objectives, yearly objectives, report cards, requests for special services, testing materials, program descriptions, time cards, field trip requests, and several profile cards for each student. . . . Teachers learn that their documentations are usually passed up the line without being read. Even when they are read, administrators have no time to verify the accuracy of the statements. Morale is lowered and paperwork becomes a meaningless exercise.

Unfortunately, it is not easy to figure out what is "excessive" paperwork. No quantitative estimate can be offered. Nor can a qualitative assessment be served up with much confidence. We may begin, though, by asking in what ways paperwork might *not* be excessive—that is, what useful regulatory functions it might perform.

THE REGULATORY SYSTEM BEHIND THE PAPER

There are many good reasons to complain about regulatory paperwork, but one class of complaints that we need to exclude at the outset concerns the substantive rules and standards that paperwork is used to enforce. Regulatory standards are often too strict, or overinclusive, or ineffective and therefore wasteful of social resources. But these defects should not usually be blamed on the paperwork procedures used to enforce the standards. The Environmental Protection Agency (EPA), for example, has mandated a system of cradle-to-grave "manifests" to accompany each movement of hazardous wastes from the site of their generation to the site of their final disposal, an expensive and cumbersome process built entirely out of paper flows. These records are to be stored by private firms and kept available for inspection by state and federal officials. The manifests may be costly to develop and maintain, but their expense pales beside that of executing the actions—appropriately secure transportation of wastes to appropriately protected and approved disposal sites—which is very high indeed in some areas of the country. In the case of new drug regulation by the federal Food and Drug Administration (FDA), it is common to complain about the many cubic yards of paperwork submitted by manufacturers in support of their licensing applications. The real problem of excessiveness, however—if there is one—is not with paperwork but with the extensive and costly and time-consuming mandated testing procedures that the paperwork simply mirrors.

In the overall system of protective regulation, paperwork functions as an enforcement mechanism in very much the same way as do inspectors who look directly into matters under their jurisdiction, and this mutual substitutability cannot be emphasized too strongly. It suggests an important lead into answering the question of how paperwork can be useful and therefore not excessive: to the extent that paperwork can act as an effective and efficient substitute for an enforcement regime that might otherwise be based on direct site visits, there is at least an initial presumption in its favor. This presumption can be rebutted by a demonstration that (1) even if the paperwork enforcement system is on balance beneficial, it is still poorly designed and executed and could be better; or (2) even at its best it still imposes costs in excess of benefits. Let us leave these complicating considerations aside temporarily, however, while we explore some of the advantages paperwork has over direct inspection.

From the regulatory agency's point of view, it is easy to see why enforcement through paperwork is often more attractive than enforcement through site visits: for a given expenditure of agency funds, paperwork can greatly extend and deepen the reach of regulatory surveillance compared with what could be done with inspectors. Inspectors must be paid by the agency, but paperwork imposes a burden of self-inspection and self-certification on the regulated parties themselves. Secondly, the time and transportation costs of site visits are much larger than the costs of sending reports and other documents through the mails. True, the agency must incur costs for printing, collecting, storing, and auditing the paper flow that it has mandated, and these can be substantial. Yet in many cases the cost advantage still lies decisively with enforcement through paperwork.

It may also be noted that paperwork and site visits can usefully be combined. Nursing homes in California, for example, are required to maintain extensive records on patient care and financial practices that are regularly audited by inspectors on their occasional visits to the facilities. And California state-sponsored school-site evaluation teams typically prepare themselves for their visits by reviewing the paperwork files of the schools they are to visit.

Another advantage of enforcement via paperwork over direct inspection is that the latter method simply cannot monitor many of the things that the former can—at least at a reasonable cost to those who must comply. Direct inspection is best suited to enforcing rules that bear on the physical environment—e.g., machine guards—but it is much less suited to enforcing rules that govern less tangible yet no less real features of the social world, such as decision processes, motives, intentions, understandings, and so on. Let us catalogue some of the situations in which paperwork seems particularly appropriate.

The past and the future

Compliance with regulations is frequently a process rather than a one-time affair: next year's plans almost always include reports on last year's activities. Plans and reports figure in the ongoing compliance process primarily because they become elements in a continuing negotiating process between applicant and funding source. The applicant points to past accomplishments, while the funding source points to past discrepancies between promise and performance. The applicant points to promises to do better next time; the funding source asks for better assurance that the promises will be kept this next time, and so forth. Of course, inspectors can negotiate in the same way; but plans and reports have the added advantage of creating a documentary record of negotiations, mimicking the legal and moral symbols of private-party contracting, and intensifying personal responsibility by fixing individual signatures to paper promises.

Explanations and justifications

Every regulatory system, whether driven mainly by direct inspection or by the auditing of paperwork, has a way to grant variances and exemptions; and these variances and exemptions must typically be justified by some sort of written explanation. Hence all regulation inevitably has a paperwork and documentation component. And the more flexibility that the system permits, the greater the paperwork and documentation burden.

Consider, for example, the Title 24 energy conservation standards adopted for new residential construction by the California Energy Commission (CEC) in 1978. A builder can meet the standards by following either the "prescriptive" or the "performance" route. The former entails installing certain levels of insulation that the regulation writers have already calculated will achieve some maximum heat loss for the climate zone—weatherstripping windows and doors, holding glazing to 16 percent of the floor area, installing a small enough furnace to hold "design heat loss" to some calculated maximum, and so on. The builder or architect may show compliance simply by including these details in the drawings submitted to the official building department "plan checker." Alternatively, the architect or builder can purchase some design flexibility by abandoning the prescriptive standards and meeting certain "performance" standards, as measured in maximum heat loss values over a year. This route to compliance, however, is complicated by the requirement to document the projected performance characteristics of the building. To facilitate enforcement and assist designers in meeting the performance standards, the CEC developed an elaborate bundle of forms and formulas similar to an income tax return. The "documentation author," as the form puts it, moves line by line through the form doing the calculations according to a reasonably well worked-out algorithm. The sheaf of papers with the results is then submitted to the local building department along with the architectural plans and drawings. (For a good overview of Title 24 and its implementation, see Feinbaum 1981, Danielson and French 1981.)

Demonstrating procedural rationality

If the object of protective regulation is to produce more "responsible" conduct, and if cognitive clarity is often one element in such conduct, then regulatory policy might plausibly aim at getting certain key individuals to think more clearly, to be more "rational," in a word. True, rationality cannot be observed directly by inspectors or by anyone else. Indeed, in many situations it is not clear what "rationality" would be. Still, regulatory policy can construe certain plausible indicia of "rationality" and can insist that these be entered into some sort of documentary record.

For instance, guidelines for preparing environmental impact statements issued by the Council on Environmental Quality (CEQ) have stipulated that the statement must include an analysis of "alternatives" to the policy under review. A proposal to lease offshore oil and gas tracts, therefore, would have to consider a number of options such as reducing the number of tracts offered, not offering any tracts at all, developing certain tracts with stipulated mitigating measures, deferring development pending further study, and so on. In earlier years, the leasing agency (the Department of the Interior) was also obliged to consider "alternatives" to oil and gas as energy sources, including solar energy, nuclear energy, and conservation measures. The guidelines also instructed agencies to consider separately short-run and reversible and long-run and irreversible environmental impacts. While agencies were not absolutely required to adhere to the format indicated by the CEQ guidelines, agencies typically have done so in order to protect themselves against lawsuits charging one or another inadequacy in the impact statement.

Whether or not the guidelines for preparing environmental impact statements actually further "rational" analysis, the indicia of rationality in this area are admittedly not clear-cut. They are much more so in the case of, say, the procedures prescribed by the Food and Drug Administration for licensing new drugs. An elaborate sequence of tests is prescribed, moving from chemical analysis to animal tests to clinical trials with humans. At some stages, "double-blind" experimental methodologies and specific statistical designs are also specified. None of this guarantees, of course, that the drug companies or the regulatory agency will *act* "rationally" on the basis of the accumulated evidence. Nor is it certain—as William Havender points out in this volume—that the evidence will furnish a clear-cut guide to rational action. But the regulations do ensure some semblance of procedural rationality.

Consciousness raising

In an important sense, "compliance" and its close relative, "deterrence," are much too narrow definitions of the objec-

tives of many regulatory policies and programs. The idea behind protective regulation typically is not merely to banish
misbehavior but to encourage higher levels of performance,
greater commitments to acting "responsibly." We do not
want a manufacturer merely to install proper machine
guards and issue a safety manual to foremen. We want
"safety consciousness" on the part of all personnel, from the
lowest wage earner to the highest manager.

Probably paperwork is less suited to consciousness raising
than is direct inspection, which can multiply face-to-face
contacts that potentially (if not commonly, in practice) are
better able to inspire and educate than are contacts mediated by paper flows. Nevertheless, the steady, day-to-day
obligations of some sorts of paperwork might have certain
advantages. Just as inspectors can serve a reminding function, so too can the continuing obligation to fill out certain
forms and documents.

Many of the procedures and documents described above as
rationality-sustaining or exception-justifying also serve this
function, of course. In *Kleppe* v. *Sierra Club*, the Supreme
Court held that the main purpose of the environmental impact statement requirement was to make sure that an
agency took "a hard look" at what it was likely to do to the
environment. Having to fill out the Title 24 energy conservation forms, or at least to stipulate that a proposed building
should be exempted from the documentation requirement,
does serve to remind builders and architects of the public
policy goal of energy conservation. Merely having to go
through the mandated procedures for affirmative action
hiring—and documenting the telephone calls made, the ad-
vertisements placed, etc., about how one has done so—does
in fact "raise consciousness" about the social objectives
behind the requirements, however burdensome or irrelevant
the requirements themselves might seem. University
researchers who in any fashion investigate "human subjects" must obtain prior clearance for their proposed work

from a review committee of their professional peers responsible initially to the university administration and ultimately to the Department of Health and Human Services. Again, while the requirements are often experienced as burdensome and irrelevant, a number of researchers, especially in the early years of the regulations, commented that they appreciated having been forced to think more deeply about certain ethical and practical questions than they ever had before.

Due process and participation

Paperwork requirements may have an especially useful attention-focusing role when the joint action of many semi-autonomous parties is at stake. We mentioned above "plans" that made promises about future action. If the plan is to be produced and executed by only one party, the promises made in the plan perhaps have some chance of being carried out. The more parties involved in the plan, however, the less likely it is to be meaningful—at least under most conditions. Each separate interest describes what it is doing and what it proposes to do in the future, but there is usually no social or political mechanism for reconciling divergent submissions or for imposing some priority order on the several projects. As one person familiar with EPA-mandated local "transportation control plans" (aimed at reducing auto usage and therefore smog) said, "The main instrument of planning here is a staple gun."[2]

Nevertheless, there may sometimes be value in having divergent or even opposed interests, which might otherwise not have a forum, participate in the "planning" process. For example, privately sponsored social service and mental health agencies in California have often used the forum provided by the annual process of state-mandated county plan preparation to seek larger allocations at the expense of public agency service providers who normally dominate the expenditure of state and county mental health funds. The

Health Systems Agencies (HSAs) set up by the 1974 National Health Planning and Resources Development Act
were to incorporate a "consumer" majority on each board.
The framers of the act assumed that physician interests and
those of other professional or institutional providers dominated health planning, and they wanted to give more of a say
to consumers who were "broadly representative of the social,
economic, linguistic and racial populations of the area." The
structures created to accomplish this purpose were in fact
effective in this limited respect, but the overall effect on
policy outcomes was insignificant since the HSAs had only
advisory power and could be overridden by state bodies
(Morone and Marmor 1981, pp. 431−50).

THE REAL WORLD OF
REGULATORY PAPERWORK

Despite these many actual and potential uses of regulatory
paperwork, much paperwork in the real world is bound to be
useless. This occurs for the same reason that all command-
and-control regulation is bound to be excessive: it imposes
standardized prescriptions on highly varied problems, and
this necessarily produces a large number of cases in which
regulatory strictures are too costly or are inappropriate to
the true situation. In addition, many political and
bureaucratic dynamics operate to expand the scope of
regulation so as to impose excessive and inappropriate costs.
Overreaction to scandals and catastrophes is one of the most
important. As a case in point, consider what happened when
the *Washington Post* revealed in September 1979 that the
U.S. Department of Agriculture (USDA) was shipping daily
hundreds of dollars' worth of usable office furniture for
burial in the District of Columbia's Lorton dump. Notwithstanding the GAO's promises to get a better grip on things,
one month later a GAO auditor testified that he saw 2,000

pieces of furniture stored in a USDA basement and $38,000 worth of new, largely unopened cartons of furniture in the agency's attic while the department continued to buy new furniture. The result was, first, a governmentwide freeze on new furniture acquisitions, then a General Services Administration (GSA) order (issued after prodding by Congress and OMB) to every federal agency to draw up and submit an annual furniture requirements and expenditures budget. Exemptions from the freeze were virtually impossible to get, leading to the usual assortment of anomalies and inefficiencies such as expensive electric typewriters remaining unused for want of typewriter tables. The annual furniture requirements and expenditures budget quickly became a bureaucratic laughingstock because it was irrelevant to the day-to-day practical wisdom that—to the skeptics, at any rate—ought to guide furniture acquisitions.[3] It lasted only one year.

The paperwork governing the use of human subjects in university-sponsored scientific research is another case of overreaction leading to overgeneralization. Researchers must document their intended procedures and have them cleared by a central campus committee charged with protecting human subjects. Researchers must also provide the committee with detailed assurances of how they will inform subjects of their risks and their rights to withdraw from the research. In principle, this sort of regulation may be beneficial. In practice, however, it spread from biomedical research, where it was clearly appropriate, to areas where its value was dubious—e.g., administering balance beam walking tests to elementary school children. Finally, overreaction by regulators is often followed by corresponding overreaction by those who are regulated. For example, the environmental impact statement requirement was initially a fine technique for raising consciousness and for generating useful environmental analysis, but it degenerated into the production of thick tomes of environmental description lacking focus, insight, or analytic acumen (Bardach and Pugliaresi 1977, pp. 23–38). This degenerative process was inevitable because impact statement documents were vulnerable to legal challenges as to their "adequacy" and the agencies' obvious defensive counterattack was to throw in as much data and take out as much "opinion"—and perforce, analytic interpretation—as possible.

The technical problems of designing "good" paperwork are often formidable and can inspire administrators to try to compensate by imposing more and more documentation requirements. It is worth remembering that a central function of documentation is to force regulated parties to reveal truths that might otherwise have remained hidden. However, the correspondence between what documentation reveals and the underlying reality is likely to be rather weak. One reason is that devious people will attempt to hide infractions if they think they can get away with doing so. While agencies naturally try to design paperwork systems that will permit auditors to detect evasion, this task is not necessarily simple. The EPA for some time toyed with the idea of requiring extensive annual reports from all hazardous waste generators and hazardous waste disposal sites as to what materials had been sent and received, respectively. By feeding these data into a computer and instructing the computer to match the alleged inflows and outflows, staff thought that they would be able to discern discrepancies and track down violators. On further analysis, however, it turned out that such a task would have been extremely costly, even with computer assistance, and well-nigh impossible were reporting firms to take even moderate pains to disguise the truth.[4]

To conclude that there will be a great deal of misinformation, it is not even necessary to impute evil motives to those who fill out the forms. Human error plays a role. And more important, it is often very costly for reporting agencies to collect, check, and record accurate data—which they are especially disinclined to do if they believe that no one will actually pay attention to the reports. In programs for the aged, for example, we learn:

> Staff responsible for preparing the supporting documents at the AAA [Areawide Agency on Aging] and Title VII [nutritional services and congregate meals] levels, gave a general concensus [sic] that to develop the data on the unduplicated counts, dollars pooled and target groups served was time consuming. Further, they reported the data were often made up; and there was no uniform method for deriving measures of pooled resources or estimates for target groups served.
>
> Many agency responses indicated that completing the report was primarily a political exercise and the numbers had little to do with reality. Some respondents went so far as to indicate that the report required people to make up numbers and lie. Significantly, the numbers prepared are never verified (even on a sample basis) by the SUA [State Unit on Aging] or AoA [U.S. Administration on Aging); nor is substantial documentation required as to the basis for the figures presented. [Estes and Noble 1978, p. 54, and Estes 1979, chap. 7, for a shortened version of this report.]

Even truthfulness and green-eyeshade commitment to accuracy are not enough, however, to make documentation correspond adequately to the realities that underlie it. Frequently there are immense technical difficulties in representing in words and numbers a reality that often is subtle, elusive, and obscure even to the most self-scrutinizing and honorable individual.

Consider "rationality." Some people would consider a thought process "rational" only if the thinker analyzed all possible alternatives and consequences in the most comprehensive manner. Others, following the lead of Herbert Simon and the school of "bounded rationality," would consider this the utmost folly. They would say that true rationality consists of suppressing most data, which are bound to be irrelevant to the usually rather limited options available in fact, and learning how to focus on the key variables and parameters in the system at issue. On this view, comprehensiveness of the sort required in an environmental impact statement, say, is pseudorationality at best and probably undermines the genuine article.

As to the "good faith effort" required by affirmative action regulations and guidelines, while one can easily recognize the polar cases of its strong presence or glaring absence, the middle range is murky. The idea that you could tell very much about it from checking the log of an employer's telephone calls or advertising campaign is dubious at best and conducive of hypocrisy and resentment at worst.

Or consider "plans." Their only reality might be the rhetorical persuasiveness of words on paper. All plans describe some sort of collective action within a single organization or across several organizations. But the people charged with documenting the plan are normally more favorable to it than the other participants in the collectivity that is supposed to carry it out. An environmental engineer, for instance, instructed by his corporate employer to prepare a plan for compliance with state or local water pollution control regulations, is almost certain to put a better face on the plan than others in the organization whose cooperation will ultimately be required to implement it. The engineer, after all, is the specialist and committed professional, while the others, almost by definition, have less of a stake in the plan.

Consider also the inherent limits of words and numbers as descriptors. For instance, the life-cycle cost calculations of different types of heating plants required to be prepared under the Title 24 conservation standards, which are supposed to contribute to "rationality," are full of potential error. Instead of prescribing a range of possible discount rates or future energy prices, the CEC stipulates values for these parameters that are weighted to make electric resistance systems look relatively uneconomic and solar installations look relatively good. A better procedure would be to pick more realistic values; better still would be to have the documentation author prepare a range of estimates based on varying assumptions. But then the whole process would become mired in arcane theories about the statistical treatment of risk and uncertainty. The numbers simply cannot be made straightforward. As to the slipperiness of words, consider the problem of defining "minority" in affirmative action programs. It is not long before one is obliged to consider not only population proportions, but the genealogical purity of an individual with purported "minority" characteristics.

To be sure, these problems pertain to direct regulation as well as to regulation through paperwork and documentation. Since regulatory paperwork is largely self-administered, however, the burden of making sense out of all these inherent ambiguities and of contesting the use of format or definitions that give misleading or inappropriate results falls on the respondent much more than on the administering agency. It is not surprising, therefore, that the most common complaints about government paperwork are that it is "meaningless" and "frustrating."

WHAT IS TO BE DONE?

As I suggested in the preceding section, much of the problem stems from the use of data collection and display by political and regulatory officials as a defense against charges, whether current or anticipated, of insufficient knowledge or concern about some issue. "You mean to say you don't know how much old, usable furniture is thrown away?" Or, "So, if I hear you correctly, Mr. Under secretary, you don't really know what percentage of the nursing homes in which we place Medicaid patients meet local fire codes?" Or, "Do you mean to tell me that we don't really know if the money we are spending on Title VII really is improving the nutritional status of the elderly?" About this source of paperwork generation not much can be done. We could exhort investigative reporters, congressional oversight committee members,

OMB budget officials, and regulatory managers to be less unrealistic in their demands that other people be omniscient. But it is hard to see what would make such self-restraint attractive, given the political rewards of exposing the alleged ignorance or laxity of supposedly responsible figures.

Somewhat more likely than self-restraint by the attackers is improved resistance by the defenders. Given the unrealistically high expectations imposed on government officials to be able to respond rationally and "authoritatively" to virtually any question about their policy domain, officials do not usually stand up and admit that (1) they don't know about a given problem (the life cycle of every piece of furniture, the status of nursing facilities vis-à-vis their myriad local fire marshals' offices, the nutritional results obtained with Title VII money), (2) it would be extremely costly if not impossible to find out, and moreover, (3) even if the answers were available they would probably not affect *policies*, which are constrained by many outside factors. Society would be well served if more officials could learn to respond in this fashion, although encouraging such responses will not be easy.[5]

As observed above, the costs of complying with paperwork requirements, like the costs of complying with protective regulation more generally, fall not on the regulator but on private parties or other governmental agencies. Indeed, the regulating agency may face high political costs for *not* imposing requirements; that is, accusations of neglecting its duties. Is there some way, then, to redesign the incentives facing regulatory agencies so as to discourage paperwork requirements? With regard to certain kinds of paperwork, it might be possible to oblige agencies to *compensate* the parties who had to fill out the relevant forms and documents so that it would no longer be cost-free for agencies (see Morss and Rich 1980, chap. 10).[6] This solution might work with government reporting requirements for general policy purposes. But it is probably not appropriate for most regulatory programs, for which the moral burden of proof is on the respondent's being asked to show compliance with some standard or rule. The financial burden seems logically to follow the moral burden in such cases. Indeed, it would be particularly odd—and politically awkward—were the government to compensate regulated parties for submitting documentation which, in a statistically predictable proportion of cases, was eventually shown to be false or misleading. (On the other hand, this problem might be solved by imposing extra-heavy fines on the violators in order to generate revenues with which to subsidize parties with good records.)

Another method of trying to bring paperwork costs under control is to treat them like a budget item and have OMB set ceilings and allocate "expenditures" as it does for the financial budget. This is the strategy of the Paperwork Reduction Act of 1980 (see U.S. OMB 1981; Neustadt 1981, pp. 28–32). The federal Information Collection Budget prepared under this act for fiscal 1981 and approved by OMB was for 1,228.4 million respondent hours. Agencies requested about 46 million more hours than this, and OMB, following its traditional practices with financial budgeting, cut the requests by almost 4 percent. The act also required each agency to establish a central administrative unit to run paperwork control functions, and it permitted OMB to delegate the clearance of new paperwork requirements to whichever agencies could eventually satisfy OMB with the effectiveness of their internal controls.[7] Until then, OMB would continue to clear all new forms (as had been the legal requirement before the act as well) and, as an enforcement tool to be used against the agencies, no agency would be permitted to take action against any party based on information reported on a form that OMB had not authorized. According to an early report by Richard M. Neustadt (1981), many of the basic prescriptions of the act had already been put in place by an executive order of President Carter in November 1979 and were being shown effective. It remains to be seen, however, how the act itself will work. One concern is that OMB, which has an expanded role under the act, will be so deluged with work that it will clear many items too hastily and others too slowly.

The greatest potential for reducing paperwork may lie in improving the *competency* of the regulatory program managers who design and enforce the documentation and reporting requirements. Both currently and prior to the 1980 act, managers have been obliged to evaluate the "practical utility" of each form or reporting requirement they impose. This is very hard to do, and one result is that agency officials do not take the obligation very seriously. More to the point, they too readily *rationalize* information requests and reporting requirements by stipulating what is absolutely unfalsifiable: that someone, somehow, some day, *might* find some bit of reported data very useful for some purpose as yet unclear. Moreover, computers, with their apparent ability to search through massive data files and correlate everything with everything else, support this illusion. It is little noticed that computer systems cannot operate effectively on unreliable data or that the bureaucratic and human context in which computers are utilized often constrains their actual use within quite narrow limits (Malvey 1981). The EPA designers of the annual report for hazardous waste generators and disposers, for example, scarcely consulted with the computer operators in EPA to see if the data they would have obtained could have been processed usefully. Not until many months had been invested in preparing the reporting forms did they go through the exercise of imagining what they would have done with these data if they could have been processed. Among the questions they needed to ask:

- If we find an apparent discrepancy between wastes generated and wastes properly disposed of, how do we know this is not simply a case of incomplete or tardy reporting?

- How do we know we haven't lost the forms or punched the data into the wrong places?

- If we proceed with an investigation as though there were a potential violation, what backlash do we create if it turns out that there is no violation but only a bureaucratic snafu?

- How can we tell if someone is lying? What sorts of additional computer runs and other inquiries will be necessary merely to establish probable cause for further investigation? Will we have the resources to do these tasks?

- If the regulated community discovers that it is difficult for us to process and utilize these data, do we risk our credibility as enforcers of more important requirements?

Although it took the EPA staff many months to get around to posing such questions, ultimately they did so; and as a result, they scrapped the annual report requirement.

In introductory courses to graduate-level social statistics, students first planning a survey are often urged to make up "dummy tables" filled with imaginary data so as to put a check on the collection of data that will prove to be unintelligible, unreliable, unanalyzable, or unenlightening. It is a very instructive exercise, expressing a profound bit of wisdom. But even when students accept its wisdom, they find it hard to put the prescription into practice. It would be surprising if bureaucrats—for whom data collection often has the same ritual meanings as it does for social science students—were better able or more willing to go through the same sort of drill. OMB and GAO like to berate agencies for having failed to do pilot studies with data collection instruments before imposing new requirements. But a cheaper and even more effective procedure would be for agencies to *simulate* their decision and policy processes; that is, to do a bit of role playing to see how they would, or would not, be affected by the data that might—or might not—come pouring in on any particular tide of paperwork.

Unfortunately, this mental exercise is complicated by what might be thought of as the paradox of deterrence. If regulatory documents received by an agency were immediately to be shredded or burned without a glance at their contents, this fact would not necessarily prove documentation was excessive. Indeed, it might prove the reverse. A prime function of regulatory paperwork, after all, is deterrence; the best testimony to the system's deterrent effectiveness might therefore be a compliance level so high that there would be no point in the agency's auditing the paper flow in search of violators. The IRS, for instance, is alleged to destroy routinely the majority of employer- and taxpayer-submitted documents because the storage and search costs involved in auditing them would be too high relative to their yield and because taxpayers' fear that they *might* be audited induces sufficient compliance anyway.[8]

An interesting case in point is furnished by a program run from 1976 to 1979 by the U.S. Department of Agriculture to prevent the feeding of diethylstilbestrol (DES) to cows and sheep within the fourteen days before they were sent to slaughter (see U.S. GAO 1980, pp. 22–24). Each seller was to sign a certificate to that effect. Over 300,000 farmers and feedlot managers were potentially affected by this regulation. In the three-year history of the program, however, the FDA, which was charged with enforcing the regulation, used the DES certificates only *once* to identify a violator, and the USDA referred only 47 cases to the FDA for investigation. Partly on the basis of these data, the GAO concluded that DES inspection certificates were worthless. Yet it should be noted that the cost burden on the industry was not terribly high—just over $2.2 million over the three years according to USDA estimates—and it is conceivable that this cost was justifiable if it actually held the number of violations to a mere 47 from what might have been, say, 50,000 or 100,000.[9]

Besides role playing and simulation of the future, regulatory competency can also be enhanced by learning from the past. In 1980–1981 the CEC set about to revise standards and paperwork requirements under the Title 24 building energy conservation program. It held numerous and lengthy hearings and actively solicited recommendations from the many affected interests; the resulting standards were much more performance-based than previously. The CEC has also been developing a computer program to be made available at no or low cost to simulate the energy consumption of planned buildings and thus reduce the paperwork burden on builders and architects. In addition, the CEC has promised to develop a "point" system that even further simplifies prospective performance calculations. Pacific Gas & Electric Company has already developed such a system—so many points for insulation, for fireplace efficiency, for weatherization, etc.—in implementing its program of cash payments to energy-conserving builders, and the CEC has been working to adapt this system to its own needs (see Feinbaum 1981).[10]

INFORMATION FOR WHAT?

Paperwork is a form of regulatory enforcement that, in many circumstances, effectively and efficiently eliminates the need for direct field-level enforcement. It is often less costly and, as we have seen, may be more appropriate as well.

As with all forms of regulatory enforcement, however, paperwork tends to grow excessive. There are many situations in which documentation requirements, which impose standardized prescriptions on a varied world, are irrelevant or ineffective. Political pressures, technical difficulties, and a tendency among agencies to compensate for poor data by requiring more and more of it, exacerbate the paperwork problem.

Modest success at curbing the paperwork explosion can be expected from the strategy underlying the recent federal Paperwork Reduction Act, which essentially treats the expenses of the paperwork burden as direct financial costs and seeks to impose budgetary review and allocation rules on them. Possibly even more progress can be made by means of simulation exercises or plain hard thinking in challenging the fundamental, ritualistic belief that "information" is a good in itself that is possessed of near magical properties to solve problems and guide decisions (Feldman and March 1981).

IV

Conclusion

15

EUGENE BARDACH

ROBERT A. KAGAN

Conclusion: Responsibility and Accountability

Self-help and communitarian patterns of responsibility. Political dimensions of imposed communitarianism. Accountability systems. The decentralizing principle. Regulatory agencies and the ethos of responsible regulation. Reforms. The need for reason and rationality.

Public policies in the field of protective regulation can be seen as attempts to redefine and reorganize the practice of social responsibility. Responsibility can be organized in many different ways, but it helps to think about two polar patterns against which real-world specimens may be compared. One is "self-help," which allocates the responsibility for undertaking protective measures to the presumptive beneficiaries of such measures. Under a self-help regime, consumers take responsibility for checking out the safety and performance of products and for maintaining them properly after purchase; tenants control their children and repair their own dwellings; and people who care deeply about breathing clean air either move away from steel mills and smoldering coal-mine dumps or sustain the cost of suing the mill or mine owners to abate the pollution. The second polar pattern is "communitarian." It allocates most responsibility for undertaking protective measures to parties other than the likely beneficiaries. In the communitarian pattern, manufacturers design their products to be safe against all forms of use, misuse, and abuse; mill and mine owners redesign their processes or install abatement equipment to keep the ambient air clear and healthy for their neighbors; and friends and neighbors watch out for and discipline one another's children.[1]

In the past century we have drifted—at the level of law and public policy, although not in private morality—toward the communitarian model of responsibility, particularly as applied to technologies involving hidden or uncertain risks, risks against which self-help is often not very effective. The communitarian model also is reflected in laws requiring affirmative action plans for the elimination of gender- and race-related bias in employment and many other areas— again, the sort of hard-to-prove injustice against which self-help is of only limited value. This drift away from the self-help model has surely been accelerated, too, by the attitude that the presumably deep-pocketed and technologically sophisticated corporation can more efficiently exercise responsibility than can individual consumers and workers, and that those who profit from an enterprise should, on moral grounds, pay all the social costs apparently associated with it. Thus, according to the communitarian view, if motorists persist in driving recklessly and in killing and maiming each other, automobile manufacturers should take (or be compelled to take) responsibility for redesigning cars to absorb impacts as well as for installing seat belts (even if motorists do not demand them). If drivers do not take responsibility for buckling up, the responsibility lies on the manufacturer to devise warning buzzers and, if these "fail," automatic restraint systems.

The communitarian model, of course, can hardly be expected to pervade social practice in a spontaneous and thorough manner. It is too deeply at odds with traditional common law and conventional morality, which still rest predominantly on notions of individual responsibility or a much narrower concept of social responsibility—that is, the obligation to avoid only purposeful or clearly negligent harm to others. In addition, the communitarian model is sometimes (though not always) at odds with norms of efficiency and practicality. In the case of automobile safety, for instance, post-crash injury prevention is most efficiently accomplished by having people wear seat belts. But if in fact people do not buckle up—and studies show that the great majority do not—then this self-help approach may be driven out by the communitarian approach of having the government oblige automobile manufacturers to install air bags. Yet air bags are terribly costly and would almost certainly not be desired by the bulk of consumers for this reason. Nor would they be favored by the automobile manufacturers. In fact, the elaboration of the communitarian model of responsibility is frequently imposed by government rather than spontaneously generated out of the interactions of private parties. In more and more areas of everyday life, government officials—guided by the political process—assume the tasks of defining precisely what responsible behavior consists of, allocating those responsibilities through specific legal rules, and enforcing these rules strictly and evenhandedly. This political version of communitarianism also puts responsibilities *on* the government: if it neglects to promulgate and enforce appropriate laws and regulations, the citizenry is entitled to punish officials by means of public criticism, lawsuits, and removal from office.

The tenor of antiregulatory political comment in recent years reflects a growing awareness of the full implications and limits of a shift towards a communitarian and political model of organizing social responsibility. For all its own limitations, self-help, as economists keep reminding us, is generally a very efficient organizing principle. For example, it is easy to overlook the extent to which market pressures and liability law, institutions activated by self-help, can effectively induce business enterprises to invest in quality assurance, safety, and fair employment systems designed to build economically valuable goodwill by ensuring that the company will act responsibly toward others. Further, the political dimensions of imposed communitarianism have exposed it to the imperfections of bureaucratic and electoral politics. For some social problems, therefore, even an imperfect self-help regime of social responsibility may be thought to be superior to a government-imposed communitarian regime that is also bound to be rather imperfect. For other social problems, some intermediate point, reflecting more of a balance or mixture of imposed responsibility and spontaneous or self-directed forms of responsibility, may be appropriate. This, at least, is the implicit assumption of all the contributors to this volume. To see their reform proposals in this light, however, it is first necessary to distinguish between the concepts of "responsibility" and "accountability"—concepts that are central to governmental attempts to impose and reallocate responsibility.

ACCOUNTABILITY V. RESPONSIBILITY

Regulation typically arises out of the perceived failure of private parties or local government entities to act in a fully responsible manner, along with the failure of existing regulators to act effectively. The expectation and fear of additional failures of responsibility underlie the implementation of such programs. Thus, they usually rely heavily on monitoring mechanisms, reporting rules, and carefully defined specifications of responsible action. Through these rules and regulations, the regulated are made accountable to the regulators, and the regulators are made accountable to the courts, to their legislative overseers, and to the people. But mechanisms of accountability may come into conflict with the basic goal of enhancing responsibility.

Consider the case of an industrial safety engineer who is told by an inspector from the Occupational Safety and Health Administration (OSHA) that several fire exits must be cut into the wall at a cost of some $50,000. The engineer objects that the chances of fire in that area of the plant are remote, that large numbers of workers rarely congregate in the area anyway, and that the $50,000 could be much better spent on improving safety training programs for new workers in the metal grinding shop. OSHA regulations, however, make the firm accountable for failure to have fire exits but not for failure to improve safety training programs; and OSHA managers make the inspector accountable for enforcing what's in the rules, not what might be most effective or pragmatic. Moreover, the safety engineer is accountable to higher management within the firm for keeping the firm out of trouble with the government as well as for improving worker safety. In such a case the safety engineer's sense of *responsibility* probably argues for the training program, but his place in the structure of *accountability* probably dictates compliance with OSHA orders and thus investment in the fire exits. In this case, not only are responsibility and accountability conceptually distinguishable, but they are also in conflict.

By responsibility we mean, roughly speaking, the felt obligation to treat someone else's interests as though they were identical with your own; and by accountability we mean—also speaking roughly—the vulnerability to criticism or more severe sanctions imposed by others for potential failures to discharge responsibilities as the reviewing parties interpret them. To put it another way, responsibility comes from within and accountability comes from without.

Responsibility and accountability need not necessarily be at odds with each other. Indeed, regulatory programs have consciously used their leverage to hold private firms accountable in order to induce them to accept, even if not necessarily to welcome, social responsibilities. As George Eads has pointed out in chapter 13 on corporate product safety efforts, partly due to prodding by federal regulatory efforts and by new developments in product liability law, corporations have established specialized units that carry out research on how products are actually used, involve themselves in product design, and supervise quality control routines at the production level. In addition, corporate environmental affairs units have expanded dramatically as engineers, biologists, and toxicologists are put to work to keep the company out of trouble (or to discharge the firm's environmental responsibilities, as its public affairs office would have it) by researching the impacts of production and waste disposal activities and by designing cost-effective abatement measures. Corporations have expanded worker safety units as well, adding teams of industrial hygienists (experts on industrial diseases) who inventory chemicals used, establish maximum exposure levels and techniques, and monitor workers' blood, lungs, and hearing. Larger school districts now employ special education officers to help insure that physically and mentally handicapped children are tested regularly and receive an "appropriate education," as the law puts it, and that hard-to-handle children are not erroneously classified as retarded.

Specialists such as these may, of course, languish on the periphery of power within their organizations. Often they do. But often, too, they make inroads. Their initial presence may be a concession to increased demands for accountability, but after a time the host organization may begin to adopt, to a certain degree, the "responsible" outlook promoted by the specialists. The organizational ethos may change somewhat.

Whether any particular accountability regime ultimately erodes or strengthens the ethos of social responsibility, however, depends critically on how it affects the morale of this expanding "trusteeship stratum"—all those doctors, teachers, union officials, fire marshals, engineers, industrial hygienists, mayors, and so forth, whose jobs require them to take responsibility for the interests of others. Probably the most obvious and the most troublesome cause of demoralization among members of this stratum is the need on occasion to subordinate responsibility to power and interest— e.g., when a mayor with "good government" aspirations feels obliged to appease an important campaign contributor by appointing his incompetent nephew to a minor post, or when a corporate accountant is pressured to bend "accepted accounting principles" in order to brighten the balance sheet.

But a subtler and perhaps more insidious form of demoralization comes from being forced consistently to misdirect effort from objects of high priority to objects of low or dubious significance because accountability obligations do not coincide with the trustees' own considered notions of what responsibility consists of in their particular organization or decision context. Our hypothetical safety engineer who was obliged by OSHA to spend $50,000 on fire exits instead of worker training might have had his morale impaired thereby. And indeed, it is not unimaginable that the OSHA inspector might himself have acknowledged the incorrectness of the outcome and might not have completely escaped being demoralized by "the system" too. This is not to say that any single such incident has an important effect on these individuals or on the fabric of social responsibility woven daily by the trusteeship stratum. But the cumulation of such experiences across time and across many individuals is certainly more problematic.

Apart from the moral value our culture places on the idea of individual responsibility, there are practical reasons to want to design accountability systems that enhance rather than diminish responsibility. Simply put, accountability systems just cannot do the job alone. New hazards and novel policy problems will always emerge that are not covered by existing rules and standards and are unknown to those who administer them. In the case of regulatory programs, occasional or chronic budgetary strictures will often mean that many or most establishments are underinspected; and most important, the usual defect in regulation—that it is tied to concrete prohibitions and narrowly detailed prescriptions even though successful trusteeship depends on conduct motivated by more diffuse aspirations and attitudes—can be remedied only by a widely dispersed corps of responsible, as opposed to merely accountable, supervisors and other functionaries. In short, because there can be no perfect accountability system, it will always need to be supplemented by a large—even a predominant—element of individual and spontaneously exercised responsibility.[2]

ELICITING RESPONSIBILITY

Most of the essays in this volume in effect call for regulatory reforms that leave as much discretion as possible to individuals—especially those in the trusteeship stratum—to set their own priorities regarding the *means*, and to some extent even the *ends*, of "responsible" conduct.[3] The essential strategies are twofold: (1) to substitute self-help for government-defined communitarian modes of organizing responsibility wherever possible; (2) failing that, to furnish the responsible actors with as much discretion as possible in regard to means and techniques, preferably by "loosening up" the government-imposed accountability regime, reducing its degree of technical specificity.

Bacow, for instance, advocates more self-help by unions in bargaining for worker safety and health measures. Union safety representatives with knowledge of the specifics of each workplace, he suggests, would have a better sense of sources of accidents, their imminence, and how much it is worth to reduce them than would the Washington-based draftsmen of OSHA regulations that are applicable, across the board, to thousands of workplaces. Let the workers take some responsibility, he implies, for deciding what safety measures are really worth fighting for. On the other hand, Bacow suggests ways the government could assist the unions in helping themselves. O'Hare's proposals for information disclosure in regard to home construction and automobile safety amount to the same thing: help people to help themselves. Once government ensures consumers access to relevant data, let them choose not only the means but the goals also, that is, the level of protection that they themselves want.

To a lesser extent, this is also the argument of the essays on the liability system, which suggest that a strengthened and streamlined litigation process could be both more effective and more reasonable than direct governmental regulation in controlling some hazards, such as injury from toxic substances and poorly designed or manufactured products. The rules of liability law establish the boundaries of an enterprise's responsibilities to others, but the enterprise retains more discretion in estimating the seriousness of the risks its products or operations pose, and has more discretion in choosing how to reduce those risks it fears will actually lead to serious harms (and massive damage awards). The en-

terprise is held accountable by the courts for its miscalcula-
tions and acts of carelessness, but in a way that encourages
rather than overrides its own responsibility for forethought,
caution, and corporate preventive techniques (although
there are exceptions when the liability law is itself over-
controlling and thus undermining responsibility). Even the
introduction of insurance into the liability system, while it
limits discretion and gives underwriters and loss control consultants a role in the way businesses make decisions, probably reinforces business responsibility for the most part. As
Ferreira points out, if the premiums are set right, private
parties are motivated to look for the most efficient risk-
reducing measures. The prospect of premium increases is the
accountability device that, ideally, would keep automobile
manufacturers, drivers, handlers of liquefied natural gas,
and so on, behaving "responsibly."

The principle of decentralizing the choice of means is also
evident in Levin's account of the Environmental Protection
Agency's (EPA) "bubble" policy, whereby firms are exempted from agency-prescribed uniform abatement measures in favor of lower-cost measures of their own choosing,
so long as their overall emissions meet the standard. Indeed,
the decentralizing principle could readily be extended
beyond the single firm to the aggregate of pollution sources
in an airshed, and the trade-offs coordinated by means of
some pricing mechanism or "pollution rights" auction.
Similarly, Grumbly's article describes the process by which
the U.S. Department of Agriculture decided to selectively
withdraw from enforcement of detailed meat-processing regulations that required inspection of each chicken and each
carcass of beef, on condition that the meat-packing firm establish its own certifiably professional and competent quality
assurance system. The enterprise remains accountable, not
for each and every departure from the government's rule
book, but for failing to maintain and implement its own professional standards; and now the firm, not the government

rule-makers and inspectors, must take responsibility for deciding what manufacturing conditions seriously risk product contamination and for deciding how those risks can most efficiently be eliminated. Eads's chapter 13 on quality assurance practices within firms suggests still other ways in which responsibility can be decentralized even while retaining some degree of business accountability to governmental regulators and the institutions of the liability law.

CAN REGULATORS BE MADE MORE RESPONSIBLE?

It is a lot easier to think up ways to make the private sector more responsible than it is to make government abandon its concern for the strict, detailed, and uniform accountability systems that tend to displace private responsibility. Why should the governmental designers of accountability systems to be imposed on the private sector go to all the trouble of designing maximal flexibility into these systems? There is no obvious answer to this question. Danaceau shows how field-level inspectors *could* carry out their duties more creatively and more effectively, but it is evident that they do not always do so and that it is not easy to administer a far-flung inspectorate of ordinary mortals so as to bring about this result.

The problem, of course, is that government agencies themselves continue to be held accountable, by the courts and by the political system as a whole, for any departure from deeply held norms of legality, aggressive enforcement, incorruptibility, and bureaucratic regularity. As noted in our introductory chapter, an agency leader takes major legal and political risks in encouraging lower-level enforcement officials to depart from the letter of the regulations in accordance with their own discretionary judgment concerning

what is really needed. At the rule-making level, the essays by
Sullivan and Pape show how a certain degree of flexibility
can be, and has been, introduced by "tiering" regulatory
targets with regard to their potential for creating serious
hazards or to some other principle. But they also show how
easy it is for agencies to get bogged down in factual detail and
technical disputes in devising regulatory subclasses, and
that those difficulties often stem from reasons beyond their
control. Here, too, the culprit is not merely the factual complexity of the world, but the problem of governmental accountability, as reflected in the heavily judicialized norms of
rationality, equal treatment, and formal proof that now pervade the administrative rule-making process.

Bardach's chapter on regulatory paperwork explains a
common pathology that afflicts regulatory efforts to decen-
tralize responsibility. Since the government regulators can
be called to account for any serious instance of irresponsibil-
ity on the part of regulated enterprises granted some discretion, they insist that the regulated report and explain and
justify their every move, that they document their acts of responsibility via endless tests, signatures, release forms, impact statements, statistics, and promises about the future.
Any successful effort to substitute true responsibility for
accountability, Bardach's chapter suggests, can occur only
through the growth of consciousness within regulatory agencies and lawmakers of the dubious benefits of too much
accountability.

Some governmental initiatives, such as the recent paperwork reform measures and the cost-benefit analysis institutions described by Eads's chapter 8 on regulatory oversight,
seek to instill just such a consciousness. The truly "responsible" regulator, these reforms imply, is concerned not
merely with formal accountability, measured in terms of
departures from strict laws and ambitious reform goals, but
is attentive to all the direct and indirect effects of regulatory
requirements, their potential harm to the social and economic

fabric, and their potential inadequacy in providing protection to those who cannot protect themselves. But, as we pointed out with respect to the regulation of businesses, the development of an ethos of responsible regulation is no easy matter, for regulatory agencies suffer from rapid turnover, short-term and often highly politicized leadership, and a turbulent and mistrustful political environment in which they can be attacked one day from the Left, another from the Right. Thus even devices to instill a higher level of economic thought and professionalism, such as the Carter and Reagan review mechanisms described by Eads, can easily be attacked—as Eads himself does with respect to the Reagan administration's plan—for allowing too much back-room bargaining and not enough public accountability. Another risk is that regulatory review processes will develop into little more than a constant demand for formal cost-benefit analysis (yet another accountability requirement) without inculcating in the agencies themselves a spirit of efficiency-conscious responsibility.

REASON, AUTONOMY, AND SPONTANEITY

The difficulties of loosening up accountability to make room for increased responsibility can easily produce an attitude of resignation. "Because people do make errors and do lapse into arrogance or corruption," it might be argued, "the excesses of accountability are the price we pay for having systems of governmental regulation. And because no humane society can do without regulation of a very large number of technological hazards and social problems, no humane society can do without excesses of accountability." Such resignation, while resting on a large element of truth, is wrong, we think, both because the underlying "truth" is somewhat overstated—there *are* ways of loosening up accountability, at least to some extent, without giving up on regulatory goals, and the chapters by Levin and Grumbly provide concrete lessons on how this can be done at the bureaucratic and political levels—and because too much is at stake in numbly accommodating ourselves to an ever-increasing volume of centrally formulated rules and account-ability regimes. Efficiency—getting the socially desired level of protection at the lowest cost—is only one reason for preferring accountability regimes with a light touch, that is, regimes that nurture reflective responsibility as well as legalistic compliance. Important cultural values are also at stake.

Consider first the value we place on reason and rationality. While we do not want or expect reason to govern all our ac-tions, we do want it to govern in areas like business decisions, scientific and engineering debates, and most areas of public policy. Yet a certain amount of unreasonableness inheres in every regulatory regime, and especially in those that rely on detailed general rules to establish legal rights and duties, or that prescribe in dense regulatory prose the specific kinds of applications, forms, reports, plans, and statistics that must be submitted by the regulated. As we pointed out in our in-troduction, unreasonableness is inevitable because centrally formulated general regulations will always be either over-inclusive or underinclusive as applied to the diversity of the world; hence, following the rules (or being punished for not following them) will not appear to "make sense" in a large number of particular cases. Of course, as a society we may gradually be learning to expect that the bureaucrats we must deal with will be guided less by reason than by rigid pro-cedures, or by the inclination to expand and exploit their authority, or by interagency rivalry, or by sheer incompe-tence and indifference. But we surely do not want the pre-serves for unreason to grow any larger than necessary or, worse yet, for the portion of the trusteeship stratum located in regulated enterprises to lapse.

A second problem with accountability systems, of whatever variety, is their antagonism to values of autonomy and privacy and individualism. To be accountable is to be reviewable, and to be reviewable means that one must open oneself to others, one must anticipate what others want and think, one must adopt a language and idiom that is responsive to the language and idiom of others. Even if there were never any actual dispute between the reviewer and the reviewed, the simple requirement that the reviewed be willing to explain himself, so to speak, is a burden of a sort. Idiosyncratic reasoning, sloppy or nonexistent documentation, impulsive or intuitive leaps into action—accountability frowns on these things. Accountability instead calls for rationalization and bureaucratization.

The progressive rationalization of life in the modern and bureaucratic world is a more encompassing process, of course, than the simple extension of accountability. Romantic critics of modernity have deplored this rationalizing thrust. Obviously they are right, up to a point. But where is that point?

The point we have in mind is the "right" balance, or mix, between order and spontaneity, between rationality and impulsiveness. Individuals will differ on where the point should be in their private lives, and they will differ as well on where it should lie for the society as a whole. More precisely, perhaps, most people will not even know where the point *is*, either in their own lives or in the society, because there is no standard metric against which to measure its movements, and we get used to the blessings and curses of increasingly extensive accountability systems. Doctors are getting used to keeping more detailed records of patient treatment and billing; professors are getting used to being evaluated by their students. Public school principals are well socialized now into the routines of reporting to school district officials and to federal and state officials and to parent councils; and they have learned to assemble masses of documentation about every conceivable element of their school's life, from pupil absentee notes to teacher ethnic identification. And all citizens who file itemized tax returns have had to adjust their outlook on record keeping and tax planning (including the mix of activities one engages in and their timing) to take account of the tax cuts. Modernity makes us into minions in the bureaucratic organization of the social welfare state, whether as taxpayers or as service recipients or as objects of regulation. Personally, we believe that this rationalizing and bureaucratizing tendency has been too strong and that the ethos of accountability that nurtures it ought therefore to be resisted.

Finally, we may note that a social preference for more elaborate accountability systems is, on the whole, a preference for conservatism over innovation and change; not to act is safe, while action exposes one to the burden of reporting and justification, and to the risks of error, being found at fault, and exposure to subsequent penalties. Adhering to legally specific obligations that codify the experience of the *past* tends to inhibit present action. While many commentators have proposed that OSHA move away from enforcing specific input standards in favor of the act's "general duty" clause requiring employers to furnish a safe and healthy work environment, neither employers nor labor unions nor the agency found this congenial. Both regulators and regulated seem to prefer to have specific duties spelled out, to be held to these, and not to be responsible for the general run of socially beneficial things that *might* be done.

The conservatism inherent in the accountability ethos of recent years is perhaps best illustrated by the inclusion of "social impacts" in various environmental impact statements of one or another kind. Might coal development affect the traditional life-styles of Wyoming ranchers? If so, it is an "impact" that federal coal-leasing agencies must take account of if not always mitigate. Will the construction of a high-rise hotel in downtown San Francisco drive up neighborhood rents and indirectly displace from several hundred to several thousand low-income residents? Yes, said the San Francisco City Planning Commission, and proceeded to compel the developers to put up a kitty to alleviate the impact on the residents as a condition of granting the required use permit. No longer is the society content to say simply, "Hard luck!" and go on about its business. It is almost as though the new accountability ethos has created a quasi—property right in something like "security" or "living conditions to be taken for granted." This right is not yet fully enforceable at law, but it acquires more and more moral strength and, in some cases, legal validity.

When government is involved, the conservative bias is especially pronounced. As Charles Schultze observed in his Godkin lectures six years ago, the first commandment for government is to do no direct harm. Thus, the Food and Drug Administration cannot balance the harms to persons who might experience adverse side effects from a proposed new drug against the harms to persons whose health would deteriorate in its absence. The "no direct harm" rule protects the first class extremely well, but there is no comparable rule to protect the second class at all. Hence, caution bordering on inaction is the agency's traditional, and rational, attitude. Nor can the Environmental Protection Agency (EPA) bring itself to register new biological pesticides that would displace less safe and possibly less effective chemical pesticides until the new pesticides have undergone extensive and expensive tests—a requirement that has excluded or slowed down the superior substitute. When government must play a role, the presumption is normally with the status quo.

It is possible that the newer conservative attitude is more beneficial than the earlier ethos of letting the engines of change run free, while letting people in the way take their lumps and letting society take its chances. Again, it is a question of judgment as to what the right balance point should be; and people will legitimately differ. However, it should make us wonder if we may not have gone too far when we recognize that an FDA of yesteryear applying today's rules would probably not have approved aspirin, and that a correct prediction of today's astonishing number of automobile-related deaths and serious injuries—not to mention the automobile's effect on family cohesiveness, community, the corner grocery store, and sexual mores—would have made an environmental impact statement on the automobile in the 1920s dismiss the new technology out of hand.

In sum, then, too much accountability is injurious to social well-being. For all that we value it, accountability comes with a price: economic inefficiency, an abridged role for reason and rationality, an erosion of individual autonomy and privacy, the progressive bureaucratization of life, and the stifling of social change. Even an imperfect ethos of responsibility—which of course carries its own price—will often be preferable to an ethos of accountability. To the extent that protective regulation displaces responsibility with accountability, it thereby imposes an important, if often concealed, social cost, a cost that the architects of regulatory policies ought to bear in mind. The ancient Romans asked, "Who will guard the guardians?" We would ask, "Who will protect us from our protectors?" and answer that the protectors must assume at least some of the responsibility themselves.

16

EUGENE BARDACH

ROBERT A. KAGAN

Postscript: The Yuletide Regulatory Reform Wish List

As this volume goes to press in December 1981, we observe in many a newspaper and magazine the published ruminations of various celebrities and better-known intellectuals touching on their favorite books of the past year or their predictions for the future or their hopes for the coming year. In the spirit of the season, therefore, we invite ourselves to offer more of our own ruminations in the form of our own wish list.

Our list concerns practical steps that we *think* governmental officials should and could take towards improving protective regulation. We emphasize "think" for two reasons. First, we are uncomfortably aware of how deceptively plausible certain measures can appear from the heights of an ivory tower, the defects of which are either well known to the soldiers involved in the day-to-day trench warfare against regulatory dilemmas or will soon be discovered by them or by other academics sitting in their own ivory towers. Second, we cannot know at this distance whether the recommended measures really could be taken in the near future—although we do believe that, with a certain amount of political courage and energy, they could be. While ours is a wish list for the Christmas season, we are not counting on Santa Claus to make the wishes come true. Here and there an administrator alone could do the trick. In other cases a much more fundamental and far-reaching consensus would need building, certainly at the elite level and conceivably at the popular level as well. But even in such cases, measures to begin building the consensus can be taken right away.

CLEAN AIR

We wish the Environmental Protection Agency (EPA) would proceed as rapidly as possible to extend the excellent principles underlying its present "bubble" policy (for which see Levin's chapter 3 in this volume) to polluting sources owned by different firms. The bubble concept permits managers within a firm to do less abatement than the law requires for certain sources—those that would be very costly to abate—provided that they adopt more stringent abatement measures for sources that would be less costly to abate. So long as the total emissions coming out of a hypothetical bubble atop the plant do not exceed a certain amount, managers thus have flexibility to find the lowest-cost mix of abatement strategies. The problem with extending the bubble concept across firms with different owners is that the low-cost abaters would obviously want compensation (most obviously from the high-cost abaters) in exchange for their willingness to take on extra cleanup obligations that would otherwise be equally shared. There is a need to fit such compensation or trading arrangements not only into the system of regulatory law (the Clean Air Act and all its associated regulations), but into the common law of property and contracts as well.

The institutional and technical problems of shifting in this direction are more or less soluble, and indeed, progress has already been made towards "controlled trading" in the form of EPA's "offsets" policy and its policy of permitting the "banking" of certain emissions rights.[1] Perhaps one of the most important things the EPA could do immediately — probably through state and local environmental agencies in most states — is to improve the inventory of current emissions and to develop a system for tracking changes in the inventory. After all, the controlled trading of obligations to clean up (and corollary rights not to have to do so) can work only if it is known who is discharging what amounts of what pollutants and might therefore have such obligations.

Another important step would be to loosen up the standards applied to newly constructed sources, especially those in very dirty or very clean areas, which are now obliged under the law to implement something like the "best" or "most stringent" control technology, in exchange for imposing tighter controls on existing sources. Although controlling new sources is often cheaper than retrofitting controls on old sources, this is not uniformly so. In many cases, equivalent reductions of emissions could cost only a fraction as much if carried out by old sources rather than by new ones forced to abide by the "best technology" sort of requirement. Arguably, the EPA even now has the discretion to move in this direction by taking economic costs more into consideration.

It would be helpful, to be sure, and probably legally necessary, for the EPA to have the backing of Congress for these changes. Fortunately, the Clean Air Act is due for reauthorization, and potentially fundamental redesign, this year. Although the act has helped clean up the air in many localities, or at least has prevented it from getting worse under the impact of economic growth, it has been and promises to be extremely costly. The 1979 report of the U.S. Council on Environmental Quality (1980, p. 666) projects the total direct costs of air pollution abatement under the act in the decade 1978–1987 to be $278.9 billion. In addition, there are indirect costs. The act is filled with anticompetitive restrictions that benefit special interests, and its addiction to tight deadlines and "technology-forcing" standards has led to furious and costly evasive strategies on the part of industry, followed by countermeasures by government, and ending with uncertainty and confusion on the part of everyone. The Clean Air Act's command-and-control approach is fundamentally mismatched with the problem it is supposed to solve. Or more precisely, it is matched only halfway correctly. The correct half is that governmental command is required to establish pollution reduction goals and to impose duties on polluters to clean up. The mistaken half is that the control system is run by relatively centralized bureaucratic means.

We do not, of course, imagine that Congress will do much about the anticompetitive elements in the act that serve special interests—and it could even make them worse—but we certainly wish it would rewrite the law to permit more conscious balancing of costs against benefits, to recognize the weak or nonexistent scientific foundations on which adverse health effects of air pollution are postulated, and to encourage more flexible methods of allocating abatement responsibilities. The administration has a potentially critical leadership role to play here. Last year, when the Clean Air Act was due to be reauthorized, it chose to delay the issue by encouraging Congress to continue the status quo for a year. At that time, the administration was preoccupied with budget and tax cuts. We wish the administration would move constructively and aggressively in this current year, however.

PHARMACEUTICALS AND MEDICAL DEVICES

We wish the regulatory process were quicker to clear beneficial new drugs. At present it takes years and many millions of dollars for a drug manufacturer to clear the numerous hurdles set up by the Food, Drug, and Cosmetics Act to prove that a proposed new drug is both safe and effective. Near-universal agreement reigns among experts in this area that one important adverse result is a considerable number of "orphan drugs"—unapproved drugs of potentially great value but limited to relatively small markets. Their limited marketability makes their development uneconomical to manufacturers facing the high front-end drug approval costs. For instance, the best-known antidote for plutonium poisoning, a close chemical relative of the agent used to treat lead poisoning, has not been approved by the Food and Drug Administration (FDA) and is not available for stockpiling in those few laboratories and other facilities where plutonium accidents might occur. Although the drug company whose scientists discovered the drug was willing, as a "public service," to manufacture the drug at a loss, given its potentially tiny market, it was unwilling to spend the more than $50 million required to test the drug in order to obtain FDA approval (Lasagna 1979, pp. 27–32).

One solution would permit the marketing of these highly specialized drugs without FDA approval. Warning labels could be affixed to containers proclaiming that the drug had not been approved by the FDA and emphasizing the need for the continuing supervision of a physician.

There is less agreement that FDA regulation has unduly slowed the introduction of beneficial new drugs more generally, although we are inclined to line up with the critics. An orphan drug exemption could have an important secondary benefit in our opinion, therefore, in that it could open the door to greater flexibility for all drugs. For this very reason, to be sure, an exemption for orphan drugs would be opposed by advocacy groups that oppose great flexibility or, in some cases, would like even tighter control of new drugs (and the companies that manufacture them).

In the case of orphan drugs, at least, we are ready to assume that a desire to maintain their reputations for safety and quality, along with the fear of expensive liability awards, would sufficiently motivate manufacturers to regulate themselves adequately without FDA supervision.[2] Patient protection would be further enhanced by the likely greater exposure of prescribing physicians to malpractice liability should the patient suffer bad side effects. In some cases, indeed, the liability system might impose too great a risk on drug companies and physicians; it might be desirable to invent a system whereby patients could voluntarily assume some of the risk themselves by signing appropriate waivers.

Liability law and concern for reputation are also powerful protections against the development and marketing of unsafe new medical devices. In addition, most purchases of such devices are mediated by sophisticated professionals like hospital administrators or physicians. We therefore wish that Congress would repeal the Medical Devices Act or, failing that, that the FDA would start to enforce it much more selectively. "Class I" devices like bedpans, tongue depressors, and arm slings clearly should not be regulated at all. Even "Class III" devices, which are life sustaining or life supporting or are implanted in the body, might not need to be regulated. As Timothy Sullivan has pointed out in his chapter 5, the tiering strategy followed by the FDA has not worked well, despite the evident good intentions behind it. Perhaps the tiering principle should be to regulate by exception: regulate only those devices that would lead to grave harm in the event of poor performance and that would not adequately be held to high safety standards by the combined forces of the marketplace, the liability law, and professionalism.

We might reiterate here a point made in our previous chapter on liability law: to provide a plausible substitute for command-and-control regulation, it might be necessary to develop new and specialized institutions to administer the liability law—to help bring down transaction costs, to facilitate proof of claims, and to rationalize compensation awards. We mentioned specifically David Leo Weimer's proposal to develop such an institution to handle pharmaceuticals in lieu of the FDA. We wish the idea would be picked up by some governmental body, such as the President's Task Force on Regulatory Relief (chaired by Vice-President Bush), and given further study and greater legitimacy.

CHEMICALS

While we are on the subject of designing new institutions to administer the liability law, we will mention once again Stephen Soble's interesting proposal to substitute liability for the regulation of toxic substances under the Toxic Substances Control Act (TOSCA; see above, chapter 11). Again, this is an idea that deserves both more legitimacy and further elaboration of the details. The governmental body that wins the competition over Weimer's proposal probably deserves to win the honors to study this one, too.

We wish we could wish that the EPA would drastically improve the administration of TOSCA. For years it has been haphazard, ineffective, and immensely burdensome to both industry and the government. However, the design of the present system is so fundamentally flawed that there may be no point in raising anyone's hopes for it. The basic problem with the act is that it forces regulators to pretend to have knowledge about supposed gaps in the knowledge of chemical manufacturers, based on their own research and tests.[3] But this is inherently absurd; for, as the saying goes, we don't know what we don't know. The only solution is to give the parties with the greatest advantage in generating relevant knowledge the incentive to do so, and to combine it with the incentive to continue to generate such knowledge (usually through more and more testing) until the point where the risks of "foreseeable" harm are just balanced against the costs (including delays in the introduction of useful products) of doing even more testing. The Soble scheme attempts to do this, and therein lies its great advantage.

FOOD ADDITIVES

We wish the Delaney clause, which forbids the use of food additives known to cause even the slightest degree of cancer in animals or humans, would disappear. Although it has not been invoked very often in the past as the rationale for banning or attempting to ban certain substances, it could well become much more important in the future as the number of known carcinogens increases apace with the growth of scientific knowledge and with the improvement of techniques for detecting various pesticide residues or other contaminants in foods. In addition, new conventions for interpreting test data are emerging that make it easier to infer carcinogenicity from inherently uncertain statistical data. As Stuart Pape observes in his chapter 7, the Delaney clause might have been tolerable decades ago at the time of its adoption, when carcinogens were seemingly uncommon and prohibitive measures aimed at them were in no danger of landing on substances that one might have regrets about prohibiting. But nowadays, even though it is very unlikely that the actual prevalence of carcinogens in the environment has changed much, our enhanced ability—and willingness—to see them practically everywhere makes the Delaney clause a very clumsy weapon indeed.

Certainly there are political problems with repealing the Delaney clause outright. Opponents would charge that the proponents favored causing cancer. A possible strategy to avoid this pitfall might be to require the FDA to balance the health risks of a possible carcinogen against its possible health benefits. In the case of nitrites, for example, the anti-botulism benefits of this additive could have been balanced against the supposedly increased risks of cancer.[4]

OCCUPATIONAL SAFETY

We wish the occupational safety area were less conflict ridden or, at any rate, that the government were less involved in the conflicts. Some conflict is inevitable, of course, since in the short run workers benefit from Occupational Safety and Health Administration (OSHA) regulation (at least to the degree that OSHA regulations do in fact produce safety benefits) while employers bear the costs. Probably the most fruitful area for cooperation is in the technical debate over the efficacy of various standards, a debate that occurs each time OSHA wishes to adopt or repeal a standard. Although OSHA does have an advisory committee structure, it does not appear to have been hospitable to consensus building. Admittedly, the creation and maintenance of consensus-building mechanisms is a subtle and difficult task, and we would best refrain from offering specific suggestions on the details.[5]

Lawrence Bacow's proposals to mobilize unions and the

leverage of collective bargaining, described in more detail in his chapter 9, seem to us sound and amenable to almost immediate implementation. In particular, we would put at the top of our wish list the proposals to expedite the training and installation of union safety stewards.

We also wish OSHA could be rid of its statutory mandate to levy fines for first-instance citations. These fines are low, and seem mainly to make OSHA immensely unpopular rather than to deter accidents; and they clearly destroy the opportunities for OSHA to elicit cooperation by acting as a "consultant" (when appropriate) rather than as a "cop." To make this proposal more acceptable politically, it might be linked to a proposal to raise the penalty levels for willful and serious violations.

We wish Congress would amend the Occupational Safety and Health Act to empower and oblige OSHA to balance compliance costs against safety and health benefits. Exactly how this balancing should be done ought to be left to OSHA to decide, along with the discretion to impose regulations for which estimated costs exceed estimated benefits if and when hazards are concentrated on relatively few workers or redistributive goals are thought to be very important.

An interesting idea recently proposed by Robert S. Smith (1981, pp. 311–38) would substitute for OSHA safety (but not health) regulation a $500 deductible for every successful workers' compensation claim, that deductible to be paid by the employer. This would be equivalent to a partial injury tax, which has been advocated by many economists as superior to regulation in inducing employers to institute aggressive safety programs while at the same time leaving employers flexibility in their choice of such programs. The deductible payment would be even better than an injury tax in at least one important respect, however: it would lead to lower workers' compensation premium payments and would therefore be less costly in the aggregate to employers. The deductible would also be better than another popular proposal: improved merit rating of workers' compensation insurance premiums, a program that would be saddled by high administrative costs if it were to be carried out effectively.

At present, the federal government has no direct authority over workers' compensation insurance, which is state regulated. However, OSHA could offer the inducement that a state with an adequate workers' compensation—related program of injury prevention would be absolved from some or all of the obligation under the Occupational Safety and Health Act to mount its own occupational safety regulatory program or to accept the federal OSHA's doing the job instead.

PRODUCT PERFORMANCE

We wish the Federal Trade Commission (FTC) would come to think of itself more as a facilitator than a regulator of market transactions. An appropriate and venerable governmental function is the standardization of weights and measures, without which commerce would be greatly impeded. In the current era, we have a need for standardized measures that go beyond pounds (or kilograms) and feet (or meters). We need measures that capture elusive performance characteristics, like energy efficiency (for home building materials, say) or durability under prolonged exposure to sunlight (for exterior paints, say). Very often trade associations manage to develop useful standardized measures of such characteristics and to induce their members to employ them. But very often they do not, or there are no trade associations active in the industry in the first place. In such cases, the FTC could act like a trade association and facilitate the development of standard performance measures. The commission has done this already with regard to home insulation—by most accounts, relatively successfully. The FDA, building on methods pioneered in Europe, did the same for sunscreen and suntan products.

Not all manufacturers initially would have an incentive to describe their products using these standardized measures, though of course some would. In the long run, market pressures would probably force most manufacturers to fall in step. But governmental agencies could reinforce the process by allowing manufacturers to advertise that their products had been tested and rated by government-approved procedures.

It could even be made unlawful to make product claims about certain performance characteristics without using the approved standardized measures. This last strategy seems highly appropriate for the tire quality grading program now administered by the National Highway Traffic Safety Administration (NHTSA). It is now mandatory, very costly, and of dubious efficacy. Were it to be made voluntary (a step that might require congressional action) on the terms described here, the system might be improved. Manufacturers would have an incentive to develop a comparative performance rating system that would not only satisfy the government's requirements but would also satisfy their own desires to have a useful promotional tool. O'Hare argues in chapter 10 that this is a convergence very much to be desired.

Simple informational strategies might not be sufficient to deal with the problems of product safety regulation. If there are fairly homogeneous consumer preferences about the level of safety desired in a product—and often this is not a bad assumption, we believe—the variety of choices allowed by mere informational strategies is not especially beneficial. Standards are preferable. Industry groups and professional associations have been more active in recent years, under the prodding of the Consumer Product Safety Commission (CPSC), in setting needed safety standards for certain products. The CPSC has an appropriate but limited role to play in the standards-setting process—a fact that it has indeed acknowledged—but there is probably a greater role for it as an epidemiologist of product-related hazards. We wish the

CPSC would improve its system of collecting and interpreting product-related injury statistics, and would focus its limited analytic resources on a handful of its higher-priority projects, e.g., those concerning chain saws, urea formaldehyde foam insulation, and upholstered furniture.

In a similar vein, we wish the NHTSA would sponsor more research aimed at identifying the relative crashworthiness of different automobile makes and models. Such knowledge would permit insurance companies to furnish stronger incentives, through the premium structure, to increase auto safety. As Ferreira argues in chapter 12, this development is a precondition for having the insurance industry substitute for the NHTSA as a "regulator" in this field.

INSPECTORS

In conclusion, we have a wish that applies to no agency in particular but to all agencies that employ inspectors and auditors. We wish agencies would use these resources more efficiently, concentrating them on the sites and hazards where these personnel would do the most good.

The "value added" principle would provide a useful guide to the deployment of a reduced inspectorial staff. For many risks and many enterprises, infrequent government inspections can add very little to the level of protection already provided by liability law, consumer pressure, labor unions, insurance company inspectors, or in-house professionals, often acting in combination with government regulations and closely relying on them. Thus, inspections by OSHA or its state equivalents can add comparatively little in terms of ordinary *accident prevention*, especially in factories with strong unions and active, professionalized, worker safety programs. On the other hand, OSHA inspections can probably provide a considerable measure of extra protection in detecting and abating occupational *health* problems that result, after long latency periods, from exposure to invisible fumes and particles; for in this area workers and unions are less adept at recognizing risks, workers' compensation law provides less of a deterrent, less sophisticated managements may be ignorant of the problems, and abatement is costly.

Recent reforms in meat inspection, as described in Grumbly's chapter 4, provide possible models for cutbacks and redeployment of inspectors in other federal and state agencies. The U.S. Department of Agriculture (USDA) stopped enforcing enormously detailed regulations in those plants that had installed competent, professionalized, and organizationally powerful quality assurance systems. Similarly, the FDA and related state agencies might substitute audits of company quality control systems, their powers, and their operations, for detailed enforcement by government inspectors of "good manufacturing practice" regulations, at least for the more sophisticated food and drug manufacturers and with respect to products for which the threat of expensive lawsuits provides a strong inducement to quality control.

For some agencies, targeting inspectors at only the worst risks—or transforming inspectors from detailed rule enforcers into auditors of intracorporate protective systems—is impeded by laws or policies that require immediate inspections in response to each and every citizen complaint; for many, if not most, complaints divert inspectors to lower priority problems and places. We wish, therefore, that agencies, with legislative support if necessary, would devote more energy to devising methods of prior screening or less labor-intensive ways of dealing with complaints, such as using the telephone or using intermediary organizations to verify that the problem complained of is indeed serious. One model, currently being picked up by OSHA in Washington, is provided by the agreement worked out between California's Division of Occupational Safety, Bechtel Engineering, and the labor unions at a major construction site: safety complaints are first routed to a special management/labor safety committee, and state inspectors do not make routine inspections (as contrasted with responding to alleged emergencies) and enforce detailed OSHA rules as long as the joint committee periodically demonstrates that it is doing a good, aggressive, accident prevention job.

Finally, we wish that all enforcement chiefs would take seriously Paul Danaceau's description (in chapter 6) of the good inspector and try to provide training and institutional support for enforcement officials who can use some judgment in rule enforcement and thereby elicit cooperation more effectively. To this end, agency leaders would have to devise ways of rewarding inspectors for being reasonable and constructive rather than for issuing large numbers of citations.

POST-POSTSCRIPTUM (P.P.S.)

Santa, you may think this is a pretty long wish list. By North Pole standards, maybe it is. But down here in the lower forty-eight, we and others know that it could be made a lot longer. We've said nothing about aviation safety, for instance, though the Federal Aviation Administration has been both underregulating and overregulating for many years. But this is an area in which you no doubt have a personal stake and perhaps some ideas of your own. What we'd like to know is this: to whom do you send *your* regulatory wish lists? And what can be done about naughty legislators, chief executives, and regulators who ignore them?

V

Notes
References
About the Authors
Index

NOTES

1. Eugene Bardach and Robert A. Kagan: "Introduction"

1. Environmental, health, and safety regulations, the Commerce Department estimated, would cost copper producers $3.5 billion between 1978 and 1987 (Hartman et al. 1979; *Wall Street Journal,* 26 April 1979). More than 30 percent of iron and steel foundries' capital investment in the mid-1970s was absorbed by regulatory compliance (Miske 1979). Federal safety and pollution controls, by some estimates, added $500 to the cost of the average 1976 automobile, or $3.35 billion for all cars sold (Weidenbaum and DeFina 1978). Polyvinyl chloride producers spent $119 million, or $23,751 per exposed worker, to comply with OSHA emission reduction regulations (Northrup et al. 1978.)

2. Aggregate cost-benefit analyses, it should be emphasized, often suffer from grave methodological weaknesses. It is enormously difficult to devise a politically acceptable measure of the benefits to society of more humane nursing home care, cleaner air, a larger bald eagle population, and so forth. There is also the distributional problem: even if a regulation is calculated to produce costs in excess of benefits in the aggregate, it might still be defensible if the harms it would eliminate are concentrated in a discrete, powerless group (such as poor or uneducated consumers, nonunionized cotton mill workers, or handicapped students) and if the costs can be passed on and spread across the vast majority of citizens. On the other hand, techniques for estimating compliance costs, particularly unanticipated, indirect, and longer-term costs, are also poorly developed. Nevertheless, cost-benefit analyses, if used as devices to stimulate thought about the trade-offs involved and less costly ways of achieving regulatory goals (rather than as mechanical decision rules), are certainly useful. See, generally, Freeman 1978, Ackerman 1974.

3. By way of contrast, there have long been widely accepted, if largely untested and clearly overgeneralized, theories of why regulatory *ineffectiveness* occurs. The "symbolic politics" theory, for example, holds that once legislators can take credit for having passed legislation to "deal with" a social problem, they lose interest in giving—or never really intended to give—regulatory officials the necessary powers or resources to implement the law (see Edelman 1964). The "capture theory" (formulated primarily in the context of single-industry economic regulatory programs) holds that, regardless of legislative intent, regulatory officials over time will become dependent on regulated

firms for information, cooperation, status rewards, and later employment, and hence will become co-opted to the industry's point of view (see Bernstein 1955, Mitnick 1980). Many of the toughness-enhancing regulatory reforms referred to above were designed explicitly to counteract presumed tendencies toward capture and indifferent enforcement. As is sometimes the case in social science, the theory pointed the way to human action that would disconfirm its claim to universal validity. See Quirk 1981, Anderson 1981, Weaver 1978.

4. More precisely, perhaps, regulators are usually criticized more severely for failing to prevent certain kinds of concentrated harms that result directly from lax regulation than for the more diffuse harms to persons unknown that may result from the "unanticipated," second-order effects of "tough" regulation. For example, the Food and Drug Administration (FDA) and the congressional committees that supervised it were especially concerned, throughout the 1960s and much of the 1970s, with preventing horrifying thalidomide-type side effects from new drugs and were especially sensitive to criticisms of laxity in that regard, but were much less responsive to the criticism that a large but more diffuse group of persons was exposed to suffering or death because of the FDA's overcaution and the regulatory delay in bringing beneficial new drugs onto the market. See Seidman 1977.

2.   William R. Havender: "Assessing and Controlling Risks"

1. These agents are by no means to be equated with "chemicals" or "pollutants," a common misinterpretation. Instead, the estimate refers to the *total* sources of environmental differences, which are in the main related to cultural and personal practices. Whether or not one smokes, chews betel nut, chooses to reside in sunny climes at high altitudes, eats fibrous or fatty or pickled foods or moldy peanuts or corn, drinks alcoholic beverages such as Calvados, is sexually promiscuous or abstemious, or bears one's first child at an early or late age, are all factors that have been shown to be correlative with—and in some cases, causal to—particular cancers. Only a small fraction of all cancer in the United States is presently thought to be attributable to workplace chemicals or to general environmental pollution with man-made chemicals, namely, 4 percent and 2 percent respectively (Doll and Peto 1981, pp. 1245, 1251, and table 20).

2. There are many theoretical reasons for thinking inflection points or thresholds must frequently exist. For one, the human organism has evolved in a sea of naturally occurring carcinogens, so it is likely to have developed defenses for coping with these in normal circumstances. In fact, we have direct evidence of such a defense in skin pigmentation, the level of which determines sensitivity to ultraviolet (i.e., sunlight) induced skin cancers. Another defense is DNA repair, which can be accomplished by many identified enzyme systems. One genetically caused defect in DNA repair—namely, xeroderma pigmentosum—leads to greatly elevated proneness to sunlight induced skin cancer. Other enzymatic systems are known to be in the liver where they are constantly at work cleansing the blood of toxic materials. Any of these systems can be saturated or overloaded by sufficiently high doses, and there is little reason to expect that cancer effects seen only in animals whose normal defense mechanisms have been overloaded by high doses must necessarily be predictive, either qualitatively or proportionately, of the results to be seen at does that allow these systems to function normally. In addition, some enzyme systems are known that not only metabolically *activate* carcinogenic substances but whose level is inducible by those same substances.

For these, the dose response must be nonlinear, curving upwards at high doses. Finally, many apparent carcinogens may be acting by means of "promotion" rather than by "initiation"—that is, by enhancing the effects of true carcinogens. Practically nothing is known about the dose response of promotion; there is not the slightest theoretical reason to think that its dose response must in general be linear.

3. Only one such "megamouse" test has been carried out. In brief, the chemical used (2-acetyl amino fluorene) induced tumors in only two organs, the liver and the bladder. For liver tumors, the incidence at the lowest dose (which was only five times less than the highest dose) was excellently predictable from the incidence seen at the higher doses by a linear model; but for the bladder tumors there was a clear inflection point, and the low-dose risk would have been overpredicted manyfold by linear extrapolation from the higher doses (Littlefield et al. 1980, pp. 23, 27). Nature is not yielding her secrets easily!

4. For saccharin, see Havender 1979, pp. 17–24, Hoover and Strasser 1980, pp. 837–40, Wynder and Stellman 1980, pp. 1214–16, Morrison and Buring 1980, pp. 537–41; for hair dyes, see Clemmesen 1981, pp. 65–79; for DDT, see Laws et al. 1967, pp. 766–75, World Health Organization 1971, and Council on Occupational Health 1970, pp. 1055–56.

5. For sugar, see Hoffman LaRoche 1978; for pepper, see Concon et al. 1979, pp. 22–26; for eggs, see Nelson et al. 1954, pp. 441–45; for Vitamin D, see Gass and Alaben 1977, p. 477.

6. In fact, in the famous saccharin rat studies, males but not females developed tumors. Thus, even within a single species under uniform test conditions, males failed to predict the outcome for females (Office of Technology Assessment 1977, pp. 50–60). This weakens the basis for predicting a significant cancer risk to humans, particularly women, from these results.

7. Personal communication from John Mendeloff in 1981.

8. For a general discussion of the "knowledge" problem, see Hayek 1945, and Sowell 1980.

9. This is another instance of maximin thinking—taking the worst possible case in the population (fetuses and young children) as the basis for regulating everyone else.

3. Michael H. Levin: "Getting There: Implementing the 'Bubble' Policy"

1. Under the Clean Air Act (CAA) as amended, EPA was eventually directed to set NSPS, reflecting "the degree of emission limitation and the percentage reduction achievable through the application of the best technological system of continuous emission reduction which (taking into consideration . . . cost . . . and any nonair quality health and environmental impact and energy requirements) the Administrator determines has been adequately demonstrated" for major categories of new or altered industrial facilities that increase emissions of regulated air pollutants above certain cutoff levels (CAA Section 111, 42 U.S.C. 7411 [1979]). EPA was also directed to set still more stringent emission limits, through a preconstruction permit program, for major new "sources" seeking to commence operations in clean- or dirty-air areas. These were to reflect either Best Available Control Technology (BACT, for clean-air areas), defined as "the maximum degree of reduction . . . which the permitting authority, on a case-by-

case basis, taking into account energy, environmental, and economic impacts and other costs, determines is achievable ... through application of production processes and available methods, systems, and techniques" with applicable NSPS as minimum requirements; or Lowest Achievable Emission Rate (LAER, for dirty-air areas), defined as either "the most stringent emission limitation ... contained in the implementation plan of any State for such class or category of source, unless the owner ... demonstrates that such limitations are not achievable, or the most stringent emission limitation ... achieved in practice by such class or category of source, whichever is more stringent" (CAA sections 160–69, 171[3], 42 U.S.C. 7470–79, 7501[3] [1979]). The following passages generally refer to the act as it existed after the 1977 amendments, since the changes were progressive and integral.

2. Individual stack tests cost $5,000–$10,000, take 2 to 3 days, and require substantial advance notice to perform. For an expanded version of the points in this and the following paragraphs, see Drayton 1978.

3. Two well-known examples include bicycle-safety regulations, drafted by the American bicycle industry for the Consumer Product Safety Commission (CPSC), which would have excluded foreign-made bicycles from the domestic market; and safety rules for swimming pool slides, which conformed to the industry leader's production molds and allegedly drove domestic competitors from the field. See Cornell et al. 1976, pp. 493–94; "Taking a Dive at the CPSC," *Regulation*, July/August 1981, p. 7. See also JACA 1975.

4. See, e.g., Hahn and Noll 1981 (re marketable permits for SO_2 for the South Coast [Los Angeles] Air Quality Control District); also statement of James Smith et al., Philadelphia Air Management Services Division, to the Senate Committee on Environment and Public Works (2 June 1981; re emission fee/subsidy plan as alternative SIP for Philadelphia).

5. The principal arguments were that this bubble rested on difficult technical determinations that plantwide emissions had not increased, that it would allow plants to leave long-lived new facilities uncontrolled merely by closing old ones that would have shut anyway, and that it would reward polluters who had installed the least amount of control on existing facilities.

6. The rationale for this compromise was that operators altering existing facilities needed more flexibility than those constructing wholly new ones.

7. The court partly relied on the "purpose" of NSPS to *enhance* air quality through the narrowest reasonable definition of "source": the more narrow the definition, the more "sources" would be subject to stringent control. This was dubious reliance in light of the NSPS' primary intent to discourage flight of new industry to less-regulated areas—a purpose that did not apply to modifications. Moreover, since new facilities meeting NSPS would still *add* emissions to the plant, the bubble appeared to accomplish air quality enhancement more effectively than the court's disposition, at least over the short term.

8. This lack of use was one of the major reasons cited by the agency's Office of General Counsel for the Solicitor General's refusal to seek review of *ASARCO* in the Supreme Court. Letter, Joan Z. Bernstein, General Counsel, EPA, to William D. Nordhaus, Member, Council of Economic Advisers (undated; week of 20 June 1978).

9. Emission Offset Interpretative Ruling, 41 *Federal Register* 55524 (21 December 1976). The ruling required such sources to install LAER control technology, to obtain

more than enough reductions from existing emitters to offset their remaining emissions, and to meet several other conditions. Though it was justified within the agency as a way to compensate for states' inability or unwillingness to control existing sources more tightly, this ruling was EPA's first full-dress attempt to use market forces to obtain new emission controls. It represented a tacit admission that, at least for existing sources, direct regulation alone was not enough.

10. For similar reasons, the agency had grudgingly adopted a limited eligibility bubble, applicable only to modifications, in regulations specifying control technology requirements for plants in clean-air (PSD) areas. See 43 *Federal Register* 26380, at 26394 (19 June 1978).

11. (Revised) Emission Offset Interpretive Ruling, 44 *Federal Register* 3274, at 3276–77, 3282 (16 January 1979). The critical condition was that approved SIPs had to demonstrate both attainment of ambient standards by December 1982, and reasonable further progress towards attainment (RFP), measured in annual incremental emission reductions, during the interim.

12. The 1976 offset ruling had banned banking on the ground that "extra" reductions should accrue to the states to assure attainment "as expeditiously as practicable." See CAA Section 110(a)(2)(A), 42 U.S.C. 7410(a)(2)(A) (1979). This confiscatory approach was bound to discourage better voluntary control by existing sources. The 1977 Clean Air Act amendments removed the legal basis for this confiscation approach and paved the way for the shift. See 44 *Federal Register* at 3280.

13. Memorandum, Joan Z. Bernstein, General Counsel, EPA, to William Drayton, Jr., Assistant Administrator for Planning and Management (undated).

14. E.g., a new suggested limitation that bubbles not result in increased *concentrations* of the bubbled pollutant, rather than not create or aggravate any ambient violation. Since a bubble shifts emissions to the most cost-effective control locations, it will by definition produce some increase in ambient concentrations somewhere, unless the emission plumes from the bubbled points precisely overlap.

15. Letter, Richard Ayres and Frances Dubrowski, Natural Resources Defense Council (NRDC), to James Kamihachi, Economic Analysis Division, EPA (22 September 1978). See also NRDC, "Comments on Proposed 'Bubble Policy'" (15 March 1979).

16. See "Guidance on Modeling Involving Point or Process Sources." Memorandum from Walter C. Barber, Director, Office of Air Quality Planning and Standards, to David Kee, Director, Air and Hazardous Materials Division, EPA Region V, 19 January 1981.

17. The block here was a policy consideration. If states gave bubble credit for surplus reductions from existing sources that would later have to be controlled to Reasonably Available Control Technology (RACT) levels under approved SIPs, relied-upon reductions from those sources might be undermined, since they would *already* have been controlled to allow emission increases elsewhere. Especially for major sources with local political power, it might be difficult for state agencies to "revisit" these approved trades and require them to be undone. The solution was yet another compromise. Large plants could agree to a RACT baseline, below which further reductions could be credited towards bubbles. Smaller plants could elect either actual emissions or RACT-level emissions as their baselines, and if they chose RACT they would be granted a five-year federal immunity from further SIP requirements.

18. See EPA press releases of 16 January 1981, entitled "EPA Announces Major Changes in Bubble Policy" and "Detailed Statement on Bubble Policy Changes."

19. See, e.g., "How to Limit the Rising Costs of Stricter Regulation," *Chemical Week,* 21 January 1981, pp. 36–40; Shabecoff 1981; Hamilton 1981; Hagerty 1981; Smith 1981, pp. 796–98; Mosher 1981, p. 362; Ryan 1981, pp. 8–9; "Cutting Red Tape in Emission Rules," *Business Week,* 4 May 1981, pp. 62F–62H; Alexander 1981, pp. 234–54; Tucker 1981, pp. 31–38; Pasztor 1981, p. 29 Drayton 1981, pp. 38–52; Raufer et al. 1981, pp. 839–45; "Putting the 'Bubble' Control of Pollution to the Test," *Chemical Week,* 9 September 1981, pp. 22–24.

6.   Paul Danaceau: "Developing Successful Enforcement Programs"

1. Danaceau (1981) provides detailed descriptions of the on-site inspection activities of Limpert, Hollenbeck, and Finucane. The experience cited in this chapter comes largely from observations the author made during one week spent in the field with each of the three model inspectors. Each week also included discussion with the inspectors as well as the representatives of the companies being inspected regarding their respective roles in developing more effective and successful enforcement programs.

2. Danaceau (1980) provides a discussion of how people in a city of 50,000 perceive and respond to government regulation.

8.   George C. Eads: "White House Oversight of Executive Branch Regulation"

1. Whether the Reagan administration will seek to alter substantive statutes that forbid or discourage cost-benefit analysis remains to be seen. Its Clean Air Act proposals certainly sidestep the issue.

2. Memorandum for Heads of Executive Departments and Agencies from David A. Stockman, Director, Office of Management and Budget: "Certain Communications Pursuant to Executive Order 12291, 'Federal Regulation,' " 11 June 1981, p. 2.

3. Some agencies, to gather information required to frame intelligent regulatory options, make use of a device called the "Advance Notice of Proposed Rule Making" (ANPRM). This should be encouraged. I do not know whether OIRA extends its formal authority to ANPRMs, but it should resist any temptation to do so. It will be hard enough for OIRA to frame intelligent priorities for its activities if it concentrates on genuine NPRMs and ignores the "fishing expeditions."

4. The Supreme Court's recent "Cotton Dust" decision, *American Textile Manufacturers* v. *Donovan,* reemphasizes the need to do this.

9.   Lawrence S. Bacow: "Private Bargaining and Public Regulation"

1. For a full review of the health and safety activities of unions, see Bacow 1980, pp. 60–88.

2. *Whirlpool Corporation* v. *Marshall,* 48 LW 4189, 4194 (1980).

3. For a description of case studies of environmental regulation, see Susskind, Richardson, and Hildebrand 1978.

10. Michael O'Hare: "Information Strategies as Regulatory Surrogates"

1. This example is contaminated by arguments from externalities, like damage to the injured person's family, or the risk that he will become a public charge. I will return to these questions.

2. A concept much underappreciated in the social sciences, an operational definition defines a dimension that provides the process by which it is observed. For example, an operational definition of *the height of a building* might be "the tangent of the angle read from a transit focussed on the top of the building and located at the elevation of the building's base, times the horizontal distance from the transit to the building's nearest wall."

3. This article contains an extensive bibliography of books and articles about the economics of information. A shorter version appears as O'Hare 1981*b*.

4. The guarantees in question apply to property-value losses that may result if the plant operates as it should. If an accident were to occur, of course, the operator's liability insurance would cover the much greater damages incurred.

5. National Fire Protection Association, telephone interview, October 1981.

6. American Cancer Society, telephone interview, October 1981.

7. Karig 1981 provided some refinement of this concept in a class paper.

8. W. Kelly, *op. ignot*. It is a continuing embarrassment to the academic information retrieval industry that no concordance to the works of this sage exists.

11. Eugene Bardach and Robert A. Kagan: "Liability Law and Social Regulation"

1. See, for example, *Borel* v. *Fibreboard Paper Products*, 493 F.2d 1076 (5th Cir. 1973), opening the way for lawsuits by thousands of exposed workers who inhaled asbestos fibers over the years and apparently, as a result, contracted asbestosis (an emphysema-like disease) and mesothelioma (a lung cancer). In one such case, a jury awarded $450,000 to an insulation installer who suffered from asbestosis; in another, a widow won $3 million. See Schept 1980, p. 1, and Krieg 1979, pp. 3, 6.

2. In Soble's proposed statute, compensation for "pain and suffering" would be authorized, unlike workers' compensation, but would be limited to one-half the total award.

3. An objection to this system might arise from the fear that chemical firm managers would be tempted to gain sure profits (and credit for them) today by speeding up or cutting down on current testing while discounting the risk of damage claims ten or twenty years hence—when they personally might no longer be with the corporation, or might have moved up to another job. But that objection may underestimate the impact of the enormous liability threat posed by such a mistake, and hence the motivation of corporations to structure incentives and career lines and pension rights to avert that kind of temptation. Moreover, chemical company officials cannot be sure that a hazardous chemical will not generate certain harms and liability suits soon after it hits the market as opposed to twenty years later.

4. See *Eisen* v. *Carlisle and Jacquelin*, 417 U.S. 156 (1974 [notice must be sent by plaintiff to all members of the class]); *Sosna* v. *Iowa*, 419 U.S. 393 (1975); and "Developments in the Law: Class Actions," *Harvard Law Review* 89 (1976: 1319). The Supreme

Court has also limited the aggregation of very small claims under state law in the federal courts by holding that the $15,000 jurisdictional minimum for such "diversity of jurisdiction" actions must be met by each member of the class; *Zahn* v. *International Paper Co.*, 414 U.S. 291 (1973). A plaintiff's lawyer in a sex discrimination class action against a large manufacturing company told us that her law firm's investment in prosecuting the action would be a minimum of $200,000, including attorneys' time, fees for computer specialists and data processing, fees for other expert witnesses, and costs of identifying members of the plaintiff class.

5. For example, scores of private lawsuits by homeowners near airports, claiming both property damage and personal injury, have provided a primary impetus for control of "noise pollution" in the vicinity of airports. See Burke 1980.

6. Payment of counsel fees and litigation expenses for successful plaintiffs is authorized, for example, by the Clean Air Act (1970), the Federal Water Pollution Control Act (1972), the Noise Pollution Act (1972), the Safe Drinking Water Act (1974), the Marine Mammals Protection Act (1972), the Toxic Substances Control Act (1976), and a number of civil rights and employment discrimination laws.

7. See, for example, Work 1979, p. 3, regarding California's arbitration plan for all civil cases where the amount in controversy is less than $15,000. Arbitration also has increasingly been used in the medical malpractice area.

8. This section draws upon the summary account of doctrinal changes set forth in Epstein 1977, p. 15, and Schwartz 1979, p. 435. See also Higgins 1978, p. 299, charting the rapidity of the rise of manufacturers' strict liability in the 1960s and 1970s.

9. A survey of manufacturers of high-risk products by the president's Interagency Task Force on Product Liability revealed that between 1971 and 1976 the average product liability *claim* rose from $476,000 to $1.711 million. In 1979, according to Jury Verdict Research, Inc., the average verdict in product liability cases was $761,000, although that average was inflated considerably by a relatively small proportion of multimillion-dollar awards. Excluding $1 million verdicts, the average award was $225,000; see Bodine 1981.

10. O'Connell 1973, pp. 773, 792; see also idem 1975. A similar plan has been advocated by Havighurst and Tancredi 1973; see also Havighurst 1975, p. 1233.

11. See, for example, Birnbaum 1980*b*, p. 19, on the Model Uniform Product Liability Act developed by the U.S. Department of Commerce; Bodine 1980 on preemptive congressional product liability act.

12. Traditionally, courts have held that violation of regulatory standards is only *prima facie* proof of negligence; see cases collected in Prosser 1971, p. 196, and Mashaw and Merrill 1975, chap. 12, pt. 5. But some more recent cases have held that regulatory violations impose absolute liability. See *Van Gaasebeck* v. *Webatuck Central School District*, 21 N.Y. 234 (1967 |school bus regulations|); *Koenig* v. *Patrick Construction Corp.*, 298 N.Y. 313 (1948 |workplace safety regulation|); and *Javins* v. *First National Realty Corp.*, 428 F.2d (D.C. Cir. 1970 |housing code violations breach warranty of habitability and bar landlord's suit for possession|).

13. The failure of employers to disclose known information about job hazards could be treated as grounds for adversely affected employees to circumvent the workers' compensation system and bring much larger damage suits and punitive damage claims in the courts. Such a "nondisclosure" theory, in fact, has been employed in lawsuits against employers by workers exposed to asbestos and to cotton dust. The Toxic Sub-

stances Control Act now requires manufacturers to keep certain records and to report to the EPA (not to workers) any evidence of adverse health effects. OSHA regulations require employers to monitor worker exposures to certain chemicals, such as lead.

14. For details of the Japanese plan, see Gresser 1975, p. 92.

12. Joseph Ferreira, Jr.: "Promoting Safety through Insurance"

1. Not all incentives are lost, since the risk of personal injury remains. Also, the insurer could adjust premiums in future years to reflect past claims experience. By varying the size of the adjustment, one can trade off the safety incentive effect and the risk-spreading benefit of the insurance. Nevertheless, the two effects are working at odds with one another.

2. Note that the premiums must reflect marginal pricing—every risk one decides to take must contribute to the premium. If premiums are based on estimated annual mileage, retrospective adjustments would have to be made at a later date or the marginal incentive would be lost.

3. Note that perfect risk assessment does not imply knowing in advance when specific accidents will arise. Rather, it implies linking the odds of having an accident to the LNG handler's activities.

4. See the Paris and Vienna Conventions as reported in OECD 1976.

5. For further discussion, see Ferreira and Hill 1980.

6. There remains, of course, the personal safety incentive to select vehicles with safety equipment and design features that limit personal injury to the driver and passengers.

7. The choice is understandable since the primary purpose of pooled insurance data is for setting or reviewing aggregate rate levels.

13. George C. Eads: "Increased Corporate Product Safety Efforts: A Substitute for Regulation?"

1. The other two "causes" were liability insurance rate-making practices and uncertainties in the tort-litigation system. The task force did not attempt to rank these three causes.

2. Wheelwright's view of the importance of incentive structure to attain so-called "social objectives" is mirrored in the argument advanced by Bacon 1970, pp. 193–94.

3. For example, a 1976 survey conducted by the Machinery and Allied Products Institute (MAPI) revealed that 58 percent of its members had written corporate policies concerning the retention of safety-related records, and 76 percent of those indicated that the policy was "strictly enforced." The "never-ending battle" characterization was provided by one of the MAPI respondents. MAPI 1976, p. 18.

4. The Ford documents introduced in the *Pinto* case are often-cited examples. See Wheeler 1980, pp. 27–30.

5. Firm A in Weinstein et al. 1980a, Appendix I, pp. 86–105, is a good example. This firm, one of four whose product safety programs were studied at considerable depth by the authors, was extremely thorough, at least in evaluating new products. However, its lack of documentation (which the authors suspected was the result of a deliberate policy to minimize liability exposure) led to the loss of critical information vital to the firm.

6. Statement of Russell Hastings in MAPI 1972, p. 70.

7. The design verification processes of Weinstein's Firm B also have this defense-oriented flavor. Weinstein et al. 1980*a*, pp. 106–25.

8. The most complete presentation of this suggestion is contained in Weinstein et al. 1980*b*, pp. 347–84.

9. Henderson's view, described in other of his writings, is that courts are inherently incapable of evaluating the "reasonableness" of product design decisions due to the polycentric nature of such decisions. He urges turning the whole product liability issue over to government regulators. As we shall see below, Henderson, though perhaps properly conscious of the limitations of the legal system in dealing with complex problems, is almost certainly excessively sanguine about the ability of government regulations to do a better job.

10. CPSC is not the only federal agency conducting such accident investigations. The Bureau of Motor Carrier Safety in the Department of Transportation investigates every accident involving a truck in which there is a death, injury, or significant property damage. And, of course, the National Transportation Safety Board investigates all aircraft accidents (and certain other transportation-related accidents) and publishes detailed findings as to their cause.

11. Under the Department of Commerce's proposed Model Uniform Product Liability Act, compliance with governmental and regulatory safety standards would be admissible as a defense in product liability litigation, but this defense could be overturned by a showing that a reasonably prudent product seller could have taken additional precautions. According to Birnbaum 1980*a*, p. 24, this merely restates existing common law. Several states have gone beyond this and have made compliance with governmental safety standards an *absoluta* defense.

14. Eugene Bardach: "Self-Regulation and Regulatory Paperwork"

1. Over half the federal paperwork burden is tax related. State and local tax collection probably represents at least half the state and local paperwork burden as well, and the amount of tax reporting required by state and local governments must at least equal the amount required by the federal government, given the near universality of state income tax filings. Then, too, most regulatory permits and licenses required to operate businesses or use property are in state and local hands. In addition, many federal requirements are requests for data to state and local agencies that these agencies themselves impose on private parties.

2. There are, of course, many reasons that most of these plans, and elements within them, were never carried out. The lack of coordinating machinery and the inability to set priorities are only two of them. Their political unpopularity among the local citizenry is probably more important overall.

3. See "GSA Stops Furniture Purchases," *Washington Post*, 11 October 1979, p. F9. I am grateful to Dail Phillips and Thomas L. Arthur for bringing this story to my attention. For further details, including those on an acquisition freeze, see *OMB Bulletin*, no. 80–6 (2 February 1980).

4. I am indebted to Tim Sullivan for information on these matters.

5. For a fuller discussion of the problem of standing up to misguided or badly intentioned accusers, see Bardach and Kagan 1982, especially chaps. 7 and 11.

6. Also see Wildavsky 1980, who proposes that agencies be allowed to keep funds budgeted for, but not spent on, data acquisition and management in a "general overhead" fund to be reprogrammed.

7. This is also something that agencies might do with regulated enterprises, i.e., to target reporting requirements more on habitual offenders while reducing paperwork burdens for firms with good records.

8. Of course, there is a sense in which perfectly effective (deterrent) paperwork could also be excessive: if less paperwork can be relied on to produce the same high level of compliance, the difference between the actual amount and the minimally required amount is excessive. Compliance is a product of many factors, of which regulatory surveillance is only one. Market pressures, the pressures of the liability law, professional norms, and the sense of civic obligation also affect compliance. (See, generally, Bardach and Kagan 1982, especially chaps. 1 and 3.) Consider, for example, a company manufacturing biologics for medical use. For its own quality-control purposes it will require reams of documents and records; any slips in quality could lead to disastrous effects on the company's reputation and to a significant liability exposure. In some cases FDA regulations governing the manufacture of biologics generate more paperwork than the company would do on its own. One might consider this extra quantity "excessive" if one preferred no higher quality standards than those imposed by the marketplace and the liability law. Further, even if one did prefer higher standards, the amount of regulatory paperwork imposed by the FDA might still be considerably greater than the amount needed to produce compliance with them.

9. The actual deterrent value of the DES certificate system is hard to determine. The GAO report argued that the system's design was such that it would not readily be used to track instances of improperly treated animals back to the responsible sources; it also argued that visual tests done by inspectors were effective enough to make the certification process redundant in any case. However, some months after DES was completely banned in mid-1979 and the certificate system was also abolished, widescale violations of the ban came to light. This phenomenon suggests that the certification system might have been having some deterrent effect. See Frazier and Weiner 1980, p. 48, in which a USDA official estimates that some 10 percent "of the people in the cattle business" were ignoring the ban, and an FDA official reports that some 430,000 animals were improperly treated with DES, about 30,000 of which reached market. Alternatively, and perhaps somewhat more plausibly, it could be that the actual violation level was relatively high before the ban as well, but simply was not detected by either the certification system or visual inspection. Thomas Grumbly, then a high official in the USDA, told the *Washington Post* (5 April 1980, p. A4) that "the meat is 'no worse than any that was on the market prior to the ban.' "

10. For completeness, a word should be said about a paperwork relief strategy based on "tiering"—that is, lightening the reporting requirements for entities that are believed to present less of a problem that others. For instance, their past compliance history might be very favorable. This strategy is potentially very useful in implementing protective regulation in general (see chapter 5 by Sullivan). The strategy might be less applicable to regulatory paperwork, however, because uniform reporting requirements are themselves seen as a condition for granting "tiered" exceptions to otherwise uniform monitoring by direct inspection.

15. Eugene Bardach and Robert A. Kagan: "Conclusion: Responsibility and Accountability"

1. There are, of course, any number of intermediate patterns. In modern societies, for example, individuals often contract with specialists such as physicians and investment advisers to help them look out for their own interests, or call upon governments to appoint specialists in altruistic concern for others, such as policemen, social workers, teachers, and water-supply purifiers. All of these specialists and professionals tend to adopt a communitarian ethos, at least within the bounds of their organizational roles.

2. Another very practical reason for preferring individual responsibility to institutionalized accountability is that the former is a lot less costly to enforce and "administer."

3. The means-end distinction in the text is based on the idea that social responsibility entails these two analytically distinguishable processes: (1) learning about and deciding what potentially harmful activities should be monitored and controlled, and within that realm, how far risks should be reduced (taking into account the costs and sacrifices that would be imposed by various levels of precaution); and (2) once those realms of responsibility and general levels of protection (in short, goals) have been determined, deciding on the most efficient means of attaining them. In practice, of course, the search for and the choice of means also shape the choice of ends. For instance, as our technical ability to detect and reduce exposure to toxic substances increases from parts per million to parts per trillion, our aspirations for the higher level of purity may increase as well.

16. Eugene Bardach and Robert A. Kagan: "Postscript: The Yuletide Regulatory Reform Wish List"

1. Under the "offset" policy, a firm may be able to build new manufacturing facilities in a high pollution ("nonattainment") area if it offsets the added pollution from its new facilities by paying for the reduction of at least an equivalent amount of pollution by other firms. Under "banking," a firm can save any "extra" (more than the law requires) reductions it has achieved to use again in building new facilities, or it might sell the extra reductions to new firms.

2. Orphan drugs differ from wide-spectrum drugs to some extent in that, because of their limited markets, there is less risk that manufacturers will take testing shortcuts or require risks because of eagerness to exploit a potentially profitable breakthrough.

3. Efforts by OSHA and by the National Institute of Occupational Safety and Health (NIOSH) to regulate exposures to dangerous chemicals in the workplace suffer the same problems as do EPA's efforts to administer TOSCA.

4. In 1978 the FDA proposed to phase in a ban on nitrites after certain scientific results suggested they were indirectly carcinogenic. Two years later, after reviewing the evidence more carefully and accumulating new evidence, the agency withdrew the proposal.

5. For further discussion of approaches, see Kelman 1981, Mendeloff 1979, and Dunlop 1976, pp. 23–27.

REFERENCES

Ackerman, Bruce A., and Hassler, William. 1981. *Clean Coal/Dirty Air.* New Haven, CT: Yale University Press.

Ackerman, Bruce A.; Rose-Ackerman, Susan; Sawyer, James W., Jr.; Henderson, Dale W. 1974. *The Uncertain Search for Environmental Quality.* New York: The Free Press.

Akerlof, G. 1970. "The Market for Lemons: Qualitative Uncertainty and the Market Mechanism." *Quarterly Journal of Economics,* August.

Alexander, Tom. 1981. "A Simpler Path to a Cleaner Environment." *Fortune,* 4 May.

Altshuler, Alan, with Womack, James P., and Pucher, John R. 1979. *The Urban Transportation System: Politics and Policy Innovation.* Cambridge, MA: MIT Press.

Ames, B. N.; Hooper, N. K.; Sawyer, C. B.; Gold, L. S.; and Havender, W. R. 1982. "Carcinogenic Potency: The Data Base." In preparation.

Anderson, Douglas D. 1981. *Regulatory Politics and Electric Utilities.* Boston, MA: Auburn House Publishing.

Ashford, Nicholas. 1976. *Crisis in the Workplace.* Cambridge, MA: MIT Press.

Bacon, Joseph L. 1970. "Planning within the Firm." *American Economic Review Papers and Proceedings.* May.

Bacow, Lawrence S. 1980. *Bargaining for Job Safety and Health.* Cambridge, MA: MIT Press.

Bardach, Eugene, and Kagan, Robert A. 1982. *Going by the Book: The Problem of Regulatory Unreasonableness.* Philadelphia, PA: Temple University Press.

Bardach, Eugene, and Pugliaresi, Lucian. 1977. "The Environmental Impact Statement vs. the Real World." *The Public Interest,* Fall.

Berger, Curtis. 1978. "Away from the Courthouse and into the Field: The Odyssey of a Special Master." *Columbia Law Review* 78.

Bernstein, Marver H. 1955. *Regulating Business by Independent Commission.* Princeton, NJ: Princeton University Press.

Birnbaum, Sheila L. 1980a. "Weighing the Model Uniform Act's Proposed Evidentiary Changes." *National Law Journal,* 24 March.

———. 1980b. "Wholesale Changes Are in Store if the Model Act Becomes Law." *National Law Journal,* 17 March.

Boden, Les, and Wagman, David. 1978. "Increasing OSHA's Clout: Sixty Million New Inspectors." *Working Papers for a New Society,* May/June.

Bodine, Larry. 1980. "Product Liability Bill Gaining Support." *National Law Journal*, 22 September.

Brehm, Howard E. 1978. "Issues of the Day—Product Safety." *Research Management*, January.

Burke, Edward J. 1980. "Legal Roar over Jet Noise." *National Law Journal*, 1 December.

Calabresi, Guido. 1970. *The Costs of Accidents: Legal and Economic Analysis.* New Haven, CT: Yale University Press.

Chandran, Rajan, and Linneman, Robert. 1978. "Planning to Minimize Product Liability." *Sloan Management Review*, Fall.

Chayes, Abram. 1976. "The Role of the Judge in Public Law Litigation." *Harvard Law Review* 89.

Clemmesen, J. 1981. "Epidemiological Studies into the Possible Carcinogenicity of Hairdyes." *Mutation Research* 87.

Concon, J. M.; Newburg, D. S.; and Swerczek, T. W. 1979. "Black Pepper (*Piper Nigrum*): Evidence of Carcinogenicity." *Nutrition and Cancer* 1.

Cornell, Nina; Noll, Roger; and Weingast, Barry. 1976. "Safety Regulation." In *Setting National Priorities: The Next Ten Years*, ed. Charles L. Schultze and Henry Owen. Washington, DC: The Brookings Institution.

Coulston, F., ed. 1979. *Regulatory Aspects of Carcinogenesis and Food Additives: The Delaney Clause.* New York: Academic Press.

Council on Occupational Health. 1970. "Evaluation of the Present Status of DDT with Respect to Man." Report of the Committee on Occupational Toxicology of the Council on Occupational Health. *Journal of American Medical Association* 212.

Crecine, J. P. 1981. *Research in Public Policy and Management.* Greenwich, CT: JAI Press.

Danaceau, Paul. 1980. *Government Regulation: The View from Janesville, Wisconsin.* March. Washington, DC: U.S. Regulatory Council.

———. 1981. *Making Inspection Work: Three Case Studies.* May. Washington, DC: U.S. Regulatory Council.

Danielson, Lynn M., and French, Sandra. 1981. *California Building Standards: A Local Perspective.* Berkeley, CA: Energy and Resources Group, University of California.

DeMuth, Christopher. 1980. "The White House Review Programs." *Regulation*, January/February.

Diver, Colin. 1979. "The Judge as Political Powerbroker: Superintending Structural Change in Public Institutions." *Virginia Law Review* 65.

Djerassi, Carl. 1979. *The Politics of Contraception.* New York: Norton.

Doll, R., and Peto, R. 1981. "The Causes of Cancer: Quantitative Estimates of Avoidable Risks of Cancer in the United States Today." *Journal of the National Cancer Institute* 66.

Drayton, William, Jr. 1978. "Beyond Effluent Fees." In *Approaches to Controlling Air Pollution*, ed. Ann F. Friedlaender. Cambridge, MA: MIT Press.

——. 1981. "Getting Smarter about Regulation." *Harvard Business Review*, July/August.

Dunlop, John T. 1976. "The Limits of Legal Compulsion." *Conference Board Record*, March.

Eads, George C. 1981. "Harnessing Regulation: The Evolving Role of White House Oversight." *Regulation*, May/June.

Edelman, Murray. 1964. *The Symbolic Uses of Politics.* Urbana, IL: University of Illinois Press.

Epstein, Richard. 1977. "Products Liability: The Gathering Storm." *Regulation*, September/October.

Estes, Carroll L. 1979. *The Aging Enterprise.* San Francisco, CA: Jossey-Bass.

——, and Noble, Maureen. 1978. *Paperwork and the Older Americans Act: Problems of Implementing Accountability.* Prepared for the U.S. Senate Special Committee on Aging. Washington, DC: Government Printing Office.

Feinbaum, Robert. 1981. *The California Experience with Energy Conservation Standards for Buildings.* Berkeley, CA: Lawrence Berkeley Laboratory, University of California.

Feldman, Martha S., and March, James G. 1981. "Information in Organizations as Signal and Symbol." *Administrative Science Quarterly*, June.

Ferreira, Joseph, Jr., and Hill, S. A. 1980. *Mechanisms for Sharing the Costs of Large Accidents: An LNG Example.* Washington, DC: National Technical Information Service.

Freeman, A. Myrick. 1978. "Air and Water Pollution Policy." In *Current Issues in U.S. Environmental Policy*, ed. Paul Portney. Baltimore, MD: Johns Hopkins University Press.

Friedlaender, Ann F., ed. 1978. *Approaches to Controlling Air Pollution.* Cambridge, MA: MIT Press.

Furman, R. H. 1979. Discussion in *Regulatory Aspects of Carcinogenesis and Food Additives: The Delaney Clause*, ed. F. Coulston. New York: Academic Press.

Gardiner, John, ed. 1977. *Public Law and Public Policy.* New York: Praeger.

Gass, G. H., and Alaben, W. T. 1977. "Preliminary Report on the Carcinogenic Dose Response Curve to Oral Vitamin D_2." *IRCS Medical Science* 5.

Glazer, Nathan. 1978. "Should Judges Administer Social Services?" *The Public Interest* (Winter).

Goldberg, Victor P. 1977. "Tort Liability for Negligent Inspection by Insurers." Working paper no. 90, Department of Economics, University of California, Davis.

Graham, J. D., and Vaupel, J. W. 1981. "Value of a Life: What Difference Does It Make?" *Risk Analysis* 1.

Greenwald, Bruce C. N., and Mueller, Marnie W. 1978. "Medical Malpractice and Medical Costs." In *The Economics of Medical Malpractice,* ed. Simon Rottenberg. Washington, DC; American Enterprise Institute.

Gresser, Julian. 1975. "The 1973 Japanese Law for the Compensation of Pollution-Related Health Damage: An Introductory Assessment." *Law in Japan* 8.

Hagerty, Thomas J. 1981. "Time for a New Idea: Air Brokering." *Milwaukee Journal,* 17 February.

Hagglund, George. 1966. Doctoral thesis, Department of Industrial Relations, University of Wisconsin.

Hahn, R. W., and Noll, Roger. 1981. "Designing a Market for Tradeable Emissions Permits." Paper presented to the Conference on Reform of Environmental Regulation, Duke University, 17–18 May.

Hamilton, Martha M. 1981. "EPA Promotes Private Method of Air Cleanup." *Washington Post,* 27 January.

Harrison, David. 1977. "Controlling Automotive Emissions: How to Save More than $1 Billion per Year and Help the Poor Too." *Public Policy* 25, Fall.

Hartman, Raymond S.; Bosdogan, Kirkor; and Nadkarni, Ravindra M. 1979. "The Economic Impacts of Environmental Regulations on the U.S. Copper Industry." *Bell Journal of Economics* 10, 2, Autumn.

Havender, W. R. 1979. "Ruminations on a Rat: Saccharin and Human Risk." *Regulation,* March/April.

Havighurst, Clark. 1975. "Medical Adversity Insurance—Has Its Time Come?" *Duke Law Journal.*

———, and Tancredi, Laurence. 1973. "Medical Adversity Insurance—A No-Fault Approach to Medical Malpractice and Quality Assurance." *Milbank Memorial Fund Quarterly* 51, Spring. Reprinted in *Insurance Law Journal,* no. 613, February 1974.

Hayek, F. A. 1945. "The Use of Knowledge in Society." *The American Economic Review* 35.

Hayes, M. K. 1981. *The Health Effects of Herbicide 2,4,5–T.* New York: American Council on Science and Health.

Henderson, James A. 1982. "Should a 'Process Defense' Be Recognized in Product Design Cases?" *New York University Law Review,* forthcoming.

Herrick, Neal. 1976. "Institutional Attitudes toward Human Fulfillment through Work." Cited in *Crisis in the Workplace,* by Nicholas Ashford. Cambridge, MA: MIT Press.

Higgins, Richard. 1978. "Producers' Liability and Product-Related Accidents." *Journal of Legal Studies* 7.

Hilts, P. J. 1981. "The Day Bacon Was Declared Poison." *The Washington Post Magazine,* 26 April.

Hoffman LaRoche Co., Ltd. 1978. "Tumorigenicity and Carcinogenicity Study with Xylitol in Long-Term Dietary Administration to Mice." Study no. HLR 25/77774, 30 January, prepared by Huntingdon Research Centre, Huntingdon, Cambridgeshire, England. Available from the U.S. Food and Drug Administration, Rockville, MD.

Hollstein, M.; McCann, J.; Angelosanto, F. A.; and Nichols, W. W. 1979. "Short-Term Tests for Carcinogens and Mutagens." *Mutation Research* 65.

Hoover, R. N., and Strasser, P. H. 1980. "Artificial Sweeteners and Human Bladder Cancer." *The Lancet*, 19 April.

Institute for Contemporary Studies. 1978. *Regulating Business: The Search for an Optimum.* San Francisco, CA: Institute for Contemporary Studies.

Institute of Medicine. 1979. *Food Safety Policy, Scientific and Societal Considerations.* March. Washington, DC: National Academy of Sciences.

JACA, Inc. 1975. "Differential Impact of Pollution Control Requirements on Small versus Large Businesses in Grain and Stone Industries." Report submitted to the Small Business Administration, May. Processed.

Jason, Georgette. 1981. "Insurors Fret over Covering Pollution Costs." *The Wall Street Journal*, 17 July.

Jenkins, R. Scott, and Scheinfurth, William. 1979. "California's Medical Injury Reform Act: An Equal Protection Challenge." *University of Southern California Law Review* 52.

Karig, Phillip. 1981. "Federal Policy Options for Preventing Automobile-Caused Deaths." Unpublished paper, Massachusetts Institute of Technology School of Government.

Kaufman, Herbert. 1977. *Red Tape*, Washington, DC: The Brookings Institution.

Kelman, Steven. 1980. "Occupational and Health Administration." In *The Politics of Regulation*, ed. James Q. Wilson. New York: Basic Books.

———. 1981*a*. *Regulating America, Regulating Sweden: A Comparative Study of Occupational Safety and Health Policy.* Cambridge, MA: MIT Press.

———. 1981*b*. "Regulation and Paternalism." *Public Policy* 29, 2.

Kirschen, Dick. 1977. "The New War on Cancer—Carter Team Seeks Causes, Not Cures." *National Journal*, 6 August.

Kolata, G. B. 1980. "Love Canal: False Alarm Caused by Botched Study." *Science* 208.

Kolb, John, and Ross, Steven S. 1980. *Product Safety and Liability: A Desk Reference.* New York: McGraw-Hill.

Kreig, Andrew. 1979. "Billions Hinge on Asbestos Appeal: Insurers Fight over Who Pays Claims." *National Law Journal*, 15 October.

Lasagna, Louis. 1979. "Who Will Adopt the Orphan Drugs?" *Regulation*, November/December.

Lave, C. A. 1978. "The Costs of Going 44." *Newsweek*, 23 October.

Lave, Lester B. 1981*a*. "Conflicting Objectives in Regulating the Automobile." *Science* 212.

396 References

———. 1981*b*. *The Strategy of Social Regulation: Decision Frameworks for Policy.* Washington, DC: The Brookings Institution.

Laws, E. R.; Curley, A.; Biros, F. J. 1967. "Men with Intensive Occupational Exposure to DDT." *Archives of Environmental Health* 15.

Lee, J. E. 1981. "How to Fight Air Pollution." *Newsweek,* 14 September.

Littlefield, N. A.; Farmer, J. H.; Gaylor, D. W.; and Sheldon, W. G. 1980. "Effects of Dose and Time in a Long-Term, Low-Dose Carcinogenesis Study." *Journal of Environmental Pathology and Toxicology* 3.

McCann, J., and Ames, B. N. 1976. "Detection of Carcinogens as Mutagens in the *Salmonella* Microsome Test: Assay of 300 Chemicals: Discussion." *Proceedings of the National Academy of Sciences* (U.S.) 73.

McGuire, E. Patrick. 1979. *The Product Safety Function: Organization and Operations.* New York: The Conference Board.

McKinsey and Company. 1977. *Product Liability: Final Report of the Insurance Study.* Vol. 1. Washington, DC: U.S. Department of Commerce.

Maloney, M. T., and Yandle, Bruce. 1980. "Bubbles and Efficiency." *Regulation,* May/June.

———. 1979. "The Estimated Cost of Air Pollution Control under Various Regulatory Approaches." Report prepared for the DuPont Company under contract with the Department of Economics, Clemson University, South Carolina. Processed.

Malvey, Mari. 1981. *Simple Systems, Complex Environments: Hospital Financial Information Systems.* Beverly Hills, CA: Sage Publications.

MAPI. 1972. *Company Programs to Reduce Products Liability Hazards: A Transcript and a MAPI Seminar.* Washington, DC: Machinery and Allied Products Institute.

———. 1976. *Products Liability: A MAPI Survey.* Washington, DC: MAPI.

Martin, Douglas. 1978. "Search for Toxic Chemicals in Environment Gets a Slow Start, Is Proving Difficult and Expensive." *The Wall Street Journal,* 9 May.

Mashaw, Jerry, and Merrill, Richard. 1975. *The American Public Law System.* St. Paul, MN: West Publishing Company.

Mendeloff, John. 1979. *Regulating Safety: An Economic and Political Analysis of Occupational Safety and Health Policy.* Cambridge, MA: MIT Press.

Miller, James C. III, and Yandle, Bruce, eds. 1979. *Benefit-Cost Analyses of Social Regulation: Case Studies from the Council on Wage and Price Stability.* Washington, DC: American Enterprise Institute.

Mintzberg, Henry. 1979. *The Structuring of Organizations.* Englewood Cliffs, NJ: Prentice-Hall.

Miske, Jack. 1979. "Capital Formation and 10–5–1." *Foundry Management and Technology,* April.

Mitnick, Barry M. 1980. *The Political Economy of Regulation: Creating, Designing, and Removing Regulatory Forms.* New York: Columbia University Press.

Morone, James A., and Marmor, Theodore R. 1981. "Representing Consumer Interests: The Case of American Health Planning." *Ethics* 91, April.

Morrison, A. S., and Buring, J. E. 1980. "Artificial Sweeteners and Cancer of the Lower Urinary Tract." *The New England Journal of Medicine* 302.

Morss, Elliott R., and Rich, Robert R. 1980. *Government Information Management: A Counter-Report of the Commission on Federal Paperwork.* Boulder, CO: Westview Press.

Mosher, Lawrence. 1981. "Bottom Up or Top Down." *National Journal,* 28 February.

Nelson, D.; Szanto, P. B.; Willheim, R.; and Ivy, A. C. 1954. "Hepatic Tumors in Rats Following the Prolonged Ingestion of Milk and Egg Yolk." *Cancer Research* 14.

Nelson, Paul C. 1980. "Togetherness Is Relevant—Counsel—Corporate Counsel Teamwork" (1976). Reprinted (1980) in *Product Liability of Manufacturers: Prevention and Defense.* Washington, DC: Defense Research Institute.

Neustadt, Richard M. 1981. "Taming the Paperwork Tiger: An Experiment in Regulatory Management." *Regulation,* January/February.

Nichols, A. L., and Zeckhauser, R. 1977. "Government Comes to the Workplace: An Assessment of OSHA." *The Public Interest,* Fall.

Northrup, Herbert; Rowan, Richard; and Perry, Charles. 1978. *The Impact of OSHA.* Philadelphia, PA: The Wharton School.

O'Connell, Jeffrey. 1975. *Ending Insult to Injury: No-Fault Insurance for Products and Services.* Urbana II: University of Illinois Press.

———. 1973. "Expanding No-Fault beyond Auto Insurance." *Virginia Law Review* 39.

OECD. 1976. *Nuclear Legislation: Nuclear Third-Party Liability.* Paris: Organization for Economic Cooperation and Development.

Office of Technology Assessment (U.S. Congress). 1977. *Cancer Testing Technology and Saccharin.* Washington, DC: U.S. Government Printing Office.

O'Hare, Michael. 1981*a.* "Buckle Up, or Else . . . " *Boston Globe,* 14 September.

———. 1981*b.* "Improving the Use of Information in Environmental Decision-making." *Environmental Impact Assessment Review* 1, 3.

———. 1981*c.* "Information Management and Public Choice." In *Research in Public Policy and Management* 1, ed. J. P. Crecine. Greenwich, CT: JAI Press.

———; Bar-Cohen, A.; and Allen, E. 1979. *Enforced Disclosure for Residential Energy Conservation.* Annapolis, MD: Maryland Energy Facility Siting Council.

Pasztor, Andy. 1981. "Market Booms for 'Rights' to Pollute." *Wall Street Journal,* 18 June.

————. 1980. "Pinto Criminal Trial of Ford Motor Co. Opens Up Broad Issues." *The Wall Street Journal,* 4 January.

Peltzman, S. 1974. *Regulation of Pharmaceutical Innovation.* Washington, DC: American Enterprise Institute.

Peretti, Della. 1980. "Implementation Problems in the Standardized Testing Program." Seminar paper, University of California, Berkeley, on file with author.

Poole, Robert W., Jr., ed. 1981. *Instead of Regulation: Alternatives to Federal Regulatory Agencies.* Lexington, MA: Lexington Books.

Portney, Paul, ed. 1978*a. Current Issues in U.S. Environmental Policy.* Baltimore, MD: Johns Hopkins University Press.

Portney, Paul. 1978*b.* "Toxic Substance Policy and the Protection of Human Health." In *Current Issues in U.S. Environmental Policy,* ed. Paul Portney. Baltimore, MD: Johns Hopkins University Press.

Posner, Richard. 1972. "A Theory of Negligence." *Journal of Legal Studies* 1.

Post, Thomas R. 1974. "A Solution to the Problem of Private Compensation in Oil Discharge Situations." *University of Miami Law Review* 28.

Prosser, William. 1971. *Torts.* 4th ed. St. Paul, MN: West Publishing Company.

Quirk, Paul J. 1980. "Food and Drug Administration." In *The Politics of Regulation,* ed. James Q. Wilson. New York: Basic Books.

————. 1981. *Industry Influence in Federal Regulatory Agencies.* Princeton, NJ: Princeton University Press.

Raufer, Roger K.; Hill, Lawrence G.; and Samsa, Michael. 1981. "Emission Fees and TERA." *Journal of the Air Pollution Control Association,* August.

Resources for the Future, Inc. 1980. "Public Opinion on Environmental Issues: Results of a National Public Opinion Survey." Report prepared for the Council on Environmental Quality, Department of Energy, Environmental Protection Agency, and Department of Agriculture, 9 October. Processed.

Rottenberg, Simon, ed. 1978. *The Economics of Medical Malpractice.* Washington, DC: American Enterprise Institute.

Ryan, Dave. 1981. "A Free Enterprise Approach to Air Pollution Control." *EPA Journal,* April.

Schept, Kenneth. 1980. "New Liability Theory Tested: Asbestos Suits Catching Fire." *The National Law Journal,* 18 August.

Schultze, Charles L. 1977. *The Public Use of Private Interest.* Washington, DC: The Brookings Institution.

————, and Owen, Henry, eds. 1976. *Setting National Priorities: The Next Ten Years.* Washington, DC: The Brookings Institution.

Schwartz, Gary T. 1979. "Understanding Products Liability." *California Law Review* 67.

Seidman, David. 1977. "The Politics and Economics of Pharmaceutical Regulation." In *Public Law and Public Policy,* ed. John Gardiner. New York: Praeger.

Shabecoff, Philip. 1981. "U.S. Backs Trading in 'Credits,' Allowing New Plants to Pollute." *New York Times,* 26 January.

Smith, R. Jeffrey. 1981*a.* "Aspartame Approved Despite Risks." *Science* 213.

———. 1981*b.* "EPA and Industry Pursue Regulatory Options." *Science,* 20 February.

Smith, Robert S. 1981. "Protecting Workers' Health and Safety." In *Instead of Regulation: Alternatives to Federal Regulatory Agencies,* ed. Robert W. Poole, Jr. Lexington, MA: Lexington Books.

Soble, Stephen. 1977. "A Proposal for the Administrative Compensation of Victims of Toxic Substance Pollution." *Harvard Journal of Legislation* 14.

Sowell, Thomas. 1980. *Knowledge and Decisions.* New York: Basic Books.

Spence, Michael. 1977. "Consumer Misperceptions, Product Failure and Producer Liability." *Review of Economic Studies* 44.

Standley, David. 1979. "Report and Recommendations on the Proposed Adoption of an EPA [Bubble] Policy." Report prepared for the Office of Air, Noise, and Radiation, Environmental Protection Agency, June. Processed.

Starr, Roger. 1979. "The End of Rental Housing." *The Public Interest,* Fall.

Stewart, Richard B., and Krier, James E. 1978. *Environmental Law and Policy.* 2d ed. Indianapolis, IN: Bobbs-Merrill.

Stone, Christopher. 1977. "A Slap on the Wrist for the Kepone Mob." *Business and Society Review* 22.

———. 1975. *Where the Law Ends.* New York: Harper.

Susskind, L.; Richardson, J.; and Hildebrand, K. 1978. "Resolving Environmental Disputes: Approaches to Intervention, Negotiation, and Conflict Resolution." Laboratory of Architecture and Planning, Massachusetts Institute of Technology, June.

Taylor, S. 1981. "Trial Lawyers See Greater Role in Product Safety." *New York Times,* 30 July.

Tucker, William. 1981. "Marketing Pollution: A Proposal for the Buying and Selling of Clean Air." *Harper's,* May.

U.S. Commission on Federal Paperwork. 1977. *Summary Report.* Washington, DC: Government Printing Office.

U.S. Council on Environmental Quality. 1979. *Tenth Annual Report.* Washington, DC: U.S. Government Printing Office.

U.S. Department of Commerce. 1970, 1977. *Final Report of the Interagency Task Force on Product Liability.* Springfield, VA: National Technical Information Testing Service.

U.S. Environmental Protection Agency. 1979. "Analysis of the Cost Impact of Plantwide Emissions Control (the Bubble Concept) on Representative Steel Mills and Electric Powerplants: Summary of Results." Report prepared by Economic Analysis Division, EPA, for Office of Planning and Management, 25 September. Processed.

U.S. General Accounting Office. 1980. *Department of Agriculture: Actions Needed to Enhance Paperwork Management and Reduce Burden,* 10 March.

———. 1981. *The Trucking Industry's Federal Paperwork Burden Should Be Reduced,* 3 March.

U.S. House of Representatives. 1978. *Product Liability Insurance.* Subcommittee on Capital, Investment, and Business Opportunities of the Committee on Small Business, 95th Congress, 2d session. Washington, DC: Government Printing Office.

U.S. Office of Management and Budget. 1981. *Information Collection Budget of the United States Government Fiscal Year 1981.* Washington, DC: Government Printing Office.

U.S. Regulatory Council. 1980*a. Federal Use of Innovative Regulatory Techniques.* Draft. Washington, DC: U.S. Regulatory Council.

———. 1980*b. Regulating with Common Sense.* Washington, DC: U.S. Regulatory Council.

Vladeck, Bruce C. 1980. *Unloving Care: The Nursing Home Tragedy.* A Twentieth Century Fund Study. New York: Basic Books.

Wardell, W.M. and Lasagna, L. 1975. *Regulation and Drug Development.* Washington, DC: American Enterprise Institute.

Weaver, Paul H. 1978. "Regulation, Social Policy, and Class Conflict." In *Regulating Business: The Search for an Optimum.* San Francisco, CA: Institute for Contemporary Studies.

Weidenbaum, Murray L., and DeFina, Robert. 1978. *The Cost of Federal Regulation.* Washington, DC: American Enterprise Institute.

Weidenbaum, Murray L., and Miller, James C. III. 1981. "Deregulation HQ: An Interview on the New Executive Order with Murray L. Weidenbaum and James C. Miller III." *Regulation,* March/April.

Weimer, David Leo. 1980. "The Regulation of Therapeutic Drugs by the FDA: History, Criticism and Alternatives." Discussion paper no. 8007, Public Policy Analysis Program, University of Rochester, New York, May.

Weinstein, Alvin S.; Piehler, Henry R.; Donaher, William A.; and Twerski, Aaron. 1980*a.* "Final Report to the National Science Foundation on Process Liability: Toward a Standard for Products Liability." Reproduced manuscript, Research Grant APR−76−18490.

———. 1980*b.* "Shifting Perspectives in Products Liability: From Quality to Process Standards." *New York University Law Review,* June.

Wheeler, Malcolm E. 1980. "In Pinto's Wake, Criminal Trials Loom for More Manufacturers." *The National Law Journal,* 6 October.

Wheelwright, Steven C. 1981. "Japan—Where Operations Are Really Strategic." *Harvard Business Review,* July/August.

Wildavsky, Aaron. 1980. *Information as an Organizational Problem.* Berkeley, CA: Survey Research Center, University of California.

Wilson, James Q., ed. 1980. *The Politics of Regulation.* New York: Basic Books.

Work, Clement. 1979. "California Adopts Arbitration Plan." *National Law Journal,* 9 July.

World Health Organization. 1971. "The Place of DDT in Operations against Malaria and Other Vector-Borne Diseases." *Official Records of the World Health Organization* (Geneva), no. 90, April.

―――. 1964. *Prevention of Cancer.* Technical Report Series 276. Geneva, Switzerland: WHO.

Wynder, E., and Stellman, S. D. 1980. "Artificial Sweetener Use and Bladder Cancer: A Case Control Study." *Science* 207.

Zuesse, E. 1981. "Love Canal: The Truth Seeps Out." *Reason,* February.

ABOUT THE AUTHORS

LAWRENCE S. BACOW is assistant professor of law and environmental policy in the Department of Urban Studies and Planning at the Massachusetts Institute of Technology, and is spending 1981–1982 as visiting associate professor of environmental law at the Hebrew University of Jerusalem in Israel. He is a lecturer in environmental law on the Executive Program in Environmental Policy and Management at the Harvard School of Public Health where he participates in the Faculty Seminar on Toxic Chemical Regulation. He has written and coauthored numerous articles, and his books include *Bargaining for Job Safety and Health* (1980), and *Sticks, Carrots and the Siting Problem* (forthcoming).

EUGENE BARDACH is professor of public policy at the University of California, Berkeley. His many articles and books include *The Implementation Game: What Happens after a Bill Becomes Law* (1977), "Save Energy, Save a Soul" in *Commentary* (1976), and "The Environmental Impact Statement vs. the Real World" in *The Public Interest* (1977). For the Institute, he contributed to *The California Coastal Plan: A Critique,* and coauthored with Sotirios Angelides the monograph *Water Banking: How to Stop Wasting Agricultural Water* (1978). He has been a policy analyst in the U.S. Department of the Interior and a consultant to government agencies in the United States and Israel.

PAUL DANACEAU has held several positions on government councils and commissions, and until 1972 he was staff director for the Subcommittee on Executive Reorganization and Government Research, Senate Committee on Government Operations. A consultant and writer on drug abuse and many aspects of health, his most recent publications for the U.S. Regulatory Council include *Government Regulation: The View from Janesville, Wisconsin* (1980) and *Making Federal Inspection Work* (1981).

GEORGE C. EADS, senior economist for The Rand Corporation, until January 1981 was the member of the President's Council of Economic Advisers responsible for supervising microeconomic analysis. He has had many years of professional experience in government and academia, and his listed publications include an article on "Regulation and Technical Change: Some Largely Unexplored Influences" in *The American Economic Review* (1980).

JOSEPH FERREIRA, JR., associate professor of urban studies and operations research at the Massachusetts Institute of Technology, has consulted on insurance rate regulation and risk assessment for such clients as the Stanford Research Institute, state insurance departments, and the U.S. General Accounting Office. His many articles and scientific papers include "Accidents and the Accident Repeater" in *Driver Behavior and Accident Involvement: Implications for Tort Liability* (1970), and in *Operations Research* (1974), "The Long-Term Effects of Merit Rating Plans on Individual Motorists."

THOMAS P. GRUMBLY is a senior consultant with the firm of Temple, Barker and Sloane, Inc., in Lexington, Massachusetts. A former staff director of the Subcommittee on Investigations and Oversight, House Committee on Science and Technology, and associate administrator of the Food Safety and Quality Service at the U.S. Department of Agriculture, he was also executive assistant to the Commissioner of the Food and Drug Administration. His publications include "Regulatory Science and Public Policy" in *Toxic Substances* (March 1981), and "Preregulation Research: The Triumph of Policy Analysis" in the *American Journal of Agricultural Economics* (1979).

WILLIAM R. HAVENDER, research biochemist at the University of California, Berkeley, is a member of the board of scientific advisors, American Council on Science and Health, and contributing editor of the magazine *Regulation.* His published articles include "Ruminations on a Rat: Saccharin and Human Risk" (*Regulation* 1979), "On Human Hubris" (*Political Psychology* 1980), "The Abuse of Science in Public Policy" (*Journal of Contemporary Studies* 1981), and in *The American Spectator,* "The 'Gauze Curtain' at Harvard Medical School" (1978), "When Intelligence Passes the Test" (1980), and "Encounters of the Regulatory Kind" (1981).

ROBERT A. KAGAN, associate professor in the Department of Political Science at the University of California, Berkeley, is a lawyer with experience both in government and in business. A former member of the board of editors of the *Columbia Law Review,* he is the author of *Regulatory Justice: Implementing a Wage-Price Freeze* (1978) and coauthor of several other books and articles. His latest book, written with Eugene Bardach, is *Going by the Book: Unreasonableness in Protective Regulation* (1981).

MICHAEL H. LEVIN is Chief, Regulatory Reform Staff, Office of Policy and Resource Management in the U.S. Environmental Protection Agency. His publications include "Politics and Polarity: The Limits of OSHA Reform" (*Regulation* 1979), and "Use of (Economic) Analysis in Regulation—Decentralizing Some Analysis to the Firm" (*Current Issues in Regulatory Reform* 1980).

MICHAEL O'HARE is a lecturer in public policy at the Kennedy School of Government, Harvard University, and was previously assistant secretary of environmental affairs for policy in the Commonwealth of Massachusetts. His publications include " 'Not on My Block, You Don't'—Facilities Siting and the Strategic Importance of Compensation" (*Public Policy* 1977), and "Information Management and Public Choice" (*Research in Public Policy and Management* 1980).

STUART M. PAPE is an associate with the law firm of Patton, Boggs and Blow in Washington, D.C. Formerly in the Food and Drug Administration as associate chief counsel for food, where he earned the FDA Commendable Service Award in 1978, he became executive assistant to Donald Kennedy, Commissioner of Food and Drugs, before returning to active legal practice.

TIMOTHY J. SULLIVAN is assistant professor in the Graduate School of Public Policy at the University of California, Berkeley, with a doctorate from the Kennedy School of Government, Harvard University. As a consultant in the analysis branch of the Office of Solid Waste, Environmental Protection Agency, he worked on alternative federal policies concerning the siting of hazardous waste management facilities.

INDEX

Labor unions, 111, 135, 181,
202–19, 351, 370, 373ff
Lancet, 46
Lave, Charles, 46
Lave, Lester, 311
Levin, Michael, 13, 18, 352, 356, 362
Liability, 7, 52ff, 209, 213, 217, 230,
244–48, 251–61 passim, 268ff,
273ff, 277, 281, 290, 298, 304,
366
Liability law, 238–66, 269ff, 275ff,
316, 348, 351ff, 366f, 373
Limpert, Robert C., 139ff, 145ff
Litigation, 35, 47, 52f, 128, 132f,
213, 219f, 238–58 passim, 271,
276, 290, 294, 305ff, 310ff, 351
Louisiana, 10
Love Canal, 47, 50f
Lynn, James T., 109

McDonald Corporation, 114
Maine, 86, 264
Market factors, 7, 44, 61, 65f, 78, 89,
97ff, 202, 205, 223–31, 243f,
246f, 252, 259–64, 271, 274–78,
292ff, 298, 302–7, 310, 351,
366f, 371–74
Maryland, 86
Massachusetts, 86, 230, 282ff
Massachusetts Hazardous Waste
Facility Siting Act, 220
Massachusetts Institute of
Technology, 48
Meat and Poultry Inspection
Program, 108, 140
Medical care, 13, 235, 249f, 253–56,
260, 316, 322
Medical Device amendments, 94
Medical Devices Act, 130f, 136, 366
Michigan, 87
Miller amendments, 161
Miller, James C. III, 181f, 184f, 192
Minnesota Mining &
Manufacturing Company, 85
Mintzberg, Henry, 301f
Mississippi, 104, 134

Montana Power Company, 133
Mueller, Marnie, 254

Narragansett Electric Company, 85
National Academy of Sciences, 132,
163, 171, 175
National Cancer Institute, 33, 48
National Disaster Relief Fund, 276
National Electronic Injury
Surveillance System, 310
National Health Planning and
Resources Development Act, 328
National Highway Traffic Safety
Administration, 4, 35, 43, 260ff,
278, 309f, 372f
National Law Journal, 195
National Marine Fisheries Service,
99
Negotiation, 201–4, 207–20, 323
Neustadt, Richard M., 335
Newberne, Paul, 47f
New Drug Application, 36ff
New Jersey, 82–87, 282
New Source Performance
Standards, 62, 68ff
New York, 47, 89, 254, 284
New York Times, 52
Nixon, Richard M., 68, 178, 182, 196
Notice of Proposed Rule Making,
181f, 192f
Nuclear safety, 73, 276

Occupational Safety and Health
Act, 202, 370f
Occupational Safety and Health
Administration, 4ff, 6, 10, 35–39,
45f, 116, 123f, 128, 135f, 141,
146–51, 154, 202–5, 209–18,
241, 263, 309, 347–51, 358,
369–75 passim
O'Connell, Jeffrey, 253
Office of Consumer Affairs, 113
Office of General Counsel, 70–73
Office of Government Programs and
Regulations, 185

PUBLICATIONS LIST*

THE INSTITUTE FOR CONTEMPORARY STUDIES

260 California Street, San Francisco, California 94111

Catalog available upon request

BUREAUCRATS AND BRAINPOWER: GOVERNMENT
REGULATION OF UNIVERSITIES
$6.95. 170 pages. Publication date: June 1979
ISBN 0–917616–35–9
Library of Congress No. 79–51328
Contributors: Nathan Glazer, Robert S. Hatfield, Richard W. Lyman, Paul
Seabury, Robert L. Sproull, Miro M. Todorovich, Caspar W.
Weinberger

THE CALIFORNIA COASTAL PLAN: A CRITIQUE
$5.95. 199 pages. Publication date: March 1976
ISBN 0–917616–04–9
Library of Congress No. 76–7715
Contributors: Eugene Bardach, Daniel K. Benjamin, Thomas E.
Borcherding, Ross D. Eckert, H. Edward Frech III, M. Bruce Johnson,
Ronald N. Lafferty, Walter J. Mead, Daniel Orr, Donald M. Pach,
Michael R. Peevey

THE CRISIS IN SOCIAL SECURITY: PROBLEMS AND PROSPECTS
$6.95. 222 pages. Publication date: April 1977; 2d ed. rev., 1978, 1979
ISBN 0–917616–16–2/1977; 0–917616–25–1/1978
Library of Congress No. 77–72542
Contributors: Michael J. Boskin, George F. Break, Rita Ricardo Campbell,
Edward Cowan, Martin S. Feldstein, Milton Friedman, Douglas R.
Munro, Donald O. Parsons, Carl V. Patton, Joseph A. Pechman,
Sherwin Rosen, W. Kip Viscusi, Richard J. Zeckhauser

*Prices subject to change.

415

416

THE ECONOMY IN THE 1980s: A PROGRAM FOR
GROWTH AND STABILITY
   $7.95 (paper), 462 pages. Publication date: June 1980
   ISBN 0–917616–39–1
   Library of Congress No. 80–80647
   $17.95 (cloth). 462 pages. Publication date: August 1980.
   ISBN 0–87855–399–1. Available through Transaction Books,
   Rutgers–The State University, New Brunswick, NJ 08903
Contributors: Michael J. Boskin, George F. Break, John T. Cuddington,
   Patricia Drury, Alain Enthoven, Laurence J. Kotlikoff, Ronald I.
   McKinnon, John H. Pencavel, Henry S. Rowen, John L. Scadding,
   John B. Shoven, James L. Sweeney, David J. Teece

EMERGING COALITIONS IN AMERICAN POLITICS
   $6.95. 524 pages. Publication date: June 1978
   ISBN 0–917616–22–7
   Library of Congress No. 78–53414
Contributors: Jack Bass, David S. Broder, Jerome M. Clubb, Edward H.
   Crane III, Walter De Vries, Andrew M. Greeley, S. I. Hayakawa, Tom
   Hayden, Milton Himmelfarb, Richard Jensen, Paul Kleppner,
   Everett Carll Ladd, Jr., Seymour Martin Lipset, Robert A. Nisbet,
   Michael Novak, Gary R. Orren, Nelson W. Polsby, Joseph L. Rauh,
   Jr., Stanley Rothman, William A. Rusher, William Schneider, Jesse
   M. Unruh, Ben J. Wattenberg

THE FAIRMONT PAPERS: BLACK ALTERNATIVES CONFERENCE,
SAN FRANCISCO, DECEMBER 1980
   $5.95. 174 pages. Publication date: March 1981
   ISBN 0–917616–42–1
   Library of Congress No. 81–80735
Contributors: Bernard E. Anderson, Thomas L. Berkley, Michael J. Boskin,
   Randolph W. Bromery, Tony Brown, Milton Friedman, Wendell
   Wilkie Gunn, Charles V. Hamilton, Robert B. Hawkins, Jr., Maria
   Lucia Johnson, Martin L. Kilson, James Lorenz, Henry Lucas, Jr.,
   Edwin Meese III, Clarence M. Pendleton, Jr., Dan J. Smith, Thomas
   Sowell, Chuck Stone, Percy E. Sutton, Clarence Thomas, Gloria E. A.
   Toote, Walter E. Williams, Oscar Wright

FEDERAL TAX REFORM: MYTHS AND REALITIES
   $5.95. 270 pages. Publication date: September 1978
   ISBN 0–917616–32–4
   Library of Congress No. 78–61661
Contributors: Robert J. Barro, Michael J. Boskin, George F. Break, Jerry R.
   Green, Laurence J. Kotlikoff, Mordecai Kurz, Peter Mieszkowski,
   John B. Shoven, Paul J. Taubman, John Whalley

GOVERNMENT CREDIT ALLOCATION: WHERE DO WE GO
FROM HERE?
> $4.95. 208 pages. Publication date: November 1975
> ISBN 0−917616−02−2
> Library of Congress No. 75−32951

Contributors: George J. Benston, Karl Brunner, Dwight M. Jaffe, Omotunde
E. G. Johnson, Edward J. Kane, Thomas Mayer, Allan H. Meltzer

NATIONAL SECURITY IN THE 1980s: FROM
WEAKNESS TO STRENGTH
> $8.95 (paper). 524 pages. Publication date: May 1980
> ISBN 0−917616−38−3
> Library of Congress No. 80−80648
> $19.95 (cloth). 524 pages. Publication date: August 1980
> ISBN 0−87855−412−2. Available through Transaction Books,
> Rutgers−The State University, New Brunswick, NJ 08903

Contributors: Kenneth L. Adelman, Richard R. Burt, Miles M. Costick,
Robert F. Ellsworth, Fred Charles Ikl e, Geoffrey T. H. Kemp, Edward
N. Luttwak, Charles Burton Marshall, Paul H. Nitze, Sam Nunn,
Henry S. Rowen, Leonard Sullivan, Jr., W. Scott Thompson, William
R. Van Cleave, Francis J. West, Jr., Albert Wohlstetter, Elmo R.
Zumwalt, Jr.

NEW DIRECTIONS IN PUBLIC HEALTH CARE: A PRESCRIPTION
FOR THE 1980s
> $6.95 (paper). 279 pages. Publication date: May 1976;
> 3d ed. rev., 1980
> ISBN 0−917616−37−5
> Library of Congress No. 79−92868
> $16.95 (cloth). 290 pages. Publication date: April 1980
> ISBN 0−87855−394−0. Available through Transaction Books,
> Rutgers−The State University, New Brunswick, NJ 08903

Contributors: Alain Enthoven, W. Philip Gramm, Leon R. Kass, Keith B.
Leffler, Cotton M. Lindsay, Jack A. Meyer, Charles E. Phelps,
Thomas C. Schelling, Harry Schwartz, Arthur Seldon, David A.
Stockman, Lewis Thomas

OPTIONS FOR U.S. ENERGY POLICY
> $6.95. 317 pages. Publication date: September 1977
> ISBN 0−917616−20−0
> Library of Congress No. 77−89094

Contributors: Albert Carnesale, Stanley M. Greenfield, Fred S. Hoffman,
Edward J. Mitchell, William R. Moffat, Richard Nehring, Robert S.
Pindyck, Norman C. Rasmussen, David J. Rose, Henry S. Rowen,
James L. Sweeney, Arthur W. Wright

418

PARENTS, TEACHERS, AND CHILDREN: PROSPECTS FOR CHOICE
IN AMERICAN EDUCATION
$5.95. 336 pages. Publication date: June 1977
ISBN 0−917616−18−9
Library of Congress No. 77−79164
Contributors: James S. Coleman, John E. Coons, William H. Cornog, Denis
P. Doyle, E. Babette Edwards, Nathan Glazer, Andrew M. Greeley,
R. Kent Greenawalt, Marvin Lazerson, William C. McCready,
Michael Novak, John P. O'Dwyer, Robert Singleton, Thomas Sowell,
Stephen D. Sugarman, Richard E. Wagner

PARTY COALITIONS IN THE 1980s
$8.95 (paper). 480 pages. Publication date: November 1981
ISBN 0−917616−43−X
Library of Congress No. 81−83095
$19.95 (cloth). 480 pages. Publication date: November 1981
ISBN 0−917616−45−6.
Contributors: John B. Anderson, David S. Broder, Walter Dean Burnham,
Patrick Caddell, Jerome M. Clubb, E. J. Dionne, Jr., Alan M. Fisher,
Michael Harrington, S. I. Hayakawa, Richard Jensen, Paul Kleppner,
Everett Carll Ladd, Seymour Martin Lipset, Arthur D. Miller, Howard
Phillips, Norman Podhoretz, Nelson W. Polsby, Richard M. Scammon,
William Schneider, Martin P. Wattenberg, Richard B. Wirthlin

POLITICS AND THE OVAL OFFICE: TOWARDS
PRESIDENTIAL GOVERNANCE
$7.95 (paper). 332 pages. Publication date: February 1981
ISBN 0−917616−40−5
Library of Congress No. 80−69617
$18.95 (cloth). 300 pages. Publication date: April 1981
ISBN 0−87855−428−9. Available through Transaction Books,
Rutgers−The State University, New Brunswick, NJ 08903
Contributors: Richard K. Betts, Jack Citrin, Eric L. Davis, Robert M.
Entman, Robert E. Hall, Hugh Heclo, Everett Carll Ladd, Jr., Arnold
J. Meltsner, Charles Peters, Robert S. Pindyck, Francis E. Rourke,
Martin M. Shapiro, Peter L. Szanton

THE POLITICS OF PLANNING: A REVIEW AND CRITIQUE OF
CENTRALIZED ECONOMIC PLANNING
$5.95. 367 pages. Publication date: March 1976
ISBN 0−917616−05−7
Library of Congress No. 76−7714
Contributors: B. Bruce-Briggs, James Buchanan, A. Lawrence Chickering,
Ralph Harris, Robert B. Hawkins, Jr., George W. Hilton, Richard
Mancke, Richard Muth, Vincent Ostrom, Svetozar Pejovich, Myron
Sharpe, John Sheahan, Herbert Stein, Gordon Tullock, Ernest van
den Haag, Paul H. Weaver, Murray L. Weidenbaum, Hans
Willgerodt, Peter P. Witonski

PUBLIC EMPLOYEE UNIONS: A STUDY OF THE CRISIS IN
PUBLIC SECTOR LABOR RELATIONS
$6.95. 251 pages. Publication date: June 1976; 2d ed. rev., 1977
ISBN 0–917616–24–3
Library of Congress No. 76–18409
Contributors: A. Lawrence Chickering, Jack D. Douglas, Raymond D.
Horton, Theodore W. Kheel, David Lewin, Seymour Martin Lipset,
Harvey C. Mansfield, Jr., George Meany, Robert A. Nisbet, Daniel
Orr, A. H. Raskin, Wes Uhlman, Harry H. Wellington, Charles B.
Wheeler, Jr., Ralph K. Winter, Jr., Jerry Wurf

REGULATING BUSINESS: THE SEARCH FOR AN OPTIMUM
$6.95. 261 pages. Publication date: April 1978
ISBN 0–917616–27–8
Library of Congress No. 78–50678
Contributors: Chris Argyris, A. Lawrence Chickering, Penny Hollander
Feldman, Richard H. Holton, Donald P. Jacobs, Alfred E. Kahn, Paul
W. MacAvoy, Almarin Phillips, V. Kerry Smith, Paul H. Weaver,
Richard J. Zeckhauser

SOCIAL REGULATION: STRATEGIES FOR REFORM
$8.95 (paper). 420 pages. Publication date: March 1982
ISBN 0–917616–46–4
Library of Congress No. 81–85279
$19.95 (cloth). 420 pages. Publication date: March 1982
ISBN 0–917616–47–2
Contributors: Lawrence S. Bacow, Eugene Bardach, Paul Danaceau, George
C. Eads, Joseph Ferreira, Jr., Thomas P. Grumbly, William R.
Havender, Robert A. Kagan, Michael H. Levin, Michael O'Hare,
Stuart M. Pape, Timothy J. Sullivan

TARIFFS, QUOTAS, AND TRADE: THE POLITICS
OF PROTECTIONISM
$7.95. 332 pages. Publication date: February 1979
ISBN 0–917616–34–0
Library of Congress No. 78–66267
Contributors: Walter Adams, Ryan C. Amacher, Sven W. Arndt, Malcolm D.
Bale, John T. Cuddington, Alan V. Deardorff, Joel B. Dirlam, Roger
D. Hansen, H. Robert Heller, D. Gale Johnson, Robert O. Keohane,
Michael W. Keran, Rachel McCulloch, Ronald I. McKinnon, Gordon
W. Smith, Robert M. Stern, Richard James Sweeney, Robert D.
Tollison, Thomas D. Willett

THE THIRD WORLD: PREMISES OF U.S. POLICY
> $7.95. 334 pages. Publication date: November 1978
> ISBN 0–917616–30–8
> Library of Congress No. 78–67593

Contributors: Dennis Austin, Peter T. Bauer, Max Beloff, Richard E. Bissell, Daniel J. Elazar, S. E. Finer, Allan E. Goodman, Nathaniel H. Leff, Seymour Martin Lipset, Edward N. Luttwak, Daniel Pipes, Wilson E. Schmidt, Anthony Smith, W. Scott Thompson, Basil S. Yamey

UNION CONTROL OF PENSION FUNDS: WILL THE NORTH RISE AGAIN?
> $2.00. 41 pages. Publication date: July 1979
> ISBN 0–917616–36–7
> Library of Congress No. 78–66581

Author: George J. Borjas

WATER BANKING: HOW TO STOP WASTING AGRICULTURAL WATER
> $2.00. 56 pages. Publication date: January 1978
> ISBN 0–917616–26–X
> Library of Congress No. 78–50766

Authors: Sotirios Angelides, Eugene Bardach

WHAT'S NEWS: THE MEDIA IN AMERICAN SOCIETY
> $7.95 (paper). 296 pages. Publication date: June 1981
> ISBN 0–917616–41–3
> Library of Congress No. 81–81414
> $18.95 (cloth). 300 pages. Publication date: August 1981
> ISBN 0–87855–448–3. Available through Transaction Books,
> Rutgers–The State University, New Brunswick, NJ 08903

Contributors: Elie Abel, Robert L. Bartley, George Comstock, Edward Jay Epstein, William A. Henry III, John L. Hulteng, Theodore Peterson, Ithiel de Sola Pool, William E. Porter, Michael Jay Robinson, James N. Rosse, Benno C. Schmidt, Jr.

JOURNAL OF CONTEMPORARY STUDIES
> $15/one year, $25/two years, $4/single issue. For delivery outside the United States, add $2/year surface mail, $10/year airmail

A quarterly journal that is a forum for lively and readable studies on foreign and domestic public policy issues. Directed toward general readers as well as policymakers and academics, emphasizing debate and controversy, it publishes the highest quality articles without regard to political or ideological bent.

The Journal of Contemporary Studies is a member of the Transaction Periodicals Consortium. Institute for Contemporary Studies books are distributed by Transaction Books, Rutgers University, New Brunswick, NJ 08903